BREAD FOR THE DAY

2008

Daily Bible Readings and Prayers

Augsburg Fortress
Minneapolis

BREAD FOR THE DAY 2008
Daily Bible Readings and Prayers

Editors: Dennis Bushkofsky, Suzanne Burke, Jessica Hillstrom
Cover design: John Goodman, Paul Boenke
Interior design: John Goodman, Christy J.P. Barker
Cover photos: breaking waves, © PhotoLink/Photodisc/Getty Images; Death Valley, CA, © S. Alden/PhotoLink/Photodisc/Getty images; Iowa cornfield and Philadelphia skyline, © Scenics of America/PhotoLink/Photodisc/Getty Images; Sawtooth Mountains, ID, © C. Borland/Photodisc/ Getty Images.

Contributors to the weekday prayers: Celie Metz Addy, Columbia, South Carolina (January); Jami Hawkins, Columbia, South Carolina (February); Curt Schneider, Waverly, Iowa (March); Elizabeth Olson, Waverly, Iowa (April); Bradley Hales, Culpeper, Virginia (May); Kent Mechler, Sheffield, Iowa (June); Julie Ryan, Downers Grove, Illinois (July); Audrey Riley, River Forest, Illinois (August); Carmala Aderman, Rice Lake, Wisconsin (September); James Boline, Santa Monica, California (October); Ronald Roschke, Boulder, Colorado (November); Luke Smetters, Chicago, Illinois (December)

ACKNOWLEDGMENTS
Scripture quotations are from the New Revised Standard Version Bible © 1989 Division of Christian Education of the National Council of the Churches of Christ in the United States of America. Used by permission.

Hymn suggestions and prayers of the day for Sundays and festivals are from *Evangelical Lutheran Worship*, copyright © 2006 Evangelical Lutheran Church in America.

Materials prepared by the Consultation on Common Texts (CCT), published in *Revised Common Lectionary* © 1992 and *Revised Common Lectionary Daily Readings* © 2005. Used by permission.

Materials prepared by the English Language Liturgical Consultation (ELLC), published in *Praying Together* © 1988: "Blessed are you, Lord" and "My soul proclaims the greatness of the Lord." Used by permission.

ISBN 978-0-8006-2126-1

Manufactured in the U.S.A.

09 08 07 1 2 3 4 5

FOREWORD

Dear sisters and brothers in Christ,

Our church embraces its great heritage in God's word. Proclaimed from pulpits, freely given in the sacraments, integrated into our lives through the daily reading of scripture, sung in the hymns of the church, offered in the prayers of God's people, commemorated in the saints of every time and place, and complete in the Word become flesh, we celebrate the power of God's presence in our lives.

Bread for the Day feeds us with the word of judgment and salvation, conviction and hope, confession and forgiveness. As we are called to mission within and beyond our own context and experience, this daily feast of the word sustains us for the journey of faith.

As the Conference of Bishops, we encourage you to invest time each day in tending to God's word. Our prayer is that this resource will assist you, your family, friends, and small groups in hearing God's word for your life for the sake of your witness and service in the world.

Your partners on the journey,

Conference of Bishops
Evangelical Lutheran Church in America

INTRODUCTION

Welcome to this resource for daily prayer. *Bread for the Day* has been developed to support personal devotions and meditation and may be adapted for group use. The reflection questions printed on the accompanying bookmark and the simplified forms for morning and evening prayer on pages 393–400 are both provided as aids to prayer.

The guiding principle of this selection of daily readings is their relationship to the Sunday readings as presented in the *Revised Common Lectionary* (a system of readings in widespread use across denominations). The readings are chosen so that the days leading up to Sunday (Thursday through Saturday) prepare for the Sunday readings. The days flowing out from Sunday (Monday through Wednesday) reflect upon the Sunday readings.

How this resource is organized

- Each day's page is dated and named in relationship to the church's year. Lesser festivals are listed along with the date as part of the day heading. Commemorations are listed just below in italics. Notes on those commemorated can be found on pages 384–392.

- Several verses of one of the appointed scripture texts are printed. The full text citation is provided for those who would like to reflect on the entire text. In addition, two or three additional reading citations with short descriptions are provided.

- Two psalms are appointed for each week; one psalm for Monday through Wednesday and a second psalm for Thursday through Saturday. In this way the days leading up to Sunday or flowing out from Sunday have a distinct relationship with one another, in addition to their relationship with the Sunday readings. In this volume the psalm is ordinarily the highlighted excerpt of the day for Mondays and Thursdays.

- Following the printed scripture text is a hymn suggestion from *Evangelical Lutheran Worship* and a prayer that incorporates a theme present in one or more of the readings.

- A page for keeping a list of prayer requests or journaling is provided at the beginning of each month.

Suggestions for using this resource

- Use the questions printed on the bookmark to guide your reflection on the scripture texts each day.

- Use the pages at the beginning of each month to keep track of prayer requests.
- Use the weekday readings to prepare for and reflect on the Sunday readings.
- Use the suggested additional readings to further enrich understandings of the Sunday readings.
- Use the simplified forms for morning and evening prayer printed on pages 393–400. These forms may be used in partnership with the readings and prayers provided for each day.
- In addition to being used to guide individual prayer, this resource could also be used to guide family prayer, prayer in congregational or other settings during the week, prayer with those who are sick or homebound, or with other groups.

Notes on lesser festivals and commemorations

The Lutheran church has always considered itself as part of the holy catholic church that transcends denominational boundaries, sharing in the riches of the wider church. Among those riches is the cloud of witnesses who, over the centuries, have pointed to Christ by their lives and death. This resource makes reference to the calendar of lesser festivals and commemorations as presented in *Evangelical Lutheran Worship*. Lesser festivals are listed along with the date as part of the day heading. Commemorations are listed in italics. Short descriptions of lesser festivals and those commemorated are provided on pages 384–392.

When a lesser festival falls on a weekday, the full set of readings appointed for that day are listed. When a lesser festival occurs on a Sunday or principal festival, it is transferred to the next open weekday in order to achieve the greatest continuity between Sunday readings and the daily lectionary. Lesser festivals that fall on a Sunday in 2008 are noted, but the readings are those appointed for the appropriate "green" Sunday around which the weekday readings are chosen. The readings for Reformation Day (Oct. 31) and All Saints Day (Nov. 1) are listed on those days and not transferred to the closest Sunday, even though this is a practice observed by many congregations.

Commemorations are noted on the days when they occur, but prayers and readings for commemorations are not provided in this book. Unlike lesser festivals, commemorations are not transferred to other days when they occur on Sundays or principal festivals.

∼ Prayer list for January

_____

_____

_____

_____

_____

_____

_____

_____

_____

_____

_____

Tuesday, January 1, 2008
NAME OF JESUS

Luke 2:15-21
The child is named Jesus

When the angels had left them and gone into heaven, the shepherds said to one another, "Let us go now to Bethlehem and see this thing that has taken place, which the Lord has made known to us." So they went with haste and found Mary and Joseph, and the child lying in the manger. When they saw this, they made known what had been told them about this child; and all who heard it were amazed at what the shepherds told them. But Mary treasured all these words and pondered them in her heart. The shepherds returned, glorifying and praising God for all they had heard and seen, as it had been told them.

After eight days had passed, it was time to circumcise the child; and he was called Jesus, the name given by the angel before he was conceived in the womb. (Luke 2:15-21)

Additional Readings:

Numbers 6:22-27	Psalm 8	Galatians 4:4-7
The Aaronic blessing	*How exalted is your name*	*We are no longer slaves*

Hymn: That Boy-Child of Mary, ELW 293

Eternal Father, you gave your incarnate Son the holy name of Jesus to be a sign of our salvation. Plant in every heart the love of the Savior of the world, Jesus Christ our Lord, who lives and reigns with you and the Holy Spirit, one God, now and forever.

Hebrews 11:1-12
Abraham's faith

Now faith is the assurance of things hoped for, the conviction of things not seen. Indeed, by faith our ancestors received approval. By faith we understand that the worlds were prepared by the word of God, so that what is seen was made from things that are not visible.

By faith Abraham obeyed when he was called to set out for a place that he was to receive as an inheritance; and he set out, not knowing where he was going. By faith he stayed for a time in the land he had been promised, as in a foreign land, living in tents, as did Isaac and Jacob, who were heirs with him of the same promise. (Heb. 11:1-3, 8-9)

Additional Readings:

Genesis 12:1-7   Psalm 72
Abram and Sarai   *Prayers for the king*

Hymn: The God of Abraham Praise, ELW 831

Faithful God, your steadfast love never fails us, and your promises are true in every age. Keep us ever faithful to you. Renew our trust in you and help us to follow where you lead us, confident in your love.

Thursday, January 3, 2008
WEEK OF CHRISTMAS 1

Psalm 72
Prayers for the king

Give the king your justice, O God,
  and your righteousness to a king's son.
May he judge your people with righteousness,
  and your poor with justice.
May the mountains yield prosperity for the people,
  and the hills, in righteousness.
May he defend the cause of the poor of the people,
  give deliverance to the needy,
  and crush the oppressor. (Ps. 72:1-4)

Additional Readings:

Genesis 28:10-22   Hebrews 11:13-22
Jacob's ladder   *Abraham, Isaac, and Jacob*
                          act on faith

Hymn: Hail to the Lord's Anointed, ELW 311

*You, O Lord, are the author and source of righteousness and mercy.
Daily inspire us to advocate for justice throughout our world. Give
leaders a hunger for peace and the wisdom to work together toward that
end.*

Exodus 3:1-5
The burning bush

Moses was keeping the flock of his father-in-law Jethro, the priest of Midian; he led his flock beyond the wilderness, and came to Horeb, the mountain of God. There the angel of the LORD appeared to him in a flame of fire out of a bush; he looked, and the bush was blazing, yet it was not consumed. Then Moses said, "I must turn aside and look at this great sight, and see why the bush is not burned up." When the LORD saw that he had turned aside to see, God called to him out of the bush, "Moses, Moses!" And he said, "Here I am." Then he said, "Come no closer! Remove the sandals from your feet, for the place on which you are standing is holy ground." (Exod. 3:1-5)

Additional Readings:

Hebrews 11:23-31	Psalm 72
Moses acts on faith	*Prayers for the king*

Hymn: Bless Now, O God, the Journey, ELW 326

God of surprises, you met Moses in his normal routine and spoke to him through a burning bush. Help us to hear your voice and to put away whatever is in the way, for wherever you are is holy ground.

Joshua 1:1-9
Be strong

After the death of Moses the servant of the LORD, the LORD spoke to Joshua son of Nun, Moses' assistant, saying, "No one shall be able to stand against you all the days of your life. As I was with Moses, so I will be with you; I will not fail you or forsake you. Be strong and courageous; for you shall put this people in possession of the land that I swore to their ancestors to give them." (Josh. 1:1, 5-6)

Additional Readings:

Hebrews 11:32—12:2
Surrounded by a cloud of witnesses

Psalm 72
Prayers for the king

Hymn: On Jordan's Stormy Bank I Stand, ELW 437

Lord, you promise to bring us at last into your heavenly kingdom. Make us bold in our everyday witness here on earth, strengthened and upheld by your mighty hand, for we are surely in your presence even now.

Sunday, January 6, 2008
EPIPHANY OF OUR LORD

Matthew 2:1-12
Christ revealed to the nations

Then Herod secretly called for the wise men and learned from them the exact time when the star had appeared. Then he sent them to Bethlehem, saying, "Go and search diligently for the child; and when you have found him, bring me word so that I may also go and pay him homage." When they had heard the king, they set out; and there, ahead of them, went the star that they had seen at its rising, until it stopped over the place where the child was. When they saw that the star had stopped, they were overwhelmed with joy. On entering the house, they saw the child with Mary his mother; and they knelt down and paid him homage. Then, opening their treasure chests, they offered him gifts of gold, frankincense, and myrrh. (Matt. 2:7-11)

Additional Readings:

Isaiah 60:1-6
Nations come to the light

Psalm 72:1-7, 10-14
All shall bow down

Ephesians 3:1-12
The gospel's promise for all

Hymn: Bright and Glorious Is the Sky, ELW 301

O God, on this day you revealed your Son to the nations by the leading of a star. Lead us now by faith to know your presence in our lives, and bring us at last to the full vision of your glory, through your Son, Jesus Christ our Lord, who lives and reigns with you and the Holy Spirit, one God, now and forever.

Monday, January 7, 2008
Time after Epiphany

Psalm 72
Prayers for the king

Give the king your justice, O God,
   and your righteousness to a king's son.
Long may he live!
   May gold of Sheba be given to him.
May prayer be made for him continually,
   and blessings invoked for him all day long.
May there be abundance of grain in the land;
   may it wave on the tops of the mountains;
   may its fruit be like Lebanon;
and may people blossom in the cities
   like the grass of the field.
 May his name endure forever,
   his fame continue as long as the sun.
May all nations be blessed in him;
   may they pronounce him happy. (Ps. 72:1, 15-17)

Additional Readings:

1 Kings 10:1-13
Gifts to Solomon from Sheba

Ephesians 3:14-21
Knowing the love of Christ

Hymn: Jesus Shall Reign, ELW 434

How can we thank you, O God, for your gifts to us? Your gifts come to us new every day. Open our hearts and hands to share your bountiful goodness with all people, near and far, in your holy name.

Tuesday, January 8, 2008
TIME AFTER EPIPHANY

Ephesians 4:7, 11-16
Gifts according to Christ

But each of us was given grace according to the measure of Christ's gift.

The gifts he gave were that some would be apostles, some prophets, some evangelists, some pastors and teachers, to equip the saints for the work of ministry, for building up the body of Christ, until all of us come to the unity of the faith and of the knowledge of the Son of God, to maturity, to the measure of the full stature of Christ. (Eph. 4:7, 11-13)

Additional Readings:

1 Kings 10:14-25   Psalm 72
Solomon's splendor   *Prayers for the king*

Hymn: Lord, You Give the Great Commission, ELW 579

Sustaining Lord, you equip each of us with specific gifts for the building up of your kingdom. Grant us the wisdom to identify these gifts in ourselves and others, that your church may be empowered for service in your name.

Wednesday, January 9, 2008
TIME AFTER EPIPHANY

Luke 13:31-35
Jerusalem that kills the prophets

At that very hour some Pharisees came and said to him, "Get away from here, for Herod wants to kill you." He said to them, "Go and tell that fox for me, 'Listen, I am casting out demons and performing cures today and tomorrow, and on the third day I finish my work. Yet today, tomorrow, and the next day I must be on my way, because it is impossible for a prophet to be killed outside of Jerusalem.' Jerusalem, Jerusalem, the city that kills the prophets and stones those who are sent to it! How often have I desired to gather your children together as a hen gathers her brood under her wings, and you were not willing! See, your house is left to you. And I tell you, you will not see me until the time comes when you say, 'Blessed is the one who comes in the name of the Lord.'" (Luke 13:31-35)

Additional Readings:

Micah 5:2-9	Psalm 72
One who is to rule Israel	*Prayers for the king*

Hymn: When Twilight Comes, ELW 566

God of the ages, your word is at once powerful and gentle, ancient and new. Your children pull together and tear apart, loving each other and causing each other pain. Gather us under your wing, O Lord, and renew us.

Psalm 29
The voice of God upon the waters

Ascribe to the LORD, O heavenly beings,
  ascribe to the LORD glory and strength.
Ascribe to the LORD the glory of his name;
  worship the LORD in holy splendor.
The voice of the LORD is over the waters;
  the God of glory thunders,
  the LORD, over mighty waters.
The voice of the LORD is powerful;
  the voice of the LORD is full of majesty.
The voice of the LORD breaks the cedars;
  the LORD breaks the cedars of Lebanon.
(Ps. 29:1-5)

Additional Readings:

1 Samuel 3:1-9	Acts 9:1-9
Samuel, a boy, says	*Saul on the road to*
"Here I am"	*Damascus*

Hymn: Before You, Lord, We Bow, ELW 893

God, you called the young boy Samuel from his sleep, and you called Saul, the persecutor out his darkness—and their lives were never the same. Teach us to recognize your voice, and make us bold in following your commands.

Acts 9:10-19a
Ananias receives Saul into the church

The Lord said to him, "Get up and go to the street called Straight, and at the house of Judas look for a man of Tarsus named Saul. At this moment he is praying, and he has seen in a vision a man named Ananias come in and lay his hands on him so that he might regain his sight." But Ananias answered, "Lord, I have heard from many about this man, how much evil he has done to your saints in Jerusalem; and here he has authority from the chief priests to bind all who invoke your name." But the Lord said to him, "Go, for he is an instrument whom I have chosen to bring my name before Gentiles and kings and before the people of Israel." (Acts 9:11-15)

Additional Readings:

1 Samuel 3:10—4:1a
Samuel receives the word of God at Shiloh

Psalm 29
The voice of God upon the waters

Hymn: Amazing Grace, How Sweet the Sound, ELW 779

O God of truth, your light will always banish darkness. Let us never be afraid to speak your word in the face of opposition, for it is your power —not ours—that will save your children, through Christ our Lord.

1 Samuel 7:3-17
Samuel guides Israel to peace

Then Samuel took a stone and set it up between Mizpah and Jeshanah, and named it Ebenezer; for he said, "Thus far the LORD has helped us." So the Philistines were subdued and did not again enter the territory of Israel; the hand of the LORD was against the Philistines all the days of Samuel. The towns that the Philistines had taken from Israel were restored to Israel, from Ekron to Gath; and Israel recovered their territory from the hand of the Philistines. There was peace also between Israel and the Amorites. (1 Sam. 7:12-14)

Additional Readings:

Acts 9:19b-31
Barnabas introduces Saul/Paul in Jerusalem

Psalm 29
The voice of God upon the waters

Hymn: Come, Thou Fount of Every Blessing, ELW 807

Almighty God, you grace us with strength in the midst of turbulent days, and where you are, peace abides. Grant us the wisdom to recognize your presence in others, that we may never exclude others who also call you Lord.

Sunday, January 13, 2008
Baptism of Our Lord

Matthew 3:13-17
Christ revealed as God's servant

Then Jesus came from Galilee to John at the Jordan, to be baptized by him. John would have prevented him, saying, "I need to be baptized by you, and do you come to me?" But Jesus answered him, "Let it be so now; for it is proper for us in this way to fulfill all righteousness." Then he consented. And when Jesus had been baptized, just as he came up from the water, suddenly the heavens were opened to him and he saw the Spirit of God descending like a dove and alighting on him. And a voice from heaven said, "This is my Son, the Beloved, with whom I am well pleased." (Matt. 3:13-17)

Additional Readings:

Isaiah 42:1-9
The servant of God brings justice

Psalm 29
The voice of God upon the waters

Acts 10:34-43
Jesus' ministry after his baptism

Hymn: Christ, When for Us You Were Baptized, ELW 304

O God our Father, at the baptism of Jesus you proclaimed him your beloved Son and anointed him with the Holy Spirit. Make all who are baptized into Christ faithful to their calling to be your daughters and sons, and empower us all with your Spirit, through Jesus Christ, our Savior and Lord, who lives and reigns with you and the Holy Spirit, one God, now and forever.

Monday, January 14, 2008
Time after Epiphany

Psalm 89:5-37
God anoints David to be a son

Then you spoke in a vision to your faithful one, and said:
  "I have set the crown on one who is mighty,
  I have exalted one chosen from the people.
I have found my servant David;
  with my holy oil I have anointed him;
  my hand shall always remain with him;
my arm also shall strengthen him.
  The enemy shall not outwit him,
  the wicked shall not humble him.
I will crush his foes before him
  and strike down those who hate him."
(Ps. 89:19-23)

Additional Readings:

Genesis 35:1-15
God calls and blesses Jacob

Acts 10:44-48
*Through Peter, God calls
Gentiles to be baptized*

Hymn: Blessed Be the God of Israel, ELW 250

*All-knowing God, you raise up prophets and leaders according to your
own terms, not according to our prejudices. Grant us the discernment to
see each other through your eyes, that we may work together in harmony
as your church.*

Tuesday, January 15, 2008
TIME AFTER EPIPHANY

Martin Luther King Jr., renewer of society, martyr, 1968

Jeremiah 1:4-10
God calls Jeremiah

Now the word of the LORD came to me saying,
   "Before I formed you in the womb I knew you,
   and before you were born I consecrated you;
   I appointed you a prophet to the nations."
Then I said, "Ah, Lord GOD! Truly I do not know how to speak,
for I am only a boy." But the LORD said to me,
   "Do not say, 'I am only a boy';
   for you shall go to all to whom I send you,
   and you shall speak whatever I command you,
   Do not be afraid of them,
   for I am with you to deliver you,
   says the LORD." (Jer. 1:4-8)

Additional Readings:

Acts 8:4-13
Philip preaches and baptizes

Psalm 89:5-37
God anoints David to be a son

Hymn: Lord, Speak to Us, That We May Speak, ELW 676

You gave us your word, Father, and your great commission. Remembering the young man Stephen, the prophet Jeremiah, and the Rev. Martin Luther King Jr., we thank you for your promise to deliver your people, even when we face immense opposition.

Isaiah 51:1-16
Through water God's people cross over

Awake, awake, put on strength,
   O arm of the Lord!
Awake, as in days of old,
   the generations of long ago!
Was it not you who cut Rahab in pieces,
   who pierced the dragon?
Was it not you who dried up the sea,
   the waters of the great deep;
who made the depths of the sea a way
   for the redeemed to cross over?
So the ransomed of the Lord shall return,
   and come to Zion with singing;
everlasting joy shall be upon their heads;
   they shall obtain joy and gladness,
   and sorrow and sighing shall flee away. (Isa. 51:9-11)

Additional Readings:

Matthew 12:15-21
The words of Isaiah applied to Jesus

Psalm 89:5-37
God anoints David to be a son

Hymn: Come, We That Love the Lord, ELW 625

Compassionate God, through the ages you have delivered countless people from untold depths, always providing a way for us to come back to you. Inspire us to invite others into your welcoming arms, where they may dwell in safety.

Thursday, January 17, 2008
TIME AFTER EPIPHANY

Antony of Egypt, renewer of the church, c. 356
Pachomius, renewer of the church, 346

Psalm 40:1-11
Doing the will of God

I waited patiently for the LORD;
   he inclined to me and heard my cry.
He drew me up from the desolate pit,
   out of the miry bog,
and set my feet upon a rock,
   making my steps secure.
He put a new song in my mouth,
   a song of praise to our God.
Many will see and fear,
   and put their trust in the LORD.
You have multiplied, O LORD my God,
   your wondrous deeds and your thoughts toward us;
   none can compare with you.
Were I to proclaim and tell of them,
   they would be more than can be counted. (Ps. 40:1-3, 5)

Additional Readings:

Isaiah 22:15-25
God replaces disobedient leaders

Galatians 1:6-12
Paul's calling through a revelation of Christ

Hymn: Out of the Depths I Cry to You, ELW 600

O God, you are worthy of our thanks and praise, yet you invite us to bring you our fears and frustrations as well. We know that we are in your keeping, and there is no one better than you. Thank you for your love!

Friday, January 18, 2008
CONFESSION OF PETER

Week of Prayer for Christian Unity begins

Matthew 16:13-19
Peter confesses, You are the Messiah

He said to them, "But who do you say that I am?" Simon Peter answered, "You are the Messiah, the Son of the living God." And Jesus answered him, "Blessed are you, Simon son of Jonah! For flesh and blood has not revealed this to you, but my Father in heaven. And I tell you, you are Peter, and on this rock I will build my church, and the gates of Hades will not prevail against it. I will give you the keys of the kingdom of heaven, and whatever you bind on earth will be bound in heaven, and whatever you loose on earth will be loosed in heaven." (Matt. 16:15-19)

Additional Readings:

Acts 4:8-13
Salvation is in no one other than Jesus

Psalm 18:1-6, 16-19
My God, my rock, worthy of praise

1 Corinthians 10:1-5
Drinking from the spiritual rock of Christ

Hymn: Christ Is Made the Sure Foundation, ELW 645

Almighty God, you inspired Simon Peter to confess Jesus as the Messiah and Son of the living God. Keep your church firm on the rock of this faith, so that in unity and peace it may proclaim one truth and follow one Lord, your Son, Jesus Christ, our Savior, who lives and reigns with you and the Holy Spirit, one God, now and forever.

Saturday, January 19, 2008
TIME AFTER EPIPHANY

Henry, Bishop of Uppsala, martyr, 1156

1 Kings 19:19-21
Elijah calls Elisha to follow him

So he set out from there, and found Elisha son of Shaphat, who was plowing. There were twelve yoke of oxen ahead of him, and he was with the twelfth. Elijah passed by him and threw his mantle over him. He left the oxen, ran after Elijah, and said, "Let me kiss my father and my mother, and then I will follow you." Then Elijah said to him, "Go back again; for what have I done to you?" He returned from following him, took the yoke of oxen, and slaughtered them; using the equipment from the oxen, he boiled their flesh, and gave it to the people, and they ate. Then he set out and followed Elijah, and became his servant.
(1 Kings 19:19-21)

Additional Readings:
Luke 5:1-11 — Psalm 40:1-11
Jesus calls the first disciples — *Doing the will of God*

Hymn: Come, Follow Me, the Savior Spake, ELW 799

Welcoming God, every day you offer us your guiding hand, encouraging us to follow where you lead. Help us to rejoice in your invitation and keep our priorities in order, that we may follow you fearlessly and with willing hearts.

Sunday, January 20, 2008
SECOND SUNDAY AFTER EPIPHANY

John 1:29-42
Christ revealed as the Lamb of God

The next day he saw Jesus coming toward him and declared, "Here is the Lamb of God who takes away the sin of the world! This is he of whom I said, 'After me comes a man who ranks ahead of me because he was before me.' I myself did not know him; but I came baptizing with water for this reason, that he might be revealed to Israel." And John testified, "I saw the Spirit descending from heaven like a dove, and it remained on him. I myself did not know him, but the one who sent me to baptize with water said to me, 'He on whom you see the Spirit descend and remain is the one who baptizes with the Holy Spirit.' And I myself have seen and have testified that this is the Son of God." (John 1:29-34)

Additional Readings:

Isaiah 49:1-7
The servant brings light to the nations

Psalm 40:1-11
Doing the will of God

1 Corinthians 1:1-9
Paul's greeting to the church at Corinth

Hymn: Lamb of God, ELW 336

Holy God, our strength and our redeemer, by your Spirit hold us forever, that through your grace we may worship you and faithfully serve you, follow you and joyfully find you, through Jesus Christ, our Savior and Lord.

Monday, January 21, 2008
TIME AFTER EPIPHANY

Agnes, martyr, c. 304

Psalm 40:6-17
Not sacrifice, but divine mercy

Sacrifice and offering you do not desire,
   but you have given me an open ear.
Burnt offering and sin offering
   you have not required.
Then I said, "Here I am;
   in the scroll of the book it is written of me.
I delight to do your will, O my God;
   your law is within my heart." (Ps. 40:6-8)

Additional Readings:

Exodus 12:1-13, 21-28
The passover lamb

Acts 8:26-40
Philip teaches about the lamb

Hymn: Lord of Glory, You Have Bought Us, ELW 707

Life-giving God, when we consider the sacrifice you have made to bring us back to you, the reality brings us to our knees. How can you love us this much? You have redeemed us, and we are truly yours forever.

Hebrews 10:1-4
Animal sacrifices cannot take away sins

Since the law has only a shadow of the good things to come and not the true form of these realities, it can never, by the same sacrifices that are continually offered year after year, make perfect those who approach. Otherwise, would they not have ceased being offered, since the worshipers, cleansed once for all, would no longer have any consciousness of sin? But in these sacrifices there is a reminder of sin year after year. For it is impossible for the blood of bulls and goats to take away sins. (Heb. 10:1-4)

Additional Readings:

Isaiah 53:1-12
The one like a lamb

Psalm 40:6-17
Not sacrifice, but divine mercy

Hymn: Rock of Ages, Cleft for Me, ELW 623

Redeeming God, though we try to be self-sufficient, we know that we are helpless to save ourselves from sin. With all our hearts we thank you for providing the one sacrifice that overcomes everything that keeps us from you.

Isaiah 48:12-21
God saves the people through water

Thus says the LORD,
  your Redeemer, the Holy One of Israel:
I am the LORD your God,
  who teaches you for your own good,
  who leads you in the way you should go.
Go out from Babylon, flee from Chaldea,
  declare this with a shout of joy, proclaim it,
send it forth to the end of the earth;
  say, "The LORD has redeemed his servant Jacob!"
They did not thirst when he led them through the deserts;
  he made water flow for them from the rock;
  he split open the rock and the water gushed out. (Is. 48:17, 20-21)

Additional Readings:

Matthew 9:14-17
Christ, the bridegroom, the new wine

Psalm 40:6-17
Not sacrifice, but divine mercy

Hymn: When Peace, like a River, ELW 785

Lord, in your generosity you offer life-giving water. Inspire us to enjoy your grace and even to frolic in celebration of your goodness. May others be drenched with your gift of water as we welcome them with a joyful embrace.

Thursday, January 24, 2008
TIME AFTER EPIPHANY

Psalm 27:1-6
God is light and salvation

The LORD is my light and my salvation;
    whom shall I fear?
The LORD is the stronghold of my life;
    of whom shall I be afraid?
When evildoers assail me
    to devour my flesh—
my adversaries and foes—
    they shall stumble and fall.
Though an army encamp against me,
    my heart shall not fear;
though war rise up against me,
    yet I will be confident. (Ps. 27:1-3)

Additional Readings:

1 Samuel 1:1-20
The birth of Samuel

Galatians 1:11-24
The divine origin of Paul's gospel

Hymn: If God My Lord Be For Me, ELW 788

Loving God, our refuge and strength, we know that you are with always with us. When our world seems to crumble, keep us from doubting you. Keep us ever confident in your care, that we will never fear the future.

Friday, January 25, 2008
CONVERSION OF PAUL

Week of Prayer for Christian Unity ends

Galatians 1:11-24
Paul receives a revelation of Christ

You have heard, no doubt, of my earlier life in Judaism. I was violently persecuting the church of God and was trying to destroy it. I advanced in Judaism beyond many among my people of the same age, for I was far more zealous for the traditions of my ancestors. But when God, who had set me apart before I was born and called me through his grace, was pleased to reveal his Son to me, so that I might proclaim him among the Gentiles, I did not confer with any human being, nor did I go up to Jerusalem to those who were already apostles before me, but I went away at once into Arabia, and afterwards I returned to Damascus. (Gal. 1:13-17)

Additional Readings:

Acts 9:1-22
Saul is converted to Christ

Psalm 67
Let all the peoples praise you, O God

Luke 21:10-19
The end times will require endurance

Hymn: By All Your Saints, ELW 420 (stanza 8)

O God, *by the preaching of your apostle Paul you have caused the light of the gospel to shine throughout the world. Grant that we may follow his example and be witnesses to the truth of your Son, Jesus Christ, our Savior and Lord, who lives and reigns with you and the Holy Spirit, one God, now and forever.*

Saturday, January 26, 2008
TIME AFTER EPIPHANY

Timothy, Titus, and Silas, missionaries

Luke 5:27-32
The call of Levi

After this he went out and saw a tax collector named Levi, sitting at the tax booth; and he said to him, "Follow me." And he got up, left everything, and followed him.

Then Levi gave a great banquet for him in his house; and there was a large crowd of tax collectors and others sitting at the table with them. The Pharisees and their scribes were complaining to his disciples, saying, "Why do you eat and drink with tax collectors and sinners?" Jesus answered, "Those who are well have no need of a physician, but those who are sick; I have come to call not the righteous but sinners to repentance." (Luke 5:27-32)

Additional Readings:
1 Samuel 15:34—16:13   Psalm 27:1-6
David anointed as king to   *God is light and salvation*
replace King Saul

Hymn: Jesus Calls Us; o'er the Tumult, ELW 696

Beckoning Father, we are bombarded by voices calling us in all directions. Help us to listen for and recognize your voice. Give us wisdom to sit and hear your words, which give life to our very souls.

Sunday, January 27, 2008
THIRD SUNDAY AFTER EPIPHANY

Lydia, Dorcas, and Phoebe, witnesses to the faith

Matthew 4:12-23
Christ revealed as a prophet

Now when Jesus heard that John had been arrested, he withdrew to Galilee. He left Nazareth and made his home in Capernaum by the sea, in the territory of Zebulun and Naphtali, so that what had been spoken through the prophet Isaiah might be fulfilled:
    "Land of Zebulun, land of Naphtali,
        on the road by the sea, across the Jordan, Galilee of the
        Gentiles—
    the people who sat in darkness
        have seen a great light,
    and for those who sat in the region and shadow of death
        light has dawned." (Matt. 4:12-16)

Additional Readings:

Isaiah 9:1-4	Psalm 27:1, 4-9	1 Corinthians 1:10-18
Light shines for those in darkness	*God is light and salvation*	*An appeal for unity in the gospel*

Hymn: Light Shone in Darkness, ELW 307

Lord God, your lovingkindness always goes before us and follows after us. Summon us into your light, and direct our steps in the ways of goodness that come through the cross of your Son, Jesus Christ, our Savior and Lord.

Monday, January 28, 2008

Time after Epiphany

Thomas Aquinas, teacher, 1274

Psalm 27:7-14
Take courage in God

Teach me your way, O Lord,
   and lead me on a level path
   because of my enemies.
Do not give me up to the will of my adversaries,
   for false witnesses have risen against me,
   and they are breathing out violence.
I believe that I shall see the goodness of the Lord
   in the land of the living.
Wait for the Lord;
   be strong, and let your heart take courage;
   wait for the Lord! (Ps. 27:11-14)

Additional Readings:

Judges 6:11-24
*God calls Gideon to lead
the people*

Ephesians 5:6-14
Live as children of the light

Hymn: Lead Me, Guide Me, ELW 768

*You are our strength, O God. Without you we are lost. Remind us
daily that we are in your holy presence and that the only thing we need
fear is separation from you. Keep our eyes fixed on you.*

Tuesday, January 29, 2008
TIME AFTER EPIPHANY

Philippians 2:12-18
The call to shine like stars

Do all things without murmuring and arguing, so that you may be blameless and innocent, children of God without blemish in the midst of a crooked and perverse generation, in which you shine like stars in the world. It is by your holding fast to the word of life that I can boast on the day of Christ that I did not run in vain or labor in vain. But even if I am being poured out as a libation over the sacrifice and the offering of your faith, I am glad and rejoice with all of you— and in the same way you also must be glad and rejoice with me. (Phil. 2:14-18)

Additional Readings:

Judges 7:12-22
God leads Gideon to victory

Psalm 27:7-14
Take courage in God

Hymn: Rejoice in God's Saints, ELW 418

Father of light, through the ages your prophets, saints, and martyrs have taught us by their lives of dedication. Shine through us, too, that we may make a difference in the lives of others, encouraging them in your word.

Wednesday, January 30, 2008
Time after Epiphany

Luke 1:67-79
Christ, the light dawning

Then his father Zechariah was filled with the Holy Spirit and spoke this prophecy:

> And you, child, will be called the prophet of the Most High;
>> for you will go before the Lord to prepare his ways,
> to give knowledge of salvation to his people
>> by the forgiveness of their sins.
> By the tender mercy of our God,
>> the dawn from on high will break upon us,
> to give light to those who sit in darkness and in the shadow of death,
>> to guide our feet into the way of peace." (Luke 1:67, 76-79)

Additional Readings:

Genesis 49:1-2, 8-13, 21-26   Psalm 27:7-14
Judah, Zebulun, Naphtali,   *Take courage in God*
and Joseph blessed

Hymn: Blessed Be the God of Israel, ELW 552

Ever-living God, no darkness can overcome your light. There is no peace like that which you bestow, and no love is purer than yours. Let your truth burst forth from our lips to reach those who yearn to hear it.

Psalm 2
The one begotten of God

I will tell of the decree of the LORD:
He said to me, "You are my son;
   today I have begotten you.
Ask of me, and I will make the nations your heritage,
   and the ends of the earth your possession.
You shall break them with a rod of iron,
   and dash them in pieces like a potter's vessel."
Now therefore, O kings, be wise;
   be warned, O rulers of the earth.
Serve the LORD with fear,
   with trembling kiss his feet,
or he will be angry, and you will perish in the way;
   for his wrath is quickly kindled. (Ps. 2:7-12)

Additional Readings:

Exodus 6:2-9
God promises deliverance through Moses

Hebrews 8:1-7
Christ, the mediator

Hymn: Come, Thou Long-Expected Jesus, ELW 254

Almighty God, creator and ruler of the universe, the powers and divisions of this world melt away before your glory. We humbly thank you for calling us your children and showing us that nothing can separate us from your love.

~ Prayer list for February

Friday, February 1, 2008
Time after Epiphany

Hebrews 11:23-28
The faith of Moses

By faith Moses was hidden by his parents for three months after his birth, because they saw that the child was beautiful; and they were not afraid of the king's edict. By faith Moses, when he was grown up, refused to be called a son of Pharaoh's daughter, choosing rather to share ill-treatment with the people of God than to enjoy the fleeting pleasures of sin. He considered abuse suffered for the Christ to be greater wealth than the treasures of Egypt, for he was looking ahead to the reward. By faith he left Egypt, unafraid of the king's anger; for he persevered as though he saw him who is invisible. By faith he kept the Passover and the sprinkling of blood, so that the destroyer of the firstborn would not touch the firstborn of Israel. (Heb. 11:23-28)

Additional Readings:

Exodus 19:9b-25   Psalm 2
Israel consecrated at Sinai   *The one begotten of God*

Hymn: We've Come This Far by Faith, ELW 633

Mothering God, we turn to you for comfort and shelter when our fear is strong and our faith is weak. Guard our hearts from despair and remind us that we are participants in the ever-unfolding story of your faithful people.

Saturday, February 2, 2008
PRESENTATION OF OUR LORD

Luke 2:22-40
The child is brought to the temple

Simeon took him in his arms and praised God, saying,
"Master, now you are dismissing your servant in peace,
   according to your word;
for my eyes have seen your salvation,
   which you have prepared in the presence of all peoples,
a light for revelation to the Gentiles
   and for glory to your people Israel." (Luke 2:28-32)

Additional Readings:

Malachi 3:1-4
*My messenger, a refiner
and purifier*

Psalm 84
*How dear to me is your
dwelling, O LORD*

Hebrews 2:14-18
*Jesus shares human flesh
and sufferings*

Hymn: In His Temple Now Behold Him, ELW 417

*Almighty and ever-living God, your only-begotten Son was
presented this day in the temple. May we be presented to you with clean
and pure hearts by the same Jesus Christ our great high priest, who lives
and reigns with you and the Holy Spirit, one God, now and forever.*

Sunday, February 3, 2008
TRANSFIGURATION OF OUR LORD

Ansgar, Bishop of Hamburg, missionary to Denmark and Sweden, 865

Matthew 17:1-9
Christ revealed as God's beloved Son

Six days later, Jesus took with him Peter and James and his brother John and led them up a high mountain, by themselves. And he was transfigured before them, and his face shone like the sun, and his clothes became dazzling white. Suddenly there appeared to them Moses and Elijah, talking with him. Then Peter said to Jesus, "Lord, it is good for us to be here; if you wish, I will make three dwellings here, one for you, one for Moses, and one for Elijah." While he was still speaking, suddenly a bright cloud overshadowed them, and from the cloud a voice said, "This is my Son, the Beloved; with him I am well pleased; listen to him!" (Matt. 17:1-5)

Additional Readings:

Exodus 24:12-18	Psalm 2	2 Peter 1:16-21
Moses enters the cloud of God's glory	*The one begotten of God*	*Shining with the glory of God*

Hymn: Jesus on the Mountain Peak, ELW 317

O God, in the transfiguration of your Son you confirmed the mysteries of the faith by the witness of Moses and Elijah, and in the voice from the bright cloud declaring Jesus your beloved Son, you foreshadowed our adoption as your children. Make us heirs with Christ of your glory, and bring us to enjoy its fullness, through Jesus Christ, our Savior and Lord, who lives and reigns with you and the Holy Spirit, one God, now and forever.

Monday, February 4, 2008
TIME AFTER EPIPHANY

Psalm 78:17-20, 52-55
Israel led to God's holy mountain

Then he led out his people like sheep,
  and guided them in the wilderness like a flock.
He led them in safety, so that they were not afraid;
  but the sea overwhelmed their enemies.
And he brought them to his holy hill,
  to the mountain that his right hand had won.
He drove out nations before them;
  he apportioned them for a possession
  and settled the tribes of Israel in their tents.
(Ps. 78:52-55)

Additional Readings:

Exodus 33:7-23
Moses asks to see God's glory

Acts 7:30-34
Moses on holy ground

Hymn: O Lord, Now Let Your Servant, ELW 313

Settle us, Holy Lord. Settle us wherever we dwell: in streets, in tents, in huts, in high-rise apartments, or large houses. We ask, too, that you un-settle us so that may serve as passionate servants, reflecting your love for people without homes.

Tuesday, February 5, 2008
TIME AFTER EPIPHANY

The Martyrs of Japan, 1597

Romans 11:1-6
A remnant chosen by grace

I ask, then, has God rejected his people? By no means! I myself
am an Israelite, a descendant of Abraham, a member of the tribe
of Benjamin. God has not rejected his people whom he foreknew.
Do you not know what the scripture says of Elijah, how he pleads
with God against Israel? "Lord, they have killed your prophets,
they have demolished your altars; I alone am left, and they are
seeking my life." But what is the divine reply to him? "I have kept
for myself seven thousand who have not bowed the knee to Baal."
So too at the present time there is a remnant, chosen by grace.
(Rom. 11:1-5)

Additional Readings:

1 Kings 19:9-18   Psalm 78:17-20, 52-55
Elijah hears God   *Israel led to God's holy
                                      mountain*

Hymn: Through the Night of Doubt and Sorrow, ELW 327

*Shepherd, do we hear your gentle voice above the busy noises we make?
Grant us times of introspection to consider those whose lives speak to us
of selfless acts of service. Help us be grace-full.*

Wednesday, February 6, 2008
ASH WEDNESDAY

Matthew 6:1-6, 16-21
The practice of faith

"Do not store up for yourselves treasures on earth, where moth
and rust consume and where thieves break in and steal; but store
up for yourselves treasures in heaven, where neither moth nor
rust consumes and where thieves do not break in and steal. For
where your treasure is, there your heart will be also."
(Matt. 6:19-21)

Additional Readings:

Joel 2:1-2, 12-17
Return to God

Psalm 51:1-17
Plea for mercy

2 Corinthians 5:20b—6:10
Now is the day of salvation

Hymn: The Glory of These Forty Days, ELW 320

*Almighty and ever-living God, you hate nothing you have made,
and you forgive the sins of all who are penitent. Create in us new and
honest hearts, so that, truly repenting of our sins, we may receive from
you, the God of all mercy, full pardon and forgiveness through your Son,
Jesus Christ, our Savior and Lord, who lives and reigns with you and the
Holy Spirit, one God, now and forever.*

Thursday, February 7, 2008
Week before Lent 1

Psalm 51
Create in me a clean heart

Have mercy on me, O God,
  according to your steadfast love;
according to your abundant mercy
  blot out my transgressions.
Wash me thoroughly from my iniquity,
  and cleanse me from my sin.
For I know my transgressions,
  and my sin is ever before me.
Against you, you alone, have I sinned,
  and done what is evil in your sight,
so that you are justified in your sentence
  and blameless when you pass judgment.
Indeed, I was born guilty,
  a sinner when my mother conceived me.
(Ps. 51:1-5)

Additional Readings:

Jonah 3:1-10
*Nineveh hears Jonah's
preaching and repents*

Romans 1:1-7
*Appointed to preach the
good news of Christ*

Hymn: Lord, Teach Us How to Pray Aright, ELW 745

*O God, as we ask for mercy and forgiveness, remind us to be merciful
and forgiving to others. Thank you for this day that offers us a time to
renew our love for you and for one another. When we call on you, give
us listening hearts.*

Jonah 4:1-11
God mercifully reproves Jonah

But this was very displeasing to Jonah, and he became angry. He prayed to the LORD and said, "O LORD! Is not this what I said while I was still in my own country? That is why I fled to Tarshish at the beginning; for I knew that you are a gracious God and merciful, slow to anger, and abounding in steadfast love, and ready to relent from punishing. And now, O LORD, please take my life from me, for it is better for me to die than to live." And the LORD said, "Is it right for you to be angry?" Then Jonah went out of the city and sat down east of the city, and made a booth for himself there. He sat under it in the shade, waiting to see what would become of the city. (Jonah 4:1-5)

Additional Readings:

Romans 1:8-17
Live by faith

Psalm 51
Create in me a clean heart

Hymn: God, Whose Giving Knows No Ending, ELW 678

Holy God, despair and hopelessness hunt us down and turn our thoughts from you. When we are waiting to see your mercy and love in our darkest hours, give us faith sufficient to hold us through our doubts.

Isaiah 58:1-12
The fast that God chooses

Is not this the fast that I choose:
  to loose the bonds of injustice,
  to undo the thongs of the yoke,
to let the oppressed go free,
  and to break every yoke?
Is it not to share your bread with the hungry,
  and bring the homeless poor into your house;
when you see the naked, to cover them,
  and not to hide yourself from your own kin?
Then your light shall break forth like the dawn,
  and your healing shall spring up quickly;
your vindicator shall go before you,
  the glory of the LORD shall be your rear guard.
Then you shall call, and the LORD will answer;
  you shall cry for help, and he will say, Here I am.
(Isa. 58:6-9a)

Additional Readings:

Matthew 18:1-7   Psalm 51
The humble one is the   *Create in me a clean heart*
greatest

Hymn: To Be Your Presence, ELW 546

God of justice, this day many people are in need of your love. Help us to hear Isaiah's words and to work in our own communities to combat homelessness, poverty, and injustice. Begin your work through us today!

Sunday, February 10, 2008
FIRST SUNDAY IN LENT

Matthew 4:1-11
The temptation of Jesus

Then Jesus was led up by the Spirit into the wilderness to be
tempted by the devil. He fasted forty days and forty nights, and
afterwards he was famished. The tempter came and said to him,
"If you are the Son of God, command these stones to become
loaves of bread." But he answered, "It is written,

   'One does not live by bread alone,

      but by every word that comes from the mouth of God.'"

(Matt. 4:1-4)

Additional Readings:

Genesis 2:15-17; 3:1-7	Psalm 32	Romans 5:12-19
Eating of the tree of knowledge	*Mercy embraces us*	*Death came, life comes*

Hymn: O Lord, throughout These Forty Days, ELW 319

*Lord God, our strength, the struggle between good and evil rages within
and around us, and the devil and all the forces that defy you tempt us
with empty promises. Keep us steadfast in your word, and when we fall,
raise us again and restore us through your Son, Jesus Christ, our Savior
and Lord, who lives and reigns with you and the Holy Spirit, one God,
now and forever.*

Psalm 32
Mercy embraces us

Happy are those whose transgression is forgiven,
 whose sin is covered.
Happy are those to whom the LORD imputes no iniquity,
 and in whose spirit there is no deceit.
While I kept silence, my body wasted away
 through my groaning all day long.
For day and night your hand was heavy upon me;
 my strength was dried up as by the heat of summer.
Then I acknowledged my sin to you,
 and I did not hide my iniquity;
I said, "I will confess my transgressions to the LORD,"
 and you forgave the guilt of my sin. (Ps. 32:1-5)

Additional Readings:

1 Kings 19:1-8	Hebrews 2:10-18
An angel feeds Elijah in the wilderness	*Christ goes before us in suffering*

Hymn: God, My Lord, My Strength, ELW 795

Forgiving God, *let us welcome your love this day in the form of the angels you send to us. When we are suffering, let us appreciate you in everything that brings sanity to our chaos. Help us see you in small but precious gifts.*

Tuesday, February 12, 2008
WEEK OF LENT 1

Hebrews 4:14—5:10
Christ was tempted as we are

Since, then, we have a great high priest who has passed through the heavens, Jesus, the Son of God, let us hold fast to our confession. For we do not have a high priest who is unable to sympathize with our weaknesses, but we have one who in every respect has been tested as we are, yet without sin. Let us therefore approach the throne of grace with boldness, so that we may receive mercy and find grace to help in time of need. (Heb. 4:14-16)

Additional Readings:

Genesis 4:1-16   Psalm 32
God protects Cain   *Mercy embraces us*

Hymn: Lord Jesus, Think on Me, ELW 599

When we are tempted to be lukewarm in our faith, O God, help us to remember Jesus, whose heart blazed for you. Consider us as we journey on our way, seeking the answers we need to live and serve you boldly.

Wednesday, February 13, 2008
WEEK OF LENT 1

Matthew 18:10-14
Not one of these little ones should be lost

"Take care that you do not despise one of these little ones; for,
I tell you, in heaven their angels continually see the face of
my Father in heaven. What do you think? If a shepherd has a
hundred sheep, and one of them has gone astray, does he not
leave the ninety-nine on the mountains and go in search of
the one that went astray? And if he finds it, truly I tell you, he
rejoices over it more than over the ninety-nine that never went
astray. So it is not the will of your Father in heaven that one of
these little ones should be lost." (Matt. 18:10-14)

Additional Readings:
Exodus 34:1-9, 27-28   Psalm 32
God's revelation of mercy   *Mercy embraces us*

Hymn: Have No Fear, Little Flock, ELW 764

*Searching God, there are so many ways we feel lost. Help us to see you
in the faces of those we hate, and guide us in ways of showing kindness
to all our brothers and sisters throughout the world who are in need of
rescue.*

Thursday, February 14, 2008
WEEK OF LENT 1

Cyril, monk, 869; Methodius, bishop, 885; missionaries to the Slavs

Psalm 121
The Lord watches over you

The LORD is your keeper;
   the LORD is your shade at your right hand.
The sun shall not strike you by day,
   nor the moon by night.
The LORD will keep you from all evil;
   he will keep your life.
The LORD will keep
   your going out and your coming in
   from this time on and forevermore. (Ps. 121:5-8)

Additional Readings:

Isaiah 51:1-3	2 Timothy 1:3-7
Look to Abraham and	*Faith handed down from*
Sarah	*faithful mothers*

Hymn: Glorious Things of You Are Spoken, ELW 647

Nurturing God, this day we consider your servants Sarah and Abraham. While their faith brought forth a nation, it is Sarah's laughter that reminds us of our humanity. Bring to birth great things in us as well!

Friday, February 15, 2008
WEEK OF LENT 1

Micah 7:18-20
God's faithfulness

Who is a God like you, pardoning iniquity
   and passing over the transgression
   of the remnant of your possession?
He does not retain his anger forever,
   because he delights in showing clemency.
He will again have compassion upon us;
   he will tread our iniquities under foot.
You will cast all our sins
   into the depths of the sea.
You will show faithfulness to Jacob
   and unswerving loyalty to Abraham,
as you have sworn to our ancestors
   from the days of old. (Micah 7:18-20)

Additional Readings:

Romans 3:21-31   Psalm 121
Paul relates law and faith   The Lord watches over you

Hymn: If You But Trust in God to Guide You, ELW 769

*How thankful we are that you grant us mercy, O God! What would
we do without your compassion? What will the people in our lives do
without our compassion? Soften our hearts and inspire compassion in
us.*

Isaiah 51:4-8
God's word means justice for all

Listen to me, my people,
    and give heed to me, my nation;
for a teaching will go out from me,
    and my justice for a light to the peoples.
Listen to me, you who know righteousness,
    you people who have my teaching in your hearts;
do not fear the reproach of others,
    and do not be dismayed when they revile you.
For the moth will eat them up like a garment,
    and the worm will eat them like wool;
but my deliverance will be forever,
    and my salvation to all generations. (Isa. 51:4, 7-8)

Additional Readings:

Luke 7:1-10
Room at the table of Abraham

Psalm 121
The Lord watches over you

Hymn: O God of Light, ELW 507

Do we not have your teaching in our hearts, Lord? We give up on making a difference when we see rampant injustice. Too easily we become afraid and dismayed. Today give us the courage and spirit to bear witness to your teachings.

Sunday, February 17, 2008
SECOND SUNDAY IN LENT

John 3:1-17
The mission of Christ: saving the world

And just as Moses lifted up the serpent in the wilderness, so must the Son of Man be lifted up, that whoever believes in him may have eternal life. "For God so loved the world that he gave his only Son, so that everyone who believes in him may not perish but may have eternal life. "Indeed, God did not send the Son into the world to condemn the world, but in order that the world might be saved through him." (John 3:14-17)

Additional Readings:

Genesis 12:1-4a	Psalm 121	Romans 4:1-5, 13-17
The blessing of God upon Abram	*The Lord watches over you*	*The promise to those of Abraham's faith*

Hymn: God Loved the World, ELW 323

O God, our leader and guide, in the waters of baptism you bring us to new birth to live as your children. Strengthen our faith in your promises, that by your Spirit we may lift up your life to all the world through your Son, Jesus Christ, our Savior and Lord, who lives and reigns with you and the Holy Spirit, one God, now and forever.

Monday, February 18, 2008
WEEK OF LENT 2

Martin Luther, renewer of the church, 1546

Psalm 128
God promises life

Happy is everyone who fears the LORD,
  who walks in his ways.
You shall eat the fruit of the labor of your hands;
  you shall be happy, and it shall go well with you.
Your wife will be like a fruitful vine
  within your house;
your children will be like olive shoots
  around your table.
Thus shall the man be blessed
  who fears the LORD. (Ps. 128:1-4)

Additional Readings:

Numbers 21:4-9   Hebrews 3:1-6
Moses lifts up the serpent   *Moses the servant, Christ the son*

Hymn: What a Fellowship, What a Joy Divine, ELW 774

God, we ask your blessing on those who are not blessed with the support and care of family or friends. Help us to be servants to all those who do not yet know you or who need the fellowship and mercy of your people.

Tuesday, February 19, 2008
WEEK OF LENT 2

Isaiah 65:17-25
God promises a new creation

For I am about to create new heavens
    and a new earth;
the former things shall not be remembered
    or come to mind.
But be glad and rejoice forever
    in what I am creating;
for I am about to create Jerusalem as a joy,
    and its people as a delight.
I will rejoice in Jerusalem,
    and delight in my people;
no more shall the sound of weeping be heard in it,
    or the cry of distress. (Isa. 65:17-19)

Additional Readings:

Romans 4:6-13
Abraham saved through faith

Psalm 128
God promises life

Hymn: Jerusalem, My Happy Home, ELW 628

Life-giving God, help us listen today for the sounds of weeping and the cries of distress. Make us to be your heart and hands so that we, through your love, might be signs of your earthly presence.

John 7:53 — 8:11
Jesus does not condemn the sinner

The scribes and the Pharisees brought a woman who had been caught in adultery; and making her stand before all of them, they said to him, "Teacher, this woman was caught in the very act of committing adultery. Now in the law Moses commanded us to stone such women. Now what do you say?" They said this to test him, so that they might have some charge to bring against him. Jesus bent down and wrote with his finger on the ground. When they kept on questioning him, he straightened up and said to them, "Let anyone among you who is without sin be the first to throw a stone at her." (John 8:3-7)

Additional Readings:

Ezekiel 36:22-32   Psalm 128
God will renew the people   *God promises life*

Hymn: Softly and Tenderly Jesus Is Calling, ELW 608

Forgiving God, how is it that we are so ready to condemn others even when we are obviously convicted of wrongful behavior ourselves? Help us to refrain from questioning your mercy and imposing our own moral judgments on the lives of others.

Thursday, February 21, 2008
Week of Lent 2

Psalm 95
The rock of our salvation

O come, let us sing to the LORD;
  let us make a joyful noise to the rock of our salvation!
Let us come into his presence with thanksgiving;
  let us make a joyful noise to him with songs of praise!
For the LORD is a great God,
  and a great King above all gods.
In his hand are the depths of the earth;
  the heights of the mountains are his also.
The sea is his, for he made it,
  and the dry land, which his hands have formed.
(Ps. 95:1-5)

Additional Readings:

Exodus 16:1-8
*Israel complains of hunger
in the wilderness*

Colossians 1:15-23
*Christ, the reconciliation of
all things*

Hymn: Let All Things Now Living, ELW 881

*Creating God, give us eyes this day to see the wonder of what you have
made. Help us to appreciate the awesome beauty in everything that lives
and breathes and moves around us.*

Ephesians 2:11-22
Christ, the reconciliation of Jew and Gentile

So then, remember that at one time you Gentiles by birth, called "the uncircumcision" by those who are called "the circumcision"—a physical circumcision made in the flesh by human hands—remember that you were at that time without Christ, being aliens from the commonwealth of Israel, and strangers to the covenants of promise, having no hope and without God in the world. But now in Christ Jesus you who once were far off have been brought near by the blood of Christ. For he is our peace; in his flesh he has made both groups into one and has broken down the dividing wall, that is, the hostility between us. (Eph. 2:11-14)

Additional Readings:

Exodus 16:9-21
God gives manna and quail

Psalm 95
The rock of our salvation

Hymn: Oh, Praise the Gracious Power, ELW 651

Uniting God, how often do we build walls and encourage divisions within our own families and communities. Remind us to consider important only those issues of eternal value and to grant our restless souls peace.

Saturday, February 23, 2008
WEEK OF LENT 2

Polycarp, Bishop of Smyrna, martyr, 156

Exodus 16:27-35
Manna and the sabbath

On the seventh day some of the people went out to gather, and they found none. The LORD said to Moses, "How long will you refuse to keep my commandments and instructions? See! The LORD has given you the sabbath, therefore on the sixth day he gives you food for two days; each of you stay where you are; do not leave your place on the seventh day." So the people rested on the seventh day. (Exod. 16:27-30)

Additional Readings:

John 4:1-6
Jesus travels to Jacob's well in Samaria

Psalm 95
The rock of our salvation

Hymn: O Day of Rest and Gladness, ELW 521

Give us holy rest in you, O Merciful One. We often clutter our lives with too much doing. Help us recognize that even without our efforts you are as close to us as our breath.

Sunday, February 24, 2008
Third Sunday in Lent

John 4:5-42
The woman at the well

Jesus said to [the Samaritan woman], "Everyone who drinks of this water will be thirsty again, but those who drink of the water that I will give them will never be thirsty. The water that I will give will become in them a spring of water gushing up to eternal life." The woman said to him, "Sir, give me this water, so that I may never be thirsty or have to keep coming here to draw water." (John 4:13-15)

Additional Readings:

Exodus 17:1-7	Psalm 95	Romans 5:1-11
Water from the rock	*The rock of our salvation*	*Reconciled to God by Christ's death*

Hymn: Come to Me, All Pilgrims Thirsty, ELW 777

Merciful God, the fountain of living water, you quench our thirst and wash away our sin. Give us this water always. Bring us to drink from the well that flows with the beauty of your truth through Jesus Christ, our Savior and Lord, who lives and reigns with you and the Holy Spirit, one God, now and forever.

Monday, February 25, 2008
WEEK OF LENT 3

Elizabeth Fedde, deaconess, 1921

Psalm 81
We drink from the rock

"But my people did not listen to my voice;
  Israel would not submit to me.
So I gave them over to their stubborn hearts,
  to follow their own counsels.
O that my people would listen to me,
  that Israel would walk in my ways!
Then I would quickly subdue their enemies,
  and turn my hand against their foes.
Those who hate the LORD would cringe before him,
  and their doom would last forever.
I would feed you with the finest of the wheat,
  and with honey from the rock I would satisfy you."
(Ps. 81:11-16)

Additional Readings:

Genesis 24:1-27   2 John 1-13
Rebekah at the well   *A woman reminded to*
                           abide in Christ

Hymn: You Satisfy the Hungry Heart, ELW 484

God, we forget that we belong to a great cloud of witnesses who have kept the faith. Help us to hear your voice in the lives of our spiritual ancestors and to walk in the ways that are most fitting for us today.

1 Corinthians 10:1-4
Drinking from Christ, the spiritual rock

I do not want you to be unaware, brothers and sisters, that our ancestors were all under the cloud, and all passed through the sea, and all were baptized into Moses in the cloud and in the sea, and all ate the same spiritual food, and all drank the same spiritual drink. For they drank from the spiritual rock that followed them, and the rock was Christ. (1 Cor. 10:1-4)

Additional Readings:

Genesis 29:1-14   Psalm 81
Rachel at the well   *We drink from the rock*

Hymn: O Jesus, Joy of Loving Hearts, ELW 658

Thirst-quenching God, today we consider what we need in order for your spirit to be renewed within us. During our Lenten journey, show us your food and drink that have been set out abundantly in our midst.

Wednesday, February 27, 2008
WEEK OF LENT 3

John 7:14-31, 37-39
Drink of Jesus, the Messiah

On the last day of the festival, the great day, while Jesus was standing there, he cried out, "Let anyone who is thirsty come to me, and let the one who believes in me drink. As the scripture has said, 'Out of the believer's heart shall flow rivers of living water.'" Now he said this about the Spirit, which believers in him were to receive; for as yet there was no Spirit, because Jesus was not yet glorified. (John 7:37-39)

Additional Readings:

Jeremiah 2:4-13   Psalm 81
God, the living water   *We drink from the rock*

Hymn: As the Deer Runs to the River, ELW 331

God, how important it is that we hear when you cry out to us, rather than being distracted by petty concerns and foolish needs. Shout at us above the clamor of our daily lives so that we may find your peace.

Thursday, February 28, 2008

WEEK OF LENT 3

Psalm 23
My head anointed with oil

Even though I walk through the darkest valley,
   I fear no evil;
for you are with me;
   your rod and your staff—
   they comfort me.
You prepare a table before me
   in the presence of my enemies;
you anoint my head with oil;
   my cup overflows.
Surely goodness and mercy shall follow me
   all the days of my life,
and I shall dwell in the house of the LORD
   my whole life long. (Ps. 23:4-6)

Additional Readings:

1 Samuel 15:10-21
*The prophet Samuel
confronts the king*

Ephesians 4:25-32
*Called to honesty and
forbearance*

Hymn: My Shepherd, You Supply My Need, ELW 782

*Merciful God, we call out to you in thankfulness this day. When your
mercy and goodness seem elusive, focus our eyes on the everyday graces
to which we are blind. Thank you for the gift of faith; may it be renewed
in us every day!*

Ephesians 5:1-9
Now in the Lord you are light

Let no one deceive you with empty words, for because of these things the wrath of God comes on those who are disobedient. Therefore do not be associated with them. For once you were darkness, but now in the Lord you are light. Live as children of light—for the fruit of the light is found in all that is good and right and true. (Eph. 5:6-9)

Additional Readings:

1 Samuel 15:22-31
The king confesses his sinful disobedience

Psalm 23
My head anointed with oil

Hymn: I Want to Walk as a Child of the Light, ELW 815

The gift of your words is our delight! The promise we have as children of the light is both a blessing and a call to action. Lead us to be good and right and true, and help us to live in ways that will honor you.

Prayer list for March

Saturday, March 1, 2008
WEEK OF LENT 3

George Herbert, hymnwriter, 1633

1 Samuel 15:32-34
Samuel grieves over Saul

Then Samuel said, "Bring Agag king of the Amalekites here to me." And Agag came to him haltingly. Agag said, "Surely this is the bitterness of death." But Samuel said,

"As your sword has made women childless,
    so your mother shall be childless among women."

And Samuel hewed Agag in pieces before the LORD in Gilgal. Then Samuel went to Ramah; and Saul went up to his house in Gibeah of Saul. (1 Sam. 15:32-34)

Additional Readings:

John 1:1-9
Christ comes with light and life

Psalm 23
My head anointed with oil

Hymn: The Only Son from Heaven, ELW 309

Lord, swords of war, poverty, violence, and hunger sever children from family, home, and innocence. Grant us faith to follow the Child of Mary, who tasted the bitterness of violence and yet broke its power that nothing may sever us from you.

Sunday, March 2, 2008
Fourth Sunday in Lent

John Wesley, 1791; Charles Wesley, 1788; renewers of the church

John 9:1-41
The man born blind

Jesus heard that they had driven [out the man who had been blind], and when he found him, he said, "Do you believe in the Son of Man?" He answered, "And who is he, sir? Tell me, so that I may believe in him." Jesus said to him, "You have seen him, and the one speaking with you is he." He said, "Lord, I believe." And he worshiped him. Jesus said, "I came into this world for judgment so that those who do not see may see, and those who do see may become blind." (John 9:35-39)

Additional Readings:

1 Samuel 16:1-13	Psalm 23	Ephesians 5:8-14
David is chosen and anointed	*My head anointed with oil*	*Live as children of light*

Hymn: Be Thou My Vision, ELW 793

Bend your ear to our prayers, Lord Christ, and come among us. By your gracious life and death for us, bring light into the darkness of our hearts, and anoint us with your Spirit, for you live and reign with the Father and the Holy Spirit, one God, now and forever.

Monday, March 3, 2008
Week of Lent 4

Psalm 146
God opens the eyes of the blind

The Lord sets the prisoners free;
   the Lord opens the eyes of the blind.
The Lord lifts up those who are bowed down;
   the Lord loves the righteous.
The Lord watches over the strangers;
   he upholds the orphan and the widow,
   but the way of the wicked he brings to ruin.
The Lord will reign forever,
   your God, O Zion, for all generations.
Praise the Lord! (Ps. 146:7c-10)

Additional Readings:

Isaiah 59:9-19
The blindness of injustice

Acts 9:1-20
Saul is baptized, his sight restored

Hymn: Praise the One Who Breaks the Darkness, ELW 843

In this world where we see so much and understand so little, focus us, Lord, on your presence in word and sacrament, that we become your visible presence in places desperate for your healing and wholeness.

Tuesday, March 4, 2008
Week of Lent 4

Isaiah 42:14-21
God will heal the blind

For a long time I have held my peace,
      I have kept still and restrained myself;
now I will cry out like a woman in labor,
      I will gasp and pant.
I will lay waste mountains and hills,
      and dry up all their herbage;
I will turn the rivers into islands,
      and dry up the pools.
I will lead the blind
      by a road they do not know,
   by paths they have not known
      I will guide them.
I will turn the darkness before them into light,
      the rough places into level ground.
   These are the things I will do,
      and I will not forsake them. (Isa. 42:14-16)

Additional Readings:

Colossians 1:9-14
The inheritance of the saints in light

Psalm 146
God opens the eyes of the blind

Hymn: In Deepest Night, ELW 699

Lord, you offer us more than mere knowledge of times and seasons. You walk with us in journeys not yet taken and paths not yet charted. Guide our uncertainty to joyous trust. Surprise us and open our very lives to see what we have not seen before.

Wednesday, March 5, 2008
WEEK OF LENT 4

Matthew 9:27-34
Jesus heals the blind

As Jesus went on from there, two blind men followed him, crying loudly, "Have mercy on us, Son of David!" When he entered the house, the blind men came to him; and Jesus said to them, "Do you believe that I am able to do this?" They said to him, "Yes, Lord." Then he touched their eyes and said, "According to your faith let it be done to you." And their eyes were opened. Then Jesus sternly ordered them, "See that no one knows of this." But they went away and spread the news about him throughout that district. (Matt. 9:27-31)

Additional Readings:

Isaiah 60:17-22
God our light

Psalm 146
God opens the eyes of the blind

Hymn: You Are Mine, ELW 581

Help us, God, that when your ways are unclear and your will is clouded, we still see what you promise, walk unerringly in your commands, and open the eyes of others with our thanksgiving and praise to you.

Psalm 130
Mercy and redemption

Out of the depths I cry to you, O Lord.
    Lord, hear my voice!
Let your ears be attentive
    to the voice of my supplications!
If you, O Lord, should mark iniquities,
    Lord, who could stand?
But there is forgiveness with you,
    so that you may be revered. (Ps. 130:1-4)

Additional Readings:

Ezekiel 1:1-3; 2:8—3:3
The word of God: lamentation and sweetness

Revelation 10:1-11
The word of God: bitter and sweet

Hymn: Out of the Depths I Cry to You, ELW 600

Gracious Lord, when we are tempted to believe that the numbers of our sins, assets, years, or our problems define us, guide us to trust that what truly counts is our being your sons and daughters through your Son, Jesus Christ.

Friday, March 7, 2008
WEEK OF LENT 4

Perpetua and Felicity and companions, martyrs at Carthage, 202

Revelation 11:15-19
The word of God: thanksgiving and singing

Then the twenty-four elders who sit on their thrones before God
fell on their faces and worshiped God, singing,
    "We give you thanks, Lord God Almighty,
        who are and who were,
    for you have taken your great power
        and begun to reign.
    The nations raged,
        but your wrath has come,
        and the time for judging the dead,
    for rewarding your servants, the prophets
        and saints and all who fear your name,
        both small and great,
    and for destroying those who destroy the earth."
Then God's temple in heaven was opened, and the ark of his
covenant was seen within his temple; and there were flashes of
lightning, rumblings, peals of thunder, an earthquake, and heavy
hail. (Rev. 11:16-19)

Additional Readings:

Ezekiel 33:10-16	Psalm 130
The word of God: repent and live	*Mercy and redemption*

Hymn: Blessing and Honor, ELW 854

*Saving God, as the vision of the empty tomb sustained the early church
in times of persecution, unite believers everywhere in the hope that fires
of destruction will give way to the brilliance of your restoration through
Jesus Christ.*

Saturday, March 8, 2008
Week of Lent 4

Ezekiel 36:8-15
Blessings upon Israel

But you, O mountains of Israel, shall shoot out your branches, and yield your fruit to my people Israel; for they shall soon come home. See now, I am for you; I will turn to you, and you shall be tilled and sown; and I will multiply your population, the whole house of Israel, all of it; the towns shall be inhabited and the waste places rebuilt; and I will multiply human beings and animals upon you. They shall increase and be fruitful; and I will cause you to be inhabited as in your former times, and will do more good to you than ever before. Then you shall know that I am the Lord. I will lead people upon you—my people Israel— and they shall possess you, and you shall be their inheritance. No longer shall you bereave them of children. (Ezek. 36:8-12)

Additional Readings:

Luke 24:44-53
Jesus blesses the disciples

Psalm 130
Mercy and redemption

Hymn: Open Now Thy Gates of Beauty, ELW 533

Gracious Lord, you continually call us to return to you. Instead of shaming us, your welcome enfolds us; instead of a grudging morsel, you feed us richly; instead of exposing the wastes of our mistakes, you restore us so that all might know your love.

Sunday, March 9, 2008
Fifth Sunday in Lent

John 11:1-45
The raising of Lazarus

And Jesus looked upward and said, "Father, I thank you for having heard me. I knew that you always hear me, but I have said this for the sake of the crowd standing here, so that they may believe that you sent me." When he had said this, he cried with a loud voice, "Lazarus, come out!" The dead man came out, his hands and feet bound with strips of cloth, and his face wrapped in a cloth. Jesus said to them, "Unbind him, and let him go."

Many of the Jews therefore, who had come with Mary and had seen what Jesus did, believed in him. (John 11:41b-45)

Additional Readings:

Ezekiel 37:1-14	Psalm 130	Romans 8:6-11
The dry bones of Israel	*Mercy and redemption*	*Life in the Spirit*

Hymn: When We Are Living, ELW 639

Almighty God, your Son came into the world to free us all from sin and death. Breathe upon us the power of your Spirit, that we may be raised to new life in Christ and serve you in righteousness all our days, through Jesus Christ, our Savior and Lord, who lives and reigns with you and the Holy Spirit, one God, now and forever.

Monday, March 10, 2008
WEEK OF LENT 5

Harriet Tubman, 1913; Sojourner Truth, 1883; renewers of society

Psalm 143
Save me from death

Save me, O LORD, from my enemies;
  I have fled to you for refuge.
Teach me to do your will,
  for you are my God.
Let your good spirit lead me
  on a level path.
For your name's sake, O LORD, preserve my life.
  In your righteousness bring me out of trouble.
In your steadfast love cut off my enemies,
  and destroy all my adversaries,
  for I am your servant. (Ps. 143:9-12)

Additional Readings:

1 Kings 17:17-24	Acts 20:7-12
Elijah raises the widow's son	*Paul raises a young man*

Hymn: Lord of Our Life, ELW 766

Prince of peace, inspire us to pray for a world that holds on to harmful grievances. Guide hands folded in prayer to reach out to others in reconciliation. Shape us to do your will in the midst of danger and harm.

2 Kings 4:18-37
Elisha raises a child from death

When Elisha came into the house, he saw the child lying dead on his bed. So he went in and closed the door on the two of them, and prayed to the LORD. Then he got up on the bed and lay upon the child, putting his mouth upon his mouth, his eyes upon his eyes, and his hands upon his hands; and while he lay bent over him, the flesh of the child became warm. He got down, walked once to and fro in the room, then got up again and bent over him; the child sneezed seven times, and the child opened his eyes. Elisha summoned Gehazi and said, "Call the Shunammite woman." So he called her. When she came to him, he said, "Take your son." She came and fell at his feet, bowing to the ground; then she took her son and left. (2 Kings 4:32-37)

Additional Readings:

Ephesians 2:1-10   Psalm 143
Alive in Christ   *Save me from death*

Hymn: O God beyond All Praising, ELW 880

God, embolden us to be prophets to those who are led away from you and your gracious community. Give us words to recount stories of your presence amid our own fears, that a new generation might also live as your beloved children.

Wednesday, March 12, 2008
WEEK OF LENT 5

Gregory the Great, Bishop of Rome, 604

Jeremiah 32:1-9, 36-41
Jeremiah buys a field

Jeremiah said, The word of the LORD came to me: Hanamel son of your uncle Shallum is going to come to you and say, "Buy my field that is at Anathoth, for the right of redemption by purchase is yours." Then my cousin Hanamel came to me in the court of the guard, in accordance with the word of the LORD, and said to me, "Buy my field that is at Anathoth in the land of Benjamin, for the right of possession and redemption is yours; buy it for yourself." Then I knew that this was the word of the LORD. (Jer. 32:6-8)

Additional Readings:

Matthew 22:23-33   Psalm 143
God of the living   *Save me from death*

Hymn: Jesus, Priceless Treasure, ELW 775

We give you thanks, gracious Lord, that your Spirit inspired the life of Gregory, bishop of Rome, who chose the simple life of a monk, blessed the church with forthright preaching and music, and gave witness to his faith within the world of his day.

Psalm 31:9-16
I commend my spirit

Be gracious to me, O LORD, for I am in distress;
    my eye wastes away from grief,
    my soul and body also.
For my life is spent with sorrow,
    and my years with sighing;
my strength fails because of my misery,
    and my bones waste away.
But I trust in you, O LORD;
    I say, "You are my God."
My times are in your hand;
    deliver me from the hand of my enemies and persecutors.
Let your face shine upon your servant;
    save me in your steadfast love. (Ps. 31:9-10, 14-16)

Additional Readings:

1 Samuel 16:11-13   Philippians 1:1-11
Samuel anoints David   *Encouraged to follow*
                           Christ's righteousness

Hymn: Jesus, Still Lead On, ELW 624

Lord, through Christ's crucifixion, you know that long hours of suffering and grief test our bodies and spirits to the point of despair. When our days are dark, may your face shine like a star in our midst that we might serve you in faith and hope.

Friday, March 14, 2008
WEEK OF LENT 5

Philippians 1:21-30
Seeing Christ in this life

Only, live your life in a manner worthy of the gospel of Christ, so that, whether I come and see you or am absent and hear about you, I will know that you are standing firm in one spirit, striving side by side with one mind for the faith of the gospel, and are in no way intimidated by your opponents. For them this is evidence of their destruction, but of your salvation. And this is God's doing. For he has graciously granted you the privilege not only of believing in Christ, but of suffering for him as well—since you are having the same struggle that you saw I had and now hear that I still have. (Phil. 1:27-30)

Additional Readings:

Job 13:13-19   Psalm 31:9-16
A servant keeps silence   *I commend my spirit*

Hymn: Give Thanks for Saints, ELW 428

Lord of wisdom, where faith is ridiculed and rejected, create in us a convincing witness to the saving power of the gospel, that amid the struggles that come to all the faithful, your church may stand united in its confession of faith.

Mark 10:32-34
Going up to Jerusalem

They were on the road, going up to Jerusalem, and Jesus was walking ahead of them; they were amazed, and those who followed were afraid. He took the twelve aside again and began to tell them what was to happen to him, saying, "See, we are going up to Jerusalem, and the Son of Man will be handed over to the chief priests and the scribes, and they will condemn him to death; then they will hand him over to the Gentiles; they will mock him, and spit upon him, and flog him, and kill him; and after three days he will rise again." (Mark 10:32-34)

Additional Readings:

Lamentations 3:55-66	Psalm 31:9-16
A cry for help	*I commend my spirit*

Hymn: Tree of Life and Awesome Mystery, ELW 334

Lord, dread fills us when our identity as your daughters and sons is tested and our faith is assailed. By the presence of Jesus, keep us steadfast in your word, and feed us with your meal that offers forgiveness, life, and salvation to all who believe.

Sunday, March 16, 2008
SUNDAY OF THE PASSION

Palm Sunday

Matthew 26:14—27:66 or Matthew 27:11-54
The passion and death of Jesus

Then Jesus cried again with a loud voice and breathed his last. At that moment the curtain of the temple was torn in two, from top to bottom. The earth shook, and the rocks were split. The tombs also were opened, and many bodies of the saints who had fallen asleep were raised. After his resurrection they came out of the tombs and entered the holy city and appeared to many. Now when the centurion and those with him, who were keeping watch over Jesus, saw the earthquake and what took place, they were terrified and said, "Truly this man was God's Son!" (Matt. 27:50-54)

Additional Readings:

Isaiah 50:4-9a	Psalm 31:9-16	Philippians 2:5-11
The servant submits to suffering	*I commend my spirit*	*Death on a cross*

Hymn: Sing, My Tongue, ELW 355/356

Everlasting God, in your endless love for the human race you sent our Lord Jesus Christ to take on our nature and to suffer death on the cross. In your mercy enable us to share in his obedience to your will and in the glorious victory of his resurrection, who lives and reigns with you and the Holy Spirit, one God, now and forever.

Monday, March 17, 2008
MONDAY IN HOLY WEEK

Patrick, bishop, missionary to Ireland, 461

Psalm 36:5-11
Refuge under the shadow of your wings

Your steadfast love, O LORD, extends to the heavens,
   your faithfulness to the clouds.
Your righteousness is like the mighty mountains,
   your judgments are like the great deep;
   you save humans and animals alike, O LORD.
How precious is your steadfast love, O God!
   All people may take refuge in the shadow of your wings.
They feast on the abundance of your house,
   and you give them drink from the river of your delights.
For with you is the fountain of life;
   in your light we see light. (Ps. 36:5-9)

Additional Readings:

Isaiah 42:1-9
The servant brings forth justice

Hebrews 9:11-15
The blood of Christ redeems for eternal life

John 12:1-11
Mary of Bethany anoints Jesus

Hymn: My Song Is Love Unknown, ELW 343

O God, your Son chose the path that led to pain before joy and the cross before glory. Plant his cross in our hearts, so that in its power and love we may come at last to joy and glory, through Jesus Christ, our Savior and Lord, who lives and reigns with you and the Holy Spirit, one God, now and forever.

Tuesday, March 18, 2008
TUESDAY IN HOLY WEEK

1 Corinthians 1:18-31
The cross of Christ reveals God's power and wisdom

Where is the one who is wise? Where is the scribe? Where is the debater of this age? Has not God made foolish the wisdom of the world? For since, in the wisdom of God, the world did not know God through wisdom, God decided, through the foolishness of our proclamation, to save those who believe. For Jews demand signs and Greeks desire wisdom, but we proclaim Christ crucified, a stumbling block to Jews and foolishness to Gentiles, but to those who are the called, both Jews and Greeks, Christ the power of God and the wisdom of God. For God's foolishness is wiser than human wisdom, and God's weakness is stronger than human strength. (1 Cor. 1:20-25)

Additional Readings:

Isaiah 49:1-7
The servant brings salvation to earth's ends

Psalm 71:1-14
From my mother's womb you have been my strength

John 12:20-36
Jesus speaks of his death

Hymn: Jesus, Keep Me Near the Cross, ELW 335

Lord Jesus, you have called us to follow you. Grant that our love may not grow cold in your service, and that we may not fail or deny you in the time of trial, for you live and reign with the Father and the Holy Spirit, one God, now and forever.

Wednesday, March 19, 2008
WEDNESDAY IN HOLY WEEK

Joseph, Guardian of Jesus

Isaiah 50:4-9a
The servant is vindicated by God

The Lord GOD has opened my ear,
    and I was not rebellious,
    I did not turn backward.
The Lord GOD helps me;
    therefore I have not been disgraced;
therefore I have set my face like flint,
    and I know that I shall not be put to shame;
    he who vindicates me is near.
  Who will contend with me?
  Let us stand up together.
  Who are my adversaries?
  Let them confront me.
It is the Lord GOD who helps me;
    who will declare me guilty? (Isa. 50:5, 7-9a)

Additional Readings:

Psalm 70	Hebrews 12:1-3	John 13:21-32
Be pleased, O God, to deliver me	*Look to Jesus, who endured the cross*	*Jesus foretells his betrayal*

Hymn: Ah, Holy Jesus, ELW 349

Almighty God, your Son our Savior suffered at human hands and endured the shame of the cross. Grant that we may walk in the way of his cross and find it the way of life and peace, through Jesus Christ, our Savior and Lord, who lives and reigns with you and the Holy Spirit, one God, now and forever.

Thursday, March 20, 2008
Maundy Thursday

John 13:1-17, 31b-35
The service of Christ: footwashing and meal

After [Jesus] had washed their feet, had put on his robe, and had returned to the table, he said to them, "Do you know what I have done to you? You call me Teacher and Lord—and you are right, for that is what I am. So if I, your Lord and Teacher, have washed your feet, you also ought to wash one another's feet. For I have set you an example, that you also should do as I have done to you. (John 13:12-15)

Additional Readings:

Exodus 12:1-4 [5-10] 11-14	Psalm 116:1-2, 12-19	1 Corinthians 11:23-26
The passover of the Lord	*The cup of salvation*	*Proclaim the Lord's death*

Hymn: Great God, Your Love Has Called Us, ELW 358

Holy God, source of all love, on the night of his betrayal, Jesus gave us a new commandment, to love one another as he loves us. Write this commandment in our hearts, and give us the will to serve others as he was the servant of all, your Son, Jesus Christ, our Savior and Lord, who lives and reigns with you and the Holy Spirit, one God, now and forever.

Friday, March 21, 2008
GOOD FRIDAY

Thomas Cranmer, Bishop of Canterbury, martyr, 1556

John 18:1—19:42
The passion and death of Jesus

When Jesus saw his mother and the disciple whom he loved standing beside her, he said to his mother, "Woman, here is your son." Then he said to the disciple, "Here is your mother." And from that hour the disciple took her into his own home.

After this, when Jesus knew that all was now finished, he said (in order to fulfill the scripture), "I am thirsty." A jar full of sour wine was standing there. So they put a sponge full of the wine on a branch of hyssop and held it to his mouth. When Jesus had received the wine, he said, "It is finished." Then he bowed his head and gave up his spirit. (John 19:26-30)

Additional Readings:

Isaiah 52:13—53:12	Psalm 22	Hebrews 10:16-25
The suffering servant	*Why have you forsaken me?*	*The way to God is opened*

Hymn: There in God's Garden, ELW 342

Almighty God, look with loving mercy on your family, for whom our Lord Jesus Christ was willing to be betrayed, to be given over to the hands of sinners, and to suffer death on the cross; who now lives and reigns with you and the Holy Spirit, one God, now and forever.

Saturday, March 22, 2008
RESURRECTION OF OUR LORD

Vigil of Easter
Jonathan Edwards, teacher, missionary to American Indians, 1758

Romans 6:3-11
Dying and rising with Christ

Do you not know that all of us who have been baptized into
Christ Jesus were baptized into his death? Therefore we have
been buried with him by baptism into death, so that, just as
Christ was raised from the dead by the glory of the Father, so we
too might walk in newness of life.

For if we have been united with him in a death like his, we will
certainly be united with him in a resurrection like his.
(Rom. 6:3-5)

Additional Readings:

Isaiah 55:1-11
*Salvation freely offered
to all*

Isaiah 12:2-6
*With joy you will draw
water from the wells of
salvation*

John 20:1-18
Seeing the risen Christ

Hymn: We Are Baptized in Christ Jesus, ELW 451

*Eternal Giver of life and light, this holy night shines with the
radiance of the risen Christ. Renew your church with the Spirit given
us in baptism, that we may worship you in sincerity and truth and may
shine as a light in the world, through your Son, Jesus Christ our Lord,
who lives and reigns with you and the Holy Spirit, one God, now and
forever.*

Sunday, March 23, 2008
Resurrection of Our Lord

Easter Day

Matthew 28:1-10
Proclaim the resurrection

But the angel said to the women, "Do not be afraid; I know that
you are looking for Jesus who was crucified. He is not here; for
he has been raised, as he said. Come, see the place where he lay.
Then go quickly and tell his disciples, 'He has been raised from
the dead, and indeed he is going ahead of you to Galilee; there
you will see him.' This is my message for you." So they left the
tomb quickly with fear and great joy, and ran to tell his disciples.
(Matt. 28:5-8)

Additional Readings:

Acts 10:34-43
God raised Jesus on the third day

Psalm 118:1-2, 14-24
On this day God has acted

Colossians 3:1-4
Raised with Christ

Hymn: Christ Has Arisen, Alleluia, ELW 364

*O God, you gave your only Son to suffer death on the cross for our
redemption, and by his glorious resurrection you delivered us from the
power of death. Make us die every day to sin, that we may live with him
forever in the joy of the resurrection, through your Son, Jesus Christ our
Lord, who lives and reigns with you and the Holy Spirit, one God, now
and forever.*

Monday, March 24, 2008

JOSEPH, GUARDIAN OF JESUS

(transferred from March 19)

Oscar Arnulfo Romero, Bishop of El Salvador, martyr, 1980

Matthew 1:16, 18-21, 24a

The Lord appears to Joseph in a dream

Now the birth of Jesus the Messiah took place in this way. When his mother Mary had been engaged to Joseph, but before they lived together, she was found to be with child from the Holy Spirit. Her husband Joseph, being a righteous man and unwilling to expose her to public disgrace, planned to dismiss her quietly. But just when he had resolved to do this, an angel of the Lord appeared to him in a dream and said, "Joseph, son of David, do not be afraid to take Mary as your wife, for the child conceived in her is from the Holy Spirit. She will bear a son, and you are to name him Jesus, for he will save his people from their sins." (Matt. 1:18-21)

Additional Readings:

2 Samuel 7:4, 8-16
God makes a covenant with David

Psalm 89:1-29 (Ps. 89:2)
The Lord's steadfast love is established forever

Romans 4:13-18
The promise to those who share Abraham's faith

Hymn: By All Your Saints, ELW 420 (stanza 9)

O God, from the family of your servant David you raised up Joseph to be the guardian of your incarnate Son and the husband of his blessed mother. Give us grace to imitate his uprightness of life and his obedience to your commands, through Jesus Christ, our Savior and Lord, who lives and reigns with you and the Holy Spirit, one God, now and forever.

Tuesday, March 25, 2008
ANNUNCIATION OF OUR LORD

Luke 1:26-38
The angel greets Mary

In the sixth month the angel Gabriel was sent by God to a town in Galilee called Nazareth, to a virgin engaged to a man whose name was Joseph, of the house of David. The virgin's name was Mary. And he came to her and said, "Greetings, favored one! The Lord is with you." But she was much perplexed by his words and pondered what sort of greeting this might be. The angel said to her, "Do not be afraid, Mary, for you have found favor with God. And now, you will conceive in your womb and bear a son, and you will name him Jesus. (Luke 1:26-31)

Additional Readings:

Isaiah 7:10-14	Psalm 45	Hebrews 10:4-10
A young woman will bear a son	*Your name will be remembered*	*The offering of Jesus' body sanctifies us*

Hymn: The Angel Gabriel from Heaven Came, ELW 265

Pour your grace into our hearts, O God, that we who have known the incarnation of your Son, Jesus Christ, announced by an angel, may by his cross and passion be brought to the glory of his resurrection; for he lives and reigns with you, in the unity of the Holy Spirit, one God, now and forever.

Psalm 118:1-2, 14-24
On this day God has acted

I thank you that you have answered me
    and have become my salvation.
The stone that the builders rejected
    has become the chief cornerstone.
This is the LORD's doing;
    it is marvelous in our eyes.
This is the day that the LORD has made;
    let us rejoice and be glad in it. (Ps. 118:21-24)

Additional Readings:

Joshua 3:1-17
*Israel crosses into the
promised land*

Matthew 28:1-10
Proclaim the resurrection

Hymn: The Day of Resurrection! ELW 361

Like people who have endured long nights of anxious waiting, we joyfully proclaim the great news of the resurrection. Open our eyes, O God, to see your great love before us every day, that we might joyfully thank and praise, serve and follow you.

Psalm 16
Fullness of joy

I bless the LORD who gives me counsel;
   in the night also my heart instructs me.
I keep the LORD always before me;
   because he is at my right hand, I shall not be moved.
Therefore my heart is glad, and my soul rejoices;
   my body also rests secure.
For you do not give me up to Sheol,
   or let your faithful one see the Pit.
You show me the path of life.
   In your presence there is fullness of joy;
   in your right hand are pleasures forevermore.
(Ps. 16:7-11)

Additional Readings:

Song of Solomon 2:8-15   Colossians 4:2-5
Arise, for the winter is past   *The new life in Christ*

Hymn: In Thee Is Gladness, ELW 867

Maker of all, you created us and all that exists. You gave us bodies and souls with all their gifts. From joy born in gratitude for your divine goodness and mercy, we offer only this: to walk the path of life faithfully, assured of your presence.

Friday, March 28, 2008
WEEK OF EASTER 1

1 Corinthians 15:1-11
Witnesses to the risen Christ

For I handed on to you as of first importance what I in turn had received: that Christ died for our sins in accordance with the scriptures, and that he was buried, and that he was raised on the third day in accordance with the scriptures, and that he appeared to Cephas, then to the twelve. Then he appeared to more than five hundred brothers and sisters at one time, most of whom are still alive, though some have died. Then he appeared to James, then to all the apostles. Last of all, as to one untimely born, he appeared also to me. (1 Cor. 15:3-8)

Additional Readings:
Song of Solomon 5:9—6:3   Psalm 16
The beloved in the garden   *Fullness of joy*

Hymn: Now the Green Blade Rises, ELW 379

Link us, God, to the journeys of all the faithful who in their own times and places saw the crucified and living Jesus. Connect us to generations yet unborn, that through our legacies of faithful and sacrificial living, they too may see the risen Christ.

Saturday, March 29, 2008
WEEK OF EASTER 1

Hans Nielsen Hauge, renewer of the church, 1824

Song of Solomon 8:6-7
Love is strong as death

Set me as a seal upon your heart,
  as a seal upon your arm;
for love is strong as death,
  passion fierce as the grave.
Its flashes are flashes of fire,
  a raging flame.
Many waters cannot quench love,
  neither can floods drown it.
If one offered for love
  all the wealth of his house,
  it would be utterly scorned.
(Song of Sol. 8:6-7)

Additional Readings:

John 20:11-20
*The witness of Mary
Magdalene*

Psalm 16
Fullness of joy

Hymn: Come, My Way, My Truth, My Life, ELW 816

Your love, O Lord, holds the universe together in a single peace, and connects child and parent, lover to beloved, and sinner with forgiveness. When we hold life together imperfectly, join us to the peace of the risen Christ.

Sunday, March 30, 2008
SECOND SUNDAY OF EASTER

John 20:19-31
Beholding the wounds of the risen Christ

A week later [Jesus'] disciples were again in the house, and Thomas was with them. Although the doors were shut, Jesus came and stood among them and said, "Peace be with you." Then he said to Thomas, "Put your finger here and see my hands. Reach out your hand and put it in my side. Do not doubt but believe." Thomas answered him, "My Lord and my God!" Jesus said to him, "Have you believed because you have seen me? Blessed are those who have not seen and yet have come to believe." (John 20:26-29)

Additional Readings:

Acts 2:14a, 22-32
God fulfills the promise to David

Psalm 16
Fullness of joy

1 Peter 1:3-9
New birth to a living hope

Hymn: O Sons and Daughters, Let Us Sing, ELW 386 *(especially stanzas 5-8)*

Almighty and eternal God, the strength of those who believe and the hope of those who doubt, may we, who have not seen, have faith in you and receive the fullness of Christ's blessing, who lives and reigns with you and the Holy Spirit, one God, now and forever.

Monday, March 31, 2008
WEEK OF EASTER 2

John Donne, poet, 1631

Psalm 114
God saves through water

Why is it, O sea, that you flee?
  O Jordan, that you turn back?
O mountains, that you skip like rams?
  O hills, like lambs?
Tremble, O earth, at the presence of the LORD,
  at the presence of the God of Jacob,
who turns the rock into a pool of water,
  the flint into a spring of water. (Ps. 114:5-8)

Additional Readings:

Judges 6:36-40
Gideon and the fleece

1 Corinthians 15:12-20
*Paul teaches the
resurrection*

Hymn: We Know That Christ Is Raised, ELW 449

*When our journeys are dull and our paths are plodding, transform
us through your grace that causes mountains to dance and dry deserts
to bubble with water. Join us to all of your redeemed creation in joyous
praise and thanksgiving.*

⤳ Prayer list for April

_____

_____

_____

_____

_____

_____

_____

_____

_____

_____

_____

1 Corinthians 15:19-28
Paul teaches the resurrection

For since death came through a human being, the resurrection of the dead has also come through a human being; for as all die in Adam, so all will be made alive in Christ. But each in his own order: Christ the first fruits, then at his coming those who belong to Christ. Then comes the end, when he hands over the kingdom to God the Father, after he has destroyed every ruler and every authority and power. For he must reign until he has put all his enemies under his feet. (1 Cor. 15:21-25)

Additional Readings:

Jonah 1:1-17
Jonah saved from the sea

Psalm 114
God saves through water

Hymn: This Joyful Eastertide, ELW 391

Because both life and death are secure in your reign, mighty God, free us from all that prevents us from fully acting as your claimed and redeemed people. Remind us of your enduring power that holds the universe together.

Wednesday, April 2, 2008
WEEK OF EASTER 2

Matthew 12:38-42
Jesus speaks of the sign of Jonah

Then some of the scribes and Pharisees said to him, "Teacher, we wish to see a sign from you." But he answered them, "An evil and adulterous generation asks for a sign, but no sign will be given to it except the sign of the prophet Jonah. For just as Jonah was three days and three nights in the belly of the sea monster, so for three days and three nights the Son of Man will be in the heart of the earth. The people of Nineveh will rise up at the judgment with this generation and condemn it, because they repented at the proclamation of Jonah, and see, something greater than Jonah is here! The queen of the South will rise up at the judgment with this generation and condemn it, because she came from the ends of the earth to listen to the wisdom of Solomon, and see, something greater than Solomon is here!" (Matt. 12:38-42)

Additional Readings:

Jonah 2:1-10
Jonah's praise for deliverance

Psalm 114
God saves through water

Hymn: Come, You Faithful, Raise the Strain, ELW 363

So often, dear God, we ask for signs and yet still see only what we want to see. Forgive our foolishness. Rouse us from our slumber to live instead in the power of the cross and empty tomb.

Thursday, April 3, 2008
WEEK OF EASTER 2

Psalm 116:1-4, 12-19
I will call upon God

What shall I return to the LORD
   for all his bounty to me?
I will lift up the cup of salvation
   and call on the name of the LORD,
I will pay my vows to the LORD
   in the presence of all his people.
Precious in the sight of the LORD
   is the death of his faithful ones.
(Ps. 116:12-15)

Additional Readings:

Isaiah 25:1-5
Praise for deliverance

1 Peter 1:8b-12
The promised salvation comes

Hymn: Christ, the Life of All the Living, ELW 339

Teach us what the psalmist proclaims: The best response we can give to you, dear God, is lives of gratitude and worship. So move in us this day that we are living witnesses to your bounty and blessing.

Friday, April 4, 2008
WEEK OF EASTER 2

Benedict the African, confessor, 1589

Isaiah 26:1-4
God sets up victory like bulwarks

On that day this song will be sung in the land of Judah:
We have a strong city;
   he sets up victory
   like walls and bulwarks.
Open the gates,
   so that the righteous nation that keeps faith
   may enter in.
Those of steadfast mind you keep in peace—
   in peace because they trust in you.
Trust in the LORD forever,
   for in the LORD GOD
   you have an everlasting rock. (Isa. 26:1-4)

Additional Readings:

1 Peter 1:13-16   Psalm 116:1-4, 12-19
A holy life   *I will call upon God*

Hymn: Dear Christians, One and All, Rejoice, ELW 594

Everlasting Rock of all creation, you are already present in our world. Strengthen us to seek your will, carry out your desires, and establish the justice and peace that are hallmarks of your eternal reign.

Saturday, April 5, 2008
WEEK OF EASTER 2

Luke 14:12-14
Welcome those in need to your table

He said also to the one who had invited him, "When you give a luncheon or a dinner, do not invite your friends or your brothers or your relatives or rich neighbors, in case they may invite you in return, and you would be repaid. But when you give a banquet, invite the poor, the crippled, the lame, and the blind. And you will be blessed, because they cannot repay you, for you will be repaid at the resurrection of the righteous." (Luke 14:12-14)

Additional Readings:

Isaiah 25:6-9
The feast for all peoples

Psalm 116:1-4, 12-19
I will call upon God

Hymn: Let Us Go Now to the Banquet, ELW 523

Lord Jesus, you welcome all to your table with gracious hospitality. Though we may sometimes wonder about such generosity, embolden us to serve those waiting for someone to notice, welcome, and care for them.

Sunday, April 6, 2008
Third Sunday of Easter

*Albrecht Dürer, 1528; Matthias Grünewald, 1529;
Lucas Cranach, 1553; artists*

Luke 24:13-35
Eating with the risen Christ

As they came near the village to which they were going, [Jesus] walked ahead as if he were going on. But they urged him strongly, saying, "Stay with us, because it is almost evening and the day is now nearly over." So he went in to stay with them. When he was at the table with them, he took bread, blessed and broke it, and gave it to them. Then their eyes were opened, and they recognized him; and he vanished from their sight. They said to each other, "Were not our hearts burning within us while he was talking to us on the road, while he was opening the scriptures to us?" (Luke 24:28-32)

Additional Readings:

Acts 2:14a, 36-41	Psalm 116:1-4, 12-19	1 Peter 1:17-23
Receiving God's promise through baptism	*I will call upon God*	*Born anew*

Hymn: Day of Arising, ELW 374

O God, your Son makes himself known to all his disciples in the breaking of bread. Open the eyes of our faith, that we may see him in his redeeming work, who lives and reigns with you and the Holy Spirit, one God, now and forever.

Psalm 134
Praise God day and night

Come, bless the Lord, all you servants of the Lord,
   who stand by night in the house of the Lord!
Lift up your hands to the holy place,
   and bless the Lord.
May the Lord, maker of heaven and earth,
   bless you from Zion. (Ps. 134:1-3)

Additional Readings:

Genesis 18:1-14
Abraham and Sarah eat with God

1 Peter 1:23-25
The word of God endures

Hymn: The Trumpets Sound, the Angels Sing, ELW 531

God of all times, life often looks bleakest in the darkness. Thank you for those who watch with us through the night, for their vigils, prayers, and blessings that come because we can call on you at all hours.

Tuesday, April 8, 2008
Week of Easter 3

1 Peter 2:1-3
Long for the pure spiritual milk

Rid yourselves, therefore, of all malice, and all guile, insincerity, envy, and all slander. Like newborn infants, long for the pure, spiritual milk, so that by it you may grow into salvation—if indeed you have tasted that the Lord is good. (1 Peter 2:1-3)

Additional Readings:

Proverbs 8:32—9:6   Psalm 134
Wisdom serves a meal   *Praise God day and night*

Hymn: All Who Hunger, Gather Gladly, ELW 461

Abundant God, your son sacrificed himself to save and redeem the whole world. Empty us, we pray, of those things that create bitterness; fill us instead with the savory seasonings of your Holy Spirit.

Wednesday, April 9, 2008
WEEK OF EASTER 3

Dietrich Bonhoeffer, theologian, 1945

Exodus 24:1-11
Moses and the elders eat with God

Then Moses and Aaron, Nadab, and Abihu, and seventy of the elders of Israel went up, and they saw the God of Israel. Under his feet there was something like a pavement of sapphire stone, like the very heaven for clearness. God did not lay his hand on the chief men of the people of Israel; also they beheld God, and they ate and drank. (Exod. 24:9-11)

Additional Readings:

John 21:1-14
The risen Christ eats with the disciples

Psalm 134
Praise God day and night

Hymn: At the Lamb's High Feast We Sing, ELW 362

How awesome to behold your majesty, great and glorious God! Thank you for the glimpses of grace that surprise and delight; continue to reveal yourself through the hospitality of eucharistic fellowship and cooperative faith communities.

Thursday, April 10, 2008
WEEK OF EASTER 3

Mikael Agricola, Bishop of Turku, 1557

Psalm 23
God our shepherd

Even though I walk through the darkest valley,
  I fear no evil;
for you are with me;
  your rod and your staff—
  they comfort me.
You prepare a table before me
  in the presence of my enemies;
you anoint my head with oil;
  my cup overflows.
Surely goodness and mercy shall follow me
  all the days of my life,
and I shall dwell in the house of the LORD
  my whole life long. (Ps. 23:4-6)

Additional Readings:

Exodus 2:15b-25   1 Peter 2:9-12
Moses the shepherd   *Living as God's people*

Hymn: Shepherd Me, O God, ELW 780

Thank you, abiding Shepherd, for the solace that generations have found through the promises of your word. Comfort especially those who are restless and fearful. Guide all who wander in darkness. Bring all your children safely through tribulation.

Friday, April 11, 2008
WEEK OF EASTER 3

1 Peter 2:13-17
Living honorably in the world

For the Lord's sake accept the authority of every human institution, whether of the emperor as supreme, or of governors, as sent by him to punish those who do wrong and to praise those who do right. For it is God's will that by doing right you should silence the ignorance of the foolish. As servants of God, live as free people, yet do not use your freedom as a pretext for evil. Honor everyone. Love the family of believers. Fear God. Honor the emperor. (1 Peter 2:13-17)

Additional Readings:

Exodus 3:16-22; 4:18-20
Moses the shepherd of Israel

Psalm 23
God our shepherd

Hymn: What God Ordains Is Good Indeed, ELW 776

God, you are the ruler of the universe, yet you work through earthbound systems. Raise up wise, generous, just, and compassionate leaders who are committed to using the power entrusted to them for the benefit of all.

Ezekiel 34:1-16
God gathers the scattered flock

For thus says the Lord GOD: I myself will search for my sheep, and will seek them out. As shepherds seek out their flocks when they are among their scattered sheep, so I will seek out my sheep. I will rescue them from all the places to which they have been scattered on a day of clouds and thick darkness. I will bring them out from the peoples and gather them from the countries, and will bring them into their own land; and I will feed them on the mountains of Israel, by the watercourses, and in all the inhabited parts of the land. I will feed them with good pasture, and the mountain heights of Israel shall be their pasture; there they shall lie down in good grazing land, and they shall feed on rich pasture on the mountains of Israel. I myself will be the shepherd of my sheep, and I will make them lie down, says the Lord GOD. (Ezek. 34:11-15)

Additional Readings:

Luke 15:1-7   Psalm 23
Parable of the lost sheep   *God our shepherd*

Hymn: Savior, like a Shepherd Lead Us, ELW 789

God who searches for the lost, we give you thanks for your unending commitment to support us. Continue to feed us with your goodness, nurture us with your love, and care for us with your mercy.

Sunday, April 13, 2008
FOURTH SUNDAY OF EASTER

John 10:1-10
Christ the shepherd

So again Jesus said to them, "Very truly, I tell you, I am the gate
for the sheep. All who came before me are thieves and bandits;
but the sheep did not listen to them. I am the gate. Whoever
enters by me will be saved, and will come in and go out and find
pasture. The thief comes only to steal and kill and destroy. I came
that they may have life, and have it abundantly."
(John 10:7-10)

Additional Readings:

Acts 2:42-47
The believers' common life

Psalm 23
God our shepherd

1 Peter 2:19-25
*Follow the shepherd, even
in suffering*

Hymn: The Lord's My Shepherd, ELW 778

*O God our shepherd, you know your sheep by name and lead us
to safety through the valleys of death. Guide us by your voice, that we
may walk in certainty and security to the joyous feast prepared in your
house, through Jesus Christ, our Savior and Lord, who lives and reigns
with you and the Holy Spirit, one God, now and forever.*

Psalm 100
We are the sheep of God's pasture

Make a joyful noise to the LORD, all the earth.
   Worship the LORD with gladness;
   come into his presence with singing.
Know that the LORD is God.
   It is he that made us, and we are his;
   we are his people, and the sheep of his pasture.
Enter his gates with thanksgiving,
   and his courts with praise.
   Give thanks to him, bless his name.
For the LORD is good;
   his steadfast love endures forever,
   and his faithfulness to all generations.
(Ps. 100:1-5)

Additional Readings:

Ezekiel 34:17-23	1 Peter 5:1-5
God the true shepherd	*Tend the flock of God*

Hymn: All People That on Earth Do Dwell, ELW 883

With grateful voices and thankful hearts, we praise you, steadfast God, because we are yours. Empower our witness and strengthen our song until that day when the whole earth is filled with your praise.

Hebrews 13:20-21
God's blessing through Christ the shepherd

Now may the God of peace, who brought back from the dead our Lord Jesus, the great shepherd of the sheep, by the blood of the eternal covenant, make you complete in everything good so that you may do his will, working among us that which is pleasing in his sight, through Jesus Christ, to whom be the glory forever and ever. Amen. (Heb. 13:20-21)

Additional Readings:

Ezekiel 34:23-31
God provides perfect pasture

Psalm 100
We are the sheep of God's pasture

Hymn: Go, My Children, with My Blessing, ELW 543

God, you send us into the world with a powerful benediction; without you we are incomplete. Work among us to bring about the vision of wholeness and renewal that flows from the love you have for all creation.

Wednesday, April 16, 2008
WEEK OF EASTER 4

Jeremiah 23:1-8
God will gather the flock

Woe to the shepherds who destroy and scatter the sheep of my pasture! says the LORD. Therefore thus says the LORD, the God of Israel, concerning the shepherds who shepherd my people: It is you who have scattered my flock, and have driven them away, and you have not attended to them. So I will attend to you for your evil doings, says the LORD. Then I myself will gather the remnant of my flock out of all the lands where I have driven them, and I will bring them back to their fold, and they shall be fruitful and multiply. I will raise up shepherds over them who will shepherd them, and they shall not fear any longer, or be dismayed, nor shall any be missing, says the LORD. (Jer. 23:1-4)

Additional Readings:

Matthew 20:17-28
Jesus came to serve

Psalm 100
We are the sheep of God's pasture

Hymn: Gather Us In, ELW 532

O God, we confess that religion can be divisive and leaders more contentious than compassionate. Banish fear, engender healing, and restore trust to those who have been damaged by religious manipulation.

Thursday, April 17, 2008
WEEK OF EASTER 4

Psalm 31:1-5, 15-16
I commend my spirit

In you, O Lord, I seek refuge;
   do not let me ever be put to shame;
   in your righteousness deliver me.
Incline your ear to me;
   rescue me speedily.
Be a rock of refuge for me,
   a strong fortress to save me.
You are indeed my rock and my fortress;
   for your name's sake lead me and guide me,
take me out of the net that is hidden for me,
   for you are my refuge.
Into your hand I commit my spirit;
   you have redeemed me, O Lord, faithful God.
(Ps. 31:1-5)

Additional Readings:

Genesis 12:1-3   Acts 6:8-15
The call of Abram   *Stephen is arrested*

Hymn: Shout to the Lord, ELW 821

God of all who seek shelter, we come this day thankful for the many times you have shielded and protected us. Continue to be a source of strength and hope. Let all who look to you find peace and redemption.

Friday, April 18, 2008
WEEK OF EASTER 4

Exodus 3:1-12
Moses at the burning bush

When the LORD saw that [Moses] had turned aside to see, God called to him out of the bush, "Moses, Moses!" And he said, "Here I am." Then he said, "Come no closer! Remove the sandals from your feet, for the place on which you are standing is holy ground." He said further, "I am the God of your father, the God of Abraham, the God of Isaac, and the God of Jacob." And Moses hid his face, for he was afraid to look at God. (Exod. 3:4-6)

Additional Readings:

Acts 7:1-16
Stephen addresses the council

Psalm 31:1-5, 15-16
I commend my spirit

Hymn: Christ Is Risen! Alleluia! ELW 382

Gracious God, in baptism you call us by name and initiate an intimate relationship. Sometimes that intimacy is so overwhelming that we turn away. Break down the barriers we erect, ease our fearfulness, and console us when we are hurting.

Saturday, April 19, 2008
WEEK OF EASTER 4

Olavus Petri, priest, 1552; Laurentius Petri, Bishop of Uppsala, 1573;
renewers of the church

Jeremiah 26:20-24
A prophet of the Lord persecuted

There was another man prophesying in the name of the LORD, Uriah son of Shemaiah from Kiriath-jearim. He prophesied against this city and against this land in words exactly like those of Jeremiah. And when King Jehoiakim, with all his warriors and all the officials, heard his words, the king sought to put him to death; but when Uriah heard of it, he was afraid and fled and escaped to Egypt. Then King Jehoiakim sent Elnathan son of Achbor and men with him to Egypt, and they took Uriah from Egypt and brought him to King Jehoiakim, who struck him down with the sword and threw his dead body into the burial place of the common people. But the hand of Ahikam son of Shaphan was with Jeremiah so that he was not given over into the hands of the people to be put to death. (Jer. 26:20-24)

Additional Readings:

John 8:48-59
Jesus the greater prophet

Psalm 31:1-5, 15-16
I commend my spirit

Hymn: Faith of Our Fathers, ELW 812/813

Eternal God, history is filled with those who have boldly proclaimed your word, even in the face of certain death. Anchor us when we are tempted to flee, infuse us with your strength, and sustain us in times of persecution.

John 14:1-14
Christ the way, truth, life

Philip said to [Jesus], "Lord, show us the Father, and we will be satisfied." Jesus said to him, "Have I been with you all this time, Philip, and you still do not know me? Whoever has seen me has seen the Father. How can you say, 'Show us the Father'? Do you not believe that I am in the Father and the Father is in me? The words that I say to you I do not speak on my own; but the Father who dwells in me does his works. Believe me that I am in the Father and the Father is in me; but if you do not, then believe me because of the works themselves. Very truly, I tell you, the one who believes in me will also do the works that I do and, in fact, will do greater works than these, because I am going to the Father." (John 14:8-12)

Additional Readings:

Acts 7:55-60	Psalm 31:1-5, 15-16	1 Peter 2:2-10
Martyrdom of Stephen	*I commend my spirit*	*God's chosen people*

Hymn: You Are the Way, ELW 758

Almighty God, your Son Jesus Christ is the way, the truth, and the life. Give us grace to love one another, to follow in the way of his commandments, and to share his risen life with all the world, for he lives and reigns with you and the Holy Spirit, one God, now and forever.

Monday, April 21, 2008
Week of Easter 5

Anselm, Bishop of Canterbury, 1109

Psalm 102:1-17
Prayer for deliverance

But you, O Lord, are enthroned forever;
   your name endures to all generations.
You will rise up and have compassion on Zion,
   for it is time to favor it;
   the appointed time has come.
For your servants hold its stones dear,
   and have pity on its dust.
The nations will fear the name of the Lord,
   and all the kings of the earth your glory.
For the Lord will build up Zion;
   he will appear in his glory. (Ps. 102:12-16)

Additional Readings:
Exodus 13:17-22
God leads the way

Acts 7:17-40
Stephen addresses the council

Hymn: O God of Every Nation, ELW 713

God of space and time, thank you for the holy places where your grace has been revealed to us. Whether elaborate or simple, distant or near, may the places we hold with special affection continue to inspire us of your presence in our midst.

Tuesday, April 22, 2008
WEEK OF EASTER 5

Proverbs 3:5-12
God, the truth and life

Trust in the LORD with all your heart,
   and do not rely on your own insight.
In all your ways acknowledge him,
   and he will make straight your paths.
Do not be wise in your own eyes;
   fear the LORD, and turn away from evil.
It will be a healing for your flesh
   and a refreshment for your body.
(Prov. 3:5-8)

Additional Readings:

Acts 7:44-56
Stephen confronts the council

Psalm 102:1-17
Prayer for deliverance

Hymn: All My Hope on God Is Founded, ELW 757

It sounds so easy to trust in you, gracious God, but you see how often we wander the crooked paths instead. Bring healing and refreshment to those misaligned parts of our lives; reassure us that you are guiding our footsteps.

Wednesday, April 23, 2008
WEEK OF EASTER 5

Toyohiko Kagawa, renewer of society, 1960

John 8:31-38
Jesus, the truth of God

Jesus answered them, "Very truly, I tell you, everyone who commits sin is a slave to sin. The slave does not have a permanent place in the household; the son has a place there forever. So if the Son makes you free, you will be free indeed. I know that you are descendants of Abraham; yet you look for an opportunity to kill me, because there is no place in you for my word. I declare what I have seen in the Father's presence; as for you, you should do what you have heard from the Father." (John 8:34-38)

Additional Readings:
Proverbs 3:13-18   Psalm 102:1-17
God, the truth and life   *Prayer for deliverance*

Hymn: Awake, My Heart, with Gladness, ELW 378

Keep us vigilant, dear God, when we are tempted to equate being chosen with being entitled. Remind us that we are truly free when we trust in you alone. May we always have room in our lives for your grace.

Thursday, April 24, 2008
Week of Easter 5

Psalm 66:8-20
Be joyful in God, all you lands

Bless our God, O peoples,
   let the sound of his praise be heard,
who has kept us among the living,
   and has not let our feet slip.
For you, O God, have tested us;
   you have tried us as silver is tried.
You brought us into the net;
   you laid burdens on our backs;
you let people ride over our heads;
   we went through fire and through water;
yet you have brought us out to a spacious place.
(Ps. 66:8-12)

Additional Readings:

Genesis 6:5-22   Acts 27:1-12
God's command to Noah   *Paul sails for Rome*

Hymn: Christ Jesus Lay in Death's Strong Bands, ELW 370

God, you are present every step of the way that we travel through life. Help us to trust your leading, respond to your goodness, anticipate your deliverance, and celebrate the special times and places where we encounter you.

Friday, April 25, 2008
MARK, EVANGELIST

Mark 1:1-15
The beginning of the gospel of Jesus Christ

The beginning of the good news of Jesus Christ, the Son of God.
As it is written in the prophet Isaiah,
"See, I am sending my messenger ahead of you,
who will prepare your way;
the voice of one crying out in the wilderness:
'Prepare the way of the Lord,
make his paths straight,'"
John the baptizer appeared in the wilderness, proclaiming a
baptism of repentance for the forgiveness of sins. And people
from the whole Judean countryside and all the people of
Jerusalem were going out to him, and were baptized by him in
the river Jordan, confessing their sins. (Mark 1:1-5)

Additional Readings:

Isaiah 52:7-10	Psalm 57	2 Timothy 4:6-11, 18
The messenger announces salvation	*Be merciful to me, O God*	*The good fight of faith*

Hymn: I Bind unto Myself Today, ELW 450

Almighty God, you have enriched your church with Mark's proclamation of the gospel. Give us grace to believe firmly in the good news of salvation and to walk daily in accord with it, through Jesus Christ, our Savior and Lord, who lives and reigns with you and the Holy Spirit, one God, now and forever.

Saturday, April 26, 2008
Week of Easter 5

John 14:27-29
Peace I leave with you

"Peace I leave with you; my peace I give to you. I do not give to you as the world gives. Do not let your hearts be troubled, and do not let them be afraid. You heard me say to you, 'I am going away, and I am coming to you.' If you loved me, you would rejoice that I am going to the Father, because the Father is greater than I. And now I have told you this before it occurs, so that when it does occur, you may believe." (John 14:27-29)

Additional Readings:

Genesis 8:13-19
The flood waters subside

Psalm 66:8-20
Be joyful in God, all you lands

Hymn: Alleluia! Sing to Jesus, ELW 392

Jesus told his disciples many things so that they might believe. Keep our faith growing, dear God, that we will bear the fruits of mature discipleship expressed in ways that heal the world and build up your whole creation.

Sunday, April 27, 2008
SIXTH SUNDAY OF EASTER

John 14:15-21
Christ our advocate

"If you love me, you will keep my commandments. And I will ask the Father, and he will give you another Advocate, to be with you forever. This is the Spirit of truth, whom the world cannot receive, because it neither sees him nor knows him. You know him, because he abides with you, and he will be in you."
(John 14:15-17)

Additional Readings:

Acts 17:22-31
Paul's message to the Athenians

Psalm 66:8-20
Be joyful in God, all you lands

1 Peter 3:13-22
The days of Noah, a sign of baptism

Hymn: O Spirit of Life, ELW 405

Almighty and ever-living God, you hold together all things in heaven and on earth. In your great mercy receive the prayers of all your children, and give to all the world the Spirit of your truth and peace, through Jesus Christ, our Savior and Lord, who lives and reigns with you and the Holy Spirit, one God, now and forever.

Monday, April 28, 2008
Week of Easter 6

Psalm 93
God reigns above the floods

The Lord is king, he is robed in majesty;
   the Lord is robed, he is girded with strength.
He has established the world; it shall never be moved;
   your throne is established from of old;
   you are from everlasting.
The floods have lifted up, O Lord,
   the floods have lifted up their voice;
   the floods lift up their roaring.
More majestic than the thunders of mighty waters,
   more majestic than the waves of the sea,
   majestic on high is the Lord!
Your decrees are very sure;
   holiness befits your house,
   O Lord, forevermore. (Ps. 93:1-5)

Additional Readings:

Genesis 9:8-17
Sign of the covenant

Acts 27:39-44
*Paul and companions
come safely to land*

Hymn: Come, Thou Almighty King, ELW 408

Dear God, in a world awash with vulgarities, your holiness and majesty are oases of joy and delight. Encourage your children to create holy resting spaces where spirits are renewed, joy is multiplied, and souls are uplifted.

Tuesday, April 29, 2008
WEEK OF EASTER 6

Catherine of Siena, theologian, 1380

1 Peter 3:8-12
Seek peace and pursue it

Finally, all of you, have unity of spirit, sympathy, love for one another, a tender heart, and a humble mind. Do not repay evil for evil or abuse for abuse; but, on the contrary, repay with a blessing. It is for this that you were called—that you might inherit a blessing. For
  "Those who desire life
    and desire to see good days,
  let them keep their tongues from evil
    and their lips from speaking deceit;
  let them turn away from evil and do good;
    let them seek peace and pursue it.
  For the eyes of the Lord are on the righteous,
    and his ears are open to their prayer.
  But the face of the Lord is against those who do evil."
(1 Peter 3:8-12)

Additional Readings:

Deuteronomy 5:22-33
Moses delivers God's commandments

Psalm 93
God reigns above the floods

Hymn: We Are Called, ELW 720

In a world filled with vengeance, Lord, your Son's death and resurrection provide us with a different model for life. Challenge us to live out your new creation in ways that witness to our belief in your power to effect transformation and renewal.

John 16:16-24
A little while, and you shall see

"A little while, and you will no longer see me, and again a little while, and you will see me." Then some of his disciples said to one another, "What does he mean by saying to us, 'A little while, and you will no longer see me, and again a little while, and you will see me'; and 'Because I am going to the Father'?" They said, "What does he mean by this 'a little while'? We do not know what he is talking about." Jesus knew that they wanted to ask him, so he said to them, "Are you discussing among yourselves what I meant when I said, 'A little while, and you will no longer see me, and again a little while, and you will see me'? Very truly, I tell you, you will weep and mourn, but the world will rejoice; you will have pain, but your pain will turn into joy." (John 16:16-20)

Additional Readings:

Deuteronomy 31:1-13
Moses promises God's presence

Psalm 93
God reigns above the floods

Hymn: Lord, Thee I Love with All My Heart, ELW 750

When we do not know the way, Lord, we grow weary and impatient. Calm our anxieties and soothe our troubled spirits, so that we can trust that in your good time and because of your love all will be well.

~ Prayer list for May

Thursday, May 1, 2008
ASCENSION OF OUR LORD

Philip and James, Apostles

Luke 24:44-53
Christ present in all times and places

Then [Jesus] opened their minds to understand the scriptures, and he said to them, "Thus it is written, that the Messiah is to suffer and to rise from the dead on the third day, and that repentance and forgiveness of sins is to be proclaimed in his name to all nations, beginning from Jerusalem. You are witnesses of these things. And see, I am sending upon you what my Father promised; so stay here in the city until you have been clothed with power from on high." (Luke 24:45-49)

Additional Readings:

Acts 1:1-11
Jesus sends the apostles

Psalm 47
God has gone up with a shout

Ephesians 1:15-23
Seeing the risen and ascended Christ

Hymn: A Hymn of Glory Let Us Sing! ELW 393

Almighty God, your only Son was taken into the heavens and in your presence intercedes for us. Receive us and our prayers for all the world, and in the end bring everything into your glory, through Jesus Christ, our Sovereign and Lord, who lives and reigns with you and the Holy Spirit, one God, now and forever.

Friday, May 2, 2008

PHILIP AND JAMES, APOSTLES

(transferred from May 1)

Athanasius, Bishop of Alexandria, 373

John 14:8-14

The Son and the Father are one

Philip said to him, "Lord, show us the Father, and we will be satisfied." Jesus said to him, "Have I been with you all this time, Philip, and you still do not know me? Whoever has seen me has seen the Father. How can you say, 'Show us the Father'? Do you not believe that I am in the Father and the Father is in me? The words that I say to you I do not speak on my own; but the Father who dwells in me does his works." (John 14:8-10)

Additional Readings:

Isaiah 30:18-21	Psalm 44:1-3, 20-26	2 Corinthians 4:1-6
God's mercy and justice	*Save us for the sake of your love*	*Proclaiming Jesus Christ as Lord*

Hymn: Dearest Jesus, at Your Word, ELW 520

Almighty God, you gave to your apostles Philip and James grace and strength to bear witness to your Son. Grant that we, remembering their victory of faith, may glorify in life and death the name of our Lord Jesus Christ, who lives and reigns with you and the Holy Spirit, one God, now and forever.

Saturday, May 3, 2008
Week of Easter 6

Psalm 93
Praise to God who reigns

The Lord is king, he is robed in majesty;
   the Lord is robed, he is girded with strength.
He has established the world; it shall never be moved;
   your throne is established from of old;
   you are from everlasting.
The floods have lifted up, O Lord,
   the floods have lifted up their voice;
   the floods lift up their roaring.
More majestic than the thunders of mighty waters,
   more majestic than the waves of the sea,
   majestic on high is the Lord!
Your decrees are very sure;
   holiness befits your house,
   O Lord, forevermore. (Ps. 93:1-5)

Additional Readings:

2 Kings 2:13-15
The spirit rests on Elisha

John 8:21-30
Jesus speaks of going to the Father

Hymn: Give to Our God Immortal Praise! ELW 848

Majestic Lord, you are the everlasting king robed in majesty and strength. Through your power and promises, continue to reign over your entire creation; showing your abundant mercy upon our hearts and souls.

Sunday, May 4, 2008
SEVENTH SUNDAY OF EASTER

Monica, mother of Augustine, 387

John 17:1-11
Christ's prayer for his disciples

"I have made your name known to those whom you gave me from the world. They were yours, and you gave them to me, and they have kept your word. Now they know that everything you have given me is from you; for the words that you gave to me I have given to them, and they have received them and know in truth that I came from you; and they have believed that you sent me. I am asking on their behalf; I am not asking on behalf of the world, but on behalf of those whom you gave me, because they are yours. All mine are yours, and yours are mine; and I have been glorified in them. And now I am no longer in the world, but they are in the world, and I am coming to you. Holy Father, protect them in your name that you have given me, so that they may be one, as we are one." (John 17:6-11)

Additional Readings:

Acts 1:6-14	Psalm 68:1-10, 32-35	1 Peter 4:12-14; 5:6-11
Jesus' companions at prayer	*Sing to God*	*God sustains those who suffer*

Hymn: Lord, Who the Night You Were Betrayed, ELW 463

O God of glory, your Son Jesus Christ suffered for us and ascended to your right hand. Unite us with Christ and each other, in suffering and in joy, that all the world may be drawn into your bountiful presence, through Jesus Christ, our Savior and Lord, who lives and reigns with you and the Holy Spirit, one God, now and forever.

Monday, May 5, 2008

Psalm 99
Priests and people praise God

The LORD is king; let the peoples tremble!
   He sits enthroned upon the cherubim; let the earth quake!
The LORD is great in Zion;
   he is exalted over all the peoples.
Let them praise your great and awesome name.
   Holy is he!
Mighty King, lover of justice,
   you have established equity;
you have executed justice
   and righteousness in Jacob.
Extol the LORD our God;
   worship at his footstool.
   Holy is he! (Ps. 99:1-5)

Additional Readings:

Leviticus 9:1-11, 22-24
The high priest Aaron offers sacrifice

1 Peter 4:1-6
Live by the will of God

Hymn: Oh, Worship the King, ELW 842

Powerful God, we worship your awesome name with all praise and thanksgiving. As the lover of justice and founder of equity, embolden us to dwell in your holiness by reaching out to your children in need.

Tuesday, May 6, 2008
WEEK OF EASTER 7

1 Peter 4:7-11
Be good stewards of grace

The end of all things is near; therefore be serious and discipline yourselves for the sake of your prayers. Above all, maintain constant love for one another, for love covers a multitude of sins. Be hospitable to one another without complaining. Like good stewards of the manifold grace of God, serve one another with whatever gift each of you has received. Whoever speaks must do so as one speaking the very words of God; whoever serves must do so with the strength that God supplies, so that God may be glorified in all things through Jesus Christ. To him belong the glory and the power forever and ever. Amen. (1 Peter 4:7-11)

Additional Readings:

Numbers 16:41-50
The high priest Aaron makes atonement

Psalm 99
Priests and people praise God

Hymn: We All Are One in Mission, ELW 576

Eternal Lord, as we prepare for the fullness of your reign on earth, compel us to live lives of discipline and obedience towards you. Through love, hospitality, and service, lead us to follow the example of Christ, our redeemer, friend, and guide.

Wednesday, May 7, 2008
WEEK OF EASTER 7

1 Kings 8:54-65
Solomon offers sacrifice

Then the king, and all Israel with him, offered sacrifice before the LORD. Solomon offered as sacrifices of well-being to the LORD twenty-two thousand oxen and one hundred twenty thousand sheep. So the king and all the people of Israel dedicated the house of the LORD. The same day the king consecrated the middle of the court that was in front of the house of the LORD; for there he offered the burnt offerings and the grain offerings and the fat pieces of the sacrifices of well-being, because the bronze altar that was before the LORD was too small to receive the burnt offerings and the grain offerings and the fat pieces of the sacrifices of well-being.

So Solomon held the festival at that time, and all Israel with him—a great assembly, people from Lebo-hamath to the Wadi of Egypt—before the LORD our God, seven days. (1 Kings 8:62-65)

Additional Readings:

John 3:31-36
The Son and the Father

Psalm 99
Priests and people praise God

Hymn: Jesus Shall Reign, ELW 434

God of the ages, as King Solomon offered sacrifices to you in dedication of the temple, may we also offer ourselves as a living sacrifice, by enjoining our hearts to offer all praise and worship to you.

Thursday, May 8, 2008
WEEK OF EASTER 7

Julian of Norwich, renewer of the church, c. 1416

Psalm 33:12-22
Our help and our shield

Truly the eye of the LORD is on those who fear him,
  on those who hope in his steadfast love,
to deliver their soul from death,
  and to keep them alive in famine.
Our soul waits for the LORD;
  he is our help and shield.
Our heart is glad in him,
  because we trust in his holy name.
Let your steadfast love, O LORD, be upon us,
  even as we hope in you. (Ps. 33:18-22)

Additional Readings:

Exodus 19:1-9a
The covenant at Sinai

Acts 2:1-11
The giving of the Spirit

Hymn: Jesus Lives, My Sure Defense, ELW 621

Gracious Lord, our longing souls need you. Be our help and shield in times of sorrow and distress. Let your steadfast love pour into our hungry souls as we find hope and purpose in you.

Friday, May 9, 2008
Week of Easter 7

*Nicolaus Ludwig von Zinzendorf,
renewer of the church, hymnwriter, 1760*

Romans 8:14-17
Led by the Spirit of God

For all who are led by the Spirit of God are children of God.
For you did not receive a spirit of slavery to fall back into fear,
but you have received a spirit of adoption. When we cry, "Abba!
Father!" it is that very Spirit bearing witness with our spirit that
we are children of God, and if children, then heirs, heirs of God
and joint heirs with Christ—if, in fact, we suffer with him so that
we may also be glorified with him. (Rom. 8:14-17)

Additional Readings:

Exodus 19:16-25
Moses and Aaron meet the Lord

Psalm 33:12-22
Our help and our shield

Hymn: We All Believe in One True God, ELW 411

*Living God, lead us with your Spirit. In your Spirit we have been
adopted as your very children and made heirs through the promise of
eternal life in Jesus Christ the Savior.*

Saturday, May 10, 2008
Vigil of Pentecost

John 7:37-39
Jesus, the true living water

On the last day of the festival, the great day, while Jesus was standing there, he cried out, "Let anyone who is thirsty come to me, and let the one who believes in me drink. As the scripture has said, 'Out of the believer's heart shall flow rivers of living water.'" Now he said this about the Spirit, which believers in him were to receive; for as yet there was no Spirit, because Jesus was not yet glorified. (John 7:37-39)

Additional Readings:

Exodus 19:1-9
The covenant at Sinai

Psalm 33:12-22
The Lord is our helper and our shield

Hymn: O Holy Spirit, root of life, ELW 399

Almighty and ever-living God, you fulfilled the promise of Easter by sending the gift of your Holy Spirit. Look upon your people gathered in prayer, open to receive the Spirit's flame. May it come to rest in our hearts and heal the divisions of word and tongue, that with one voice and one song we may praise your name in joy and thanksgiving; through Jesus Christ, our Savior and Lord, who lives and reigns with you and the Holy Spirit, one God, now and forever.

John 20:19-23
The Spirit poured out

When it was evening on that day, the first day of the week, and the doors of the house where the disciples had met were locked for fear of the Jews, Jesus came and stood among them and said, "Peace be with you." After he said this, he showed them his hands and his side. Then the disciples rejoiced when they saw the Lord. Jesus said to them again, "Peace be with you. As the Father has sent me, so I send you." When he had said this, he breathed on them and said to them, "Receive the Holy Spirit. If you forgive the sins of any, they are forgiven them; if you retain the sins of any, they are retained." (John 20:19-23)

Additional Readings:

Acts 2:1-21
Filled with the Spirit

Psalm 104:24-34, 35b
Renewing the face of the earth

1 Corinthians 12:3b-13
Varieties of gifts, the same Spirit

Hymn: O Holy Spirit, Enter In, ELW 786

O God, on this day you open the hearts of your faithful people by sending into us your Holy Spirit. Direct us by the light of that Spirit, that we may have a right judgment in all things and rejoice at all times in your peace, through Jesus Christ, your Son and our Lord, who lives and reigns with you and the Holy Spirit, one God, now and forever.

Monday, May 12, 2008
TIME AFTER PENTECOST

Psalm 104:24-34, 35b
Renewing the face of the earth

O LORD, how manifold are your works!
  In wisdom you have made them all;
  the earth is full of your creatures.
These all look to you
  to give them their food in due season;
when you give to them, they gather it up;
  when you open your hand, they are filled with good things.
When you hide your face, they are dismayed;
  when you take away their breath, they die
  and return to their dust.
When you send forth your spirit, they are created;
  and you renew the face of the ground. (Ps. 104:24, 27-30)

Additional Readings:

Joel 2:18-29   Romans 8:18-24
The promised spirit of God   *We have the first fruits of the Spirit*

Hymn: All Creatures, Worship God Most High, ELW 835

*God of beauty, through your abundant wisdom you have created
and sustained every living thing. By your very own breath, there is life.
Continue to renew creation that it might continue to thrive and serve
you.*

143

Romans 8:26-27
Praying in the Spirit

Likewise the Spirit helps us in our weakness; for we do not
know how to pray as we ought, but that very Spirit intercedes
with sighs too deep for words. And God, who searches the
heart, knows what is the mind of the Spirit, because the Spirit
intercedes for the saints according to the will of God.
(Rom. 8:26-27)

Additional Readings:

Ezekiel 39:7-8, 21-29
The promised spirit of God

Psalm 104:24-34, 35b
Renewing the face of the earth

Hymn: Healer of Our Every Ill, ELW 612

*Strengthening Lord, through your goodness you have sent the Spirit
to help us in our weakness. May the Holy Spirit always intercede for
us in our prayers and may you direct the thoughts that reside in our
hearts.*

Wednesday, May 14, 2008

MATTHIAS, APOSTLE

Luke 6:12-16

Jesus calls the Twelve

Now during those days he went out to the mountain to pray; and he spent the night in prayer to God. And when day came, he called his disciples and chose twelve of them, whom he also named apostles: Simon, whom he named Peter, and his brother Andrew, and James, and John, and Philip, and Bartholomew, and Matthew, and Thomas, and James son of Alphaeus, and Simon, who was called the Zealot, and Judas son of James, and Judas Iscariot, who became a traitor. (Luke 6:12-16)

Additional Readings:

Isaiah 66:1-2
Heaven is God's throne, earth is God's footstool

Psalm 56
I am bound by the vow I made to you

Acts 1:15-26
The apostles cast lots for Matthias

Hymn: The Church of Christ, in Every Age, ELW 729

Almighty God, you chose your faithful servant Matthias to be numbered among the Twelve. Grant that your church may always be taught and guided by faithful and true pastors, through Jesus Christ our shepherd, who lives and reigns with you and the Holy Spirit, one God, now and forever.

Psalm 8
How exalted is your name

O Lord, our Sovereign,
    how majestic is your name in all the earth!
You have set your glory above the heavens.
    Out of the mouths of babes and infants
  you have founded a bulwark because of your foes,
    to silence the enemy and the avenger.
When I look at your heavens, the work of your fingers,
    the moon and the stars that you have established;
what are human beings that you are mindful of them,
    mortals that you care for them?
Yet you have made them a little lower than God,
    and crowned them with glory and honor. (Ps. 8:1-5)

Additional Readings:

Job 38:1-11	2 Timothy 1:8-12a
Creation story from Job	*Grace revealed in Christ*

Hymn: Many and Great, O God, ELW 837

God of creation, how beautiful is your name in all the earth! Through the work of your fingers you established the universe, and in your own image you formed humanity. Continue to bless and renew your vast creation.

Friday, May 16, 2008
Time after Pentecost

2 Timothy 1:12b-14
The treasure of the triune God

But I am not ashamed, for I know the one in whom I have put my trust, and I am sure that he is able to guard until that day what I have entrusted to him. Hold to the standard of sound teaching that you have heard from me, in the faith and love that are in Christ Jesus. Guard the good treasure entrusted to you, with the help of the Holy Spirit living in us. (2 Tim. 1:12b-14)

Additional Readings:

Job 38:12-21
Creation story from Job

Psalm 8
How exalted is your name

Hymn: Praise the Almighty! ELW 877

Gracious God, as the Apostle Paul counseled young Timothy to guard the good treasure, may we place our trust, faith, and love in the treasure we hold in Jesus Christ, who provides us with the riches of heaven.

Saturday, May 17, 2008
Time after Pentecost

John 14:15-17
Father, Son, Spirit

"If you love me, you will keep my commandments. And I will ask the Father, and he will give you another Advocate, to be with you forever. This is the Spirit of truth, whom the world cannot receive, because it neither sees him nor knows him. You know him, because he abides with you, and he will be in you." (John 14:15-17)

Additional Readings:

Job 38:22-38   Psalm 8
Creation story from Job   *How exalted is your name*

Hymn: Day by Day, ELW 790

Always-present Lord, through the Holy Spirit you have promised never to leave us. As the Spirit of Truth continues to abide in us, may we grow in our love and understanding of Jesus and his mission for us.

Sunday, May 18, 2008
THE HOLY TRINITY

Erik, King of Sweden, martyr, 1160

Matthew 28:16-20
Living in the community of the Trinity

Now the eleven disciples went to Galilee, to the mountain
to which Jesus had directed them. When they saw him, they
worshiped him; but some doubted. And Jesus came and said to
them, "All authority in heaven and on earth has been given to
me. Go therefore and make disciples of all nations, baptizing
them in the name of the Father and of the Son and of the
Holy Spirit, and teaching them to obey everything that I have
commanded you. And remember, I am with you always, to the
end of the age." (Matt. 28:16-20)

Additional Readings:

Genesis 1:1—2:4a	Psalm 8	2 Corinthians 13:11-13
Creation of the heavens and the earth	*How exalted is your name*	*Paul's farewell*

Hymn: Holy, Holy, Holy, Lord God Almighty! ELW 413

*Almighty Creator and ever-living God: we worship your glory, eternal
Three-in-One, and we praise your power, majestic One-in-Three. Keep
us steadfast in this faith, defend us in all adversity, and bring us at last
into your presence, where you live in endless joy and love, Father, Son,
and Holy Spirit, one God, now and forever.*

Monday, May 19, 2008
TIME AFTER PENTECOST

Psalm 29
Praise the glory of God

Ascribe to the LORD, O heavenly beings,
  ascribe to the LORD glory and strength.
Ascribe to the LORD the glory of his name;
  worship the LORD in holy splendor.
The LORD sits enthroned over the flood;
  the LORD sits enthroned as king forever.
May the LORD give strength to his people!
  May the LORD bless his people with peace!
(Ps. 29:1-2, 10-11)

Additional Readings:

Job 38:39—39:12   1 Corinthians 12:1-3
Creation story from Job   *Faith is a gift of the Spirit*

Hymn: Oh, That I Had a Thousand Voices, ELW 833

Lord, you are full of might and splendor. As you reign enthroned as king forever, may we continue to worship your glorious name. Continue to strengthen your people and bless us with peace.

Tuesday, May 20, 2008
TIME AFTER PENTECOST

1 Corinthians 12:4-13
The Spirit in the community

Now there are varieties of gifts, but the same Spirit; and there are
varieties of services, but the same Lord; and there are varieties
of activities, but it is the same God who activates all of them in
everyone. To each is given the manifestation of the Spirit for the
common good. (1 Cor. 12:4-7)

Additional Readings:

Job 39:13-25   Psalm 29
Creation story from Job   *Praise the glory of God*

Hymn: O Living Breath of God, ELW 407

*God of community, through the power of your Spirit you have given
a variety of gifts to your followers. Help us not to use these spiritual gifts
for our own gain but to build the church that is your own body.*

Wednesday, May 21, 2008
TIME AFTER PENTECOST

Helena, mother of Constantine, c. 330

John 14:25-26
Father, Son, Spirit

"I have said these things to you while I am still with you. But the Advocate, the Holy Spirit, whom the Father will send in my name, will teach you everything, and remind you of all that I have said to you." (John 14:25-26)

Additional Readings:

Job 39:26—40:5
Creation story from Job;
Job's response

Psalm 29
Praise the glory of God

Hymn: Father Most Holy, ELW 415

Holy Father, your Son Jesus promised that you would send your Holy Spirit to teach us what we need to know and to remind us of Christ's words. Open our hearts to your Spirit so we may continue to receive the everlasting truth.

Thursday, May 22, 2008
TIME AFTER PENTECOST

Psalm 131
A child upon its mother's breast

O LORD, my heart is not lifted up,
  my eyes are not raised too high;
I do not occupy myself with things
  too great and too marvelous for me.
But I have calmed and quieted my soul,
  like a weaned child with its mother;
  my soul is like the weaned child that is with me.
O Israel, hope in the LORD
  from this time on and forevermore. (Ps. 131:1-3)

Additional Readings:

Proverbs 12:22-28   Philippians 2:19-24
Anxiety burdens the heart   *Timothy's worth*

Hymn: When Peace, like a River, ELW 785

O Lord, our hope is in you. Help us not to be filled with pride and arrogance over things that should not concern us. May our souls be calmed and quieted by your nurturing care.

Friday, May 23, 2008
Time after Pentecost

Isaiah 26:1-6
Trust in God

On that day this song will be sung in the land of Judah:
We have a strong city;
  he sets up victory
  like walls and bulwarks.
Open the gates,
  so that the righteous nation that keeps faith
  may enter in.
Those of steadfast mind you keep in peace—
  in peace because they trust in you.
Trust in the Lord forever,
  for in the Lord God
  you have an everlasting rock. (Isa. 26:1-4)

Additional Readings:

Philippians 2:25-30   Psalm 131
Paul overcomes anxiety   *A child upon its mother's breast*

Hymn: Open Now Thy Gates of Beauty, ELW 533

Faithful God, we experience victory in you. As you grant us the gift of peace, help us to place our absolute trust in you, for you are our rock, our protector, our strength, and our salvation.

Saturday, May 24, 2008
Time after Pentecost

Nicolaus Copernicus, 1543; Leonhard Euler, 1783; scientists

Isaiah 31:1-9
Misplaced trust

Alas for those who go down to Egypt for help
   and who rely on horses,
who trust in chariots because they are many
   and in horsemen because they are very strong,
but do not look to the Holy One of Israel
   or consult the Lord!
Yet he too is wise and brings disaster;
   he does not call back his words,
but will rise against the house of the evildoers,
   and against the helpers of those who work iniquity.
The Egyptians are human, and not God;
   their horses are flesh, and not spirit.
When the Lord stretches out his hand,
   the helper will stumble, and the one helped will fall,
   and they will all perish together. (Isa. 31:1-3)

Additional Readings:

Luke 11:14-23
A house divided falls

Psalm 131
A child upon its mother's breast

Hymn: When Our Song Says Peace, ELW 709

Almighty Lord, like the people of Israel we have foolishly trusted in false gods of this world. Through your abundant mercy and steadfast love, forgive our erring ways and help us to trust in you alone.

Matthew 6:24-34
The teaching of Christ: trust in God

"But if God so clothes the grass of the field, which is alive today and tomorrow is thrown into the oven, will he not much more clothe you—you of little faith? Therefore do not worry, saying, 'What will we eat?' or 'What will we drink?' or 'What will we wear?' For it is the Gentiles who strive for all these things; and indeed your heavenly Father knows that you need all these things. But strive first for the kingdom of God and his righteousness, and all these things will be given to you as well." (Matt. 6:30-33)

Additional Readings:

Isaiah 49:8-16a	Psalm 131	1 Corinthians 4:1-5
God's motherly compassion	*A child upon its mother's breast*	*Servants accountable to God*

Hymn: Children of the Heavenly Father, ELW 781

God of tender care, like a mother, like a father, you never forget your children, and you know already what we need. In all our anxiety, give us the spirit of trust and faithful hearts, that in confidence we may embody the peace and justice of your Son, Jesus Christ, our Savior and Lord.

Psalm 104
God cares for all the earth

May the glory of the Lord endure forever;
   may the Lord rejoice in his works—
who looks on the earth and it trembles,
   who touches the mountains and they smoke.
I will sing to the Lord as long as I live;
   I will sing praise to my God while I have being.
May my meditation be pleasing to him,
   for I rejoice in the Lord.
Let sinners be consumed from the earth,
   and let the wicked be no more.
Bless the Lord, O my soul.
Praise the Lord! (Ps. 104:31-35)

Additional Readings:

Deuteronomy 32:1-14
God's care for the chosen people

Hebrews 10:32-39
Confidence that rewards

Hymn: How Great Thou Art, ELW 856

Caring God, because of your continued blessings upon the earth, we will sing praises to you as long as we live. May the meditation of our souls be pleasing to you always.

Tuesday, May 27, 2008
Time after Pentecost

John Calvin, renewer of the church, 1564

1 Corinthians 4:6-21
The life of an apostle

For I think that God has exhibited us apostles as last of all, as though sentenced to death, because we have become a spectacle to the world, to angels and to mortals. We are fools for the sake of Christ, but you are wise in Christ. We are weak, but you are strong. You are held in honor, but we in disrepute. To the present hour we are hungry and thirsty, we are poorly clothed and beaten and homeless, and we grow weary from the work of our own hands. When reviled, we bless; when persecuted, we endure; when slandered, we speak kindly. We have become like the rubbish of the world, the dregs of all things, to this very day. (1 Cor. 4:9-13)

Additional Readings:

1 Kings 17:1-16   Psalm 104
God feeds the widow   *God cares for all the earth*

Hymn: Just a Closer Walk with Thee, ELW 697

Lord of all blessings, your apostles experienced both persecution and joy for sharing Jesus with others. Through your strength, grant us the ability to give witness to Christ and to make the genuine riches of his life known in our world.

Wednesday, May 28, 2008
Time after Pentecost

Isaiah 66:7-13
God as a nursing mother

Rejoice with Jerusalem, and be glad for her,
   all you who love her;
rejoice with her in joy,
   all you who mourn over her—
that you may nurse and be satisfied
   from her consoling breast;
that you may drink deeply with delight
   from her glorious bosom.
For thus says the LORD:
I will extend prosperity to her like a river,
   and the wealth of the nations like an overflowing stream;
and you shall nurse and be carried on her arm,
   and dandled on her knees.
As a mother comforts her child,
   so I will comfort you;
you shall be comforted in Jerusalem. (Isa. 66:10-13)

Additional Readings:

Luke 12:22-31	Psalm 104
Do not worry	*God cares for all the earth*

Hymn: Mothering God, You Gave Me Birth, ELW 735

Nurturing God, as you promise blessing and prosperity upon Jerusalem, bless all who believe in you. Like a nursing mother who feeds her child, continue to satisfy and feed our parched souls with your love and comfort.

Thursday, May 29, 2008
Time after Pentecost

Jiří Tranovský, hymnwriter, 1637

Psalm 31:1-5, 19-24
I commit my spirit

In you, O Lord, I seek refuge;
   do not let me ever be put to shame;
   in your righteousness deliver me.
Incline your ear to me;
   rescue me speedily.
Be a rock of refuge for me,
   a strong fortress to save me.
You are indeed my rock and my fortress;
   for your name's sake lead me and guide me,
take me out of the net that is hidden for me,
   for you are my refuge.
Into your hand I commit my spirit;
   you have redeemed me, O Lord, faithful God.
(Ps. 31:1-5)

Additional Readings:

Exodus 24:1-8
The blood of the covenant

Romans 2:17-29
*Real circumcision a matter
of the heart*

Hymn: What a Friend We Have in Jesus, ELW 742

*Almighty God, as your only Son, Jesus, committed his spirit to you on
the cross, inspire us to commit our lives to you. For it is in you where we
find refuge, righteousness, and redemption.*

Friday, May 30, 2008
TIME AFTER PENTECOST

Deuteronomy 30:1-5
God's fidelity assured

When all these things have happened to you, the blessings and the curses that I have set before you, if you call them to mind among all the nations where the LORD your God has driven you, and return to the LORD your God, and you and your children obey him with all your heart and with all your soul, just as I am commanding you today, then the LORD your God will restore your fortunes and have compassion on you, gathering you again from all the peoples among whom the LORD your God has scattered you. Even if you are exiled to the ends of the world, from there the LORD your God will gather you, and from there he will bring you back. The LORD your God will bring you into the land that your ancestors possessed, and you will possess it; he will make you more prosperous and numerous than your ancestors. (Deut. 30:1-5)

Additional Readings:

Romans 9:6-13
God's election of Israel

Psalm 31:1-5, 19-24
I commit my spirit

Hymn: Oh, That the Lord Would Guide My Ways, ELW 772

God of expectation, as you commanded your chosen people to return to the Lord and obey him with their hearts and souls, help us also to come back to you; the one who faithfully promises restoration and compassion.

Saturday, May 31, 2008
VISIT OF MARY TO ELIZABETH

Luke 1:39-57
Mary greets Elizabeth

In those days Mary set out and went with haste to a Judean town in the hill country, where she entered the house of Zechariah and greeted Elizabeth. When Elizabeth heard Mary's greeting, the child leaped in her womb. And Elizabeth was filled with the Holy Spirit and exclaimed with a loud cry, "Blessed are you among women, and blessed is the fruit of your womb." (Luke 1:39-42)

Additional Readings:

1 Samuel 2:1-10
Hannah's thanksgiving

Psalm 113
God, the helper of the needy

Romans 12:9-16b
Rejoice with those who rejoice

Hymn: Unexpected and Mysterious, ELW 258

Mighty God, by whose grace Elizabeth rejoiced with Mary and greeted her as the mother of the Lord: look with favor on your lowly servants that, with Mary, we may magnify your holy name and rejoice to acclaim her Son as our Savior, who lives and reigns with you and the Holy Spirit, one God, now and forever.

∽ Prayer list for June

_____

_____

_____

_____

_____

_____

_____

_____

_____

_____

_____

Sunday, June 1, 2008
TIME AFTER PENTECOST

Justin, martyr at Rome, c. 165

Matthew 7:21-29
Doing the works of God

"Everyone then who hears these words of mine and acts on them will be like a wise man who built his house on rock. The rain fell, the floods came, and the winds blew and beat on that house, but it did not fall, because it had been founded on rock. And everyone who hears these words of mine and does not act on them will be like a foolish man who built his house on sand. The rain fell, and the floods came, and the winds blew and beat against that house, and it fell—and great was its fall!" (Matt. 7:24-27)

Additional Readings:

Deuteronomy 11:18-21, 26-28
Keeping the words of God

Psalm 31:1-5, 19-24
I commit my spirit

Romans 1:16-17; 3:22b-28 [29-31]
Justified by God's grace as a gift

Hymn: How Firm a Foundation, ELW 796

O God our rock, you offer us a covenant of mercy, and you provide the foundation of our lives. Ground us in your word, and strengthen our resolve to be your disciples, through Jesus Christ, our Savior and Lord.

Monday, June 2, 2008
TIME AFTER PENTECOST

Psalm 52
The wicked and the righteous

The righteous will see, and fear,
   and will laugh at the evildoer, saying,
"See the one who would not take
   refuge in God,
but trusted in abundant riches,
   and sought refuge in wealth!"
But I am like a green olive tree
   in the house of God.
I trust in the steadfast love of God
   forever and ever.
I will thank you forever,
   because of what you have done.
In the presence of the faithful
   I will proclaim your name, for it is good.
(Ps. 52:6-9)

Additional Readings:

Joshua 8:30-35
Joshua renews the covenant

Romans 2:1-11
The righteous judgment of God

Hymn: All Depends on Our Possessing, ELW 589

*Everything that we call our own comes from your gracious hand,
O God. Help us to put our trust in you, the giver, and not the gifts, so
that we might find refuge in your steadfast love.*

Tuesday, June 3, 2008

Time after Pentecost

The Martyrs of Uganda, 1886; John XXIII, Bishop of Rome, 1963

Joshua 24:1-2, 11-28
The Israelites renew the covenant

"Now therefore revere the LORD, and serve him in sincerity and in faithfulness; put away the gods that your ancestors served beyond the River and in Egypt, and serve the LORD. Now if you are unwilling to serve the LORD, choose this day whom you will serve, whether the gods your ancestors served in the region beyond the River or the gods of the Amorites in whose land you are living; but as for me and my household, we will serve the LORD."

Then the people answered, "Far be it from us that we should forsake the LORD to serve other gods; for it is the LORD our God who brought us and our ancestors up from the land of Egypt, out of the house of slavery, and who did those great signs in our sight. He protected us along all the way that we went, and among all the peoples through whom we passed; and the LORD drove out before us all the peoples, the Amorites who lived in the land. Therefore we also will serve the LORD, for he is our God."
(Josh. 24:14-18)

Additional Readings:

Romans 3:9-22a
All have sinned

Psalm 52
The wicked and the righteous

Hymn: O Jesus, I Have Promised, ELW 810

God, you have been faithful to your people throughout all generations, rescuing them from bondage and saving from sin. Turn our hearts to you, so that we might not forsake you but instead serve you in sincerity and faithfulness.

Wednesday, June 4, 2008
TIME AFTER PENTECOST

Matthew 7:13-20
The narrow gate

"Beware of false prophets, who come to you in sheep's clothing but inwardly are ravenous wolves. You will know them by their fruits. Are grapes gathered from thorns, or figs from thistles? In the same way, every good tree bears good fruit, but the bad tree bears bad fruit. A good tree cannot bear bad fruit, nor can a bad tree bear good fruit. Every tree that does not bear good fruit is cut down and thrown into the fire. Thus you will know them by their fruits. (Matt. 7:15-20)

Additional Readings:

Job 28:12-28
The way of wisdom

Psalm 52
The wicked and the righteous

Hymn: Spirit of Gentleness, ELW 396

Lord, there is much in this world that would lead us astray. Give us a discerning spirit so that we might love what is true, walk in your ways, and bear fruit worthy of our calling as your people.

Thursday, June 5, 2008
Time after Pentecost

Boniface, Bishop of Mainz, missionary to Germany, martyr, 754

Psalm 50:7-15
The salvation of God

"Hear, O my people, and I will speak,
  O Israel, I will testify against you.
  I am God, your God.
Offer to God a sacrifice of thanksgiving,
  and pay your vows to the Most High.
Call on me in the day of trouble;
  I will deliver you, and you shall glorify me."
(Ps. 50:7, 14-15)

Additional Readings:

Lamentations 1:7-11   2 Peter 2:17-22
Jerusalem becomes unclean   The world's entanglements

Hymn: O God beyond All Praising, ELW 880

*O God, you are always more willing to listen than we are to speak.
Let our mouths overflow with prayer, praise, and thanksgiving. Hear us
when we call upon you, and deliver us according to your mercy.*

Friday, June 6, 2008
Time after Pentecost

Acts 28:1-10
Paul in Malta heals Publius

Now in the neighborhood of that place were lands belonging to the leading man of the island, named Publius, who received us and entertained us hospitably for three days. It so happened that the father of Publius lay sick in bed with fever and dysentery. Paul visited him and cured him by praying and putting his hands on him. After this happened, the rest of the people on the island who had diseases also came and were cured. They bestowed many honors on us, and when we were about to sail, they put on board all the provisions we needed. (Acts 28:7-10)

Additional Readings:

Lamentations 3:40-58
Let us return to God

Psalm 50:7-15
The salvation of God

Hymn: Come, Ye Disconsolate, ELW 607

O God our healer, the apostles made your power known through acts of healing. Make your power known among us. Bring us wholeness of body, mind, and soul. Let your healing hand be at work in our lives.

Saturday, June 7, 2008
Time after Pentecost

Seattle, chief of the Duwamish Confederacy, 1866

Matthew 9:27-34
Jesus heals those who are blind or mute

As Jesus went on from there, two blind men followed him, crying loudly, "Have mercy on us, Son of David!" When he entered the house, the blind men came to him; and Jesus said to them, "Do you believe that I am able to do this?" They said to him, "Yes, Lord." Then he touched their eyes and said, "According to your faith let it be done to you." And their eyes were opened. Then Jesus sternly ordered them, "See that no one knows of this." But they went away and spread the news about him throughout that district. (Matt. 9:27-31)

Additional Readings:

Exodus 34:1-9
Moses makes new tablets

Psalm 50:7-15
The salvation of God

Hymn: We Come to You for Healing, Lord, ELW 617

The world is full of your wonders, and life testifies to your deeds. Heal our spiritual blindness so that we might recognize your healing power in our lives. Open our eyes of faith, Lord, to see you at work among us.

Sunday, June 8, 2008
TIME AFTER PENTECOST

Matthew 9:9-13, 18-26
Christ heals a woman and raises a girl

As Jesus was walking along, he saw a man called Matthew sitting at the tax booth; and he said to him, "Follow me." And he got up and followed him.

And as he sat at dinner in the house, many tax collectors and sinners came and were sitting with him and his disciples. When the Pharisees saw this, they said to his disciples, "Why does your teacher eat with tax collectors and sinners?" But when he heard this, he said, "Those who are well have no need of a physician, but those who are sick. Go and learn what this means, 'I desire mercy, not sacrifice.' For I have come to call not the righteous but sinners." (Matt. 9:9-13)

Additional Readings:

Hosea 5:15—6:6	Psalm 50:7-15	Romans 4:13-25
God desires steadfast love	*The salvation of God*	*The faith of Abraham*

Hymn: Come, Follow Me, the Savior Spake, ELW 799

O God, you are the source of life and the ground of our being. By the power of your Spirit heal the wounds of this hurting world, and raise us to the new life of your Son, Jesus Christ, our Savior and Lord.

Monday, June 9, 2008
TIME AFTER PENTECOST

Columba, 597; Aidan, 651; Bede, 735; renewers of the church

Psalm 40:1-8
God's will, not sacrifice

Sacrifice and offering you do not desire,
   but you have given me an open ear.
Burnt offering and sin offering
   you have not required.
Then I said, "Here I am;
   in the scroll of the book it is written of me.
I delight to do your will, O my God;
   your law is within my heart." (Ps. 40:6-8)

Additional Readings:

Leviticus 15:25-31; 22:1-9   2 Corinthians 6:14—7:2
Purity regulations   *We are the temple of God*

Hymn: The Lord Now Sends Us Forth, ELW 538

What do you want from us, Lord? Surely not sacrifices or offerings meant to appease you. What do you want from us? Our whole lives. Help us to do your will and walk in your ways.

Hosea 8:11-14; 10:1-2
God rejects Israel's sacrifice

When Ephraim multiplied altars to expiate sin,
  they became to him altars for sinning.
Though I write for him the multitude of my instructions,
  they are regarded as a strange thing.
Though they offer choice sacrifices,
  though they eat flesh,
  the LORD does not accept them.
Now he will remember their iniquity,
  and punish their sins;
  they shall return to Egypt.
Israel has forgotten his Maker,
  and built palaces;
and Judah has multiplied fortified cities;
  but I will send a fire upon his cities,
  and it shall devour his strongholds. (Hosea 8:11-14)

Hebrews 13:1-16   Psalm 40:1-8
Sacrifices pleasing to God   *God's will, not sacrifice*

Hymn: Take My Life, That I May Be, ELW 583/685

How quickly we turn from you, Lord! Often even our piety is only a mask behind which we try to hide our self-serving ways. You, Lord, see through our masks. Though we deserve punishment, we flee to you for mercy.

Wednesday, June 11, 2008
BARNABAS, APOSTLE

Acts 11:19-30; 13:1-3
Barnabas and Saul are set apart

Now in the church at Antioch there were prophets and teachers:
Barnabas, Simeon who was called Niger, Lucius of Cyrene,
Manaen a member of the court of Herod the ruler, and Saul.
While they were worshiping the Lord and fasting, the Holy Spirit
said, "Set apart for me Barnabas and Saul for the work to which I
have called them." Then after fasting and praying they laid their
hands on them and sent them off. (Acts 13:1-3)

Additional Readings:

Isaiah 42:5-12	Psalm 112	Matthew 10:7-16
The LORD calls us in righteousness	*Happy are the God-fearing*	*Jesus sends out the Twelve*

Hymn: Spread, Oh, Spread, Almighty Word, ELW 663

*We praise you, O God, for the life of your faithful servant Barnabas,
who, seeking not his own renown but the well-being of your church,
gave generously of his life and possessions for the relief of the poor and
the spread of the gospel. Grant that we may follow his example and by
our actions give glory to you, Father, Son, and Holy Spirit, now and
forever.*

Thursday, June 12, 2008
TIME AFTER PENTECOST

Exodus 4:18-23
Moses called to Egypt

And the LORD said to Moses, "When you go back to Egypt, see that you perform before Pharaoh all the wonders that I have put in your power; but I will harden his heart, so that he will not let the people go. Then you shall say to Pharaoh, 'Thus says the LORD: Israel is my firstborn son. I said to you, "Let my son go that he may worship me." But you refused to let him go; now I will kill your firstborn son.'" (Exod. 4:21-23)

Additional Readings:

Hebrews 3:1-6   Psalm 100
Moses a servant, Christ   *We are God's people*
a son

Hymn: Wade in the Water, ELW 459

The signs of your presence and power are all around us, Lord, yet we are prone to dismiss them. Open our eyes and hearts, and lead us from the bondage of our sin into the freedom of life in you.

Exodus 4:27-31
Aaron called to Moses' side

The LORD said to Aaron, "Go into the wilderness to meet Moses." So he went; and he met him at the mountain of God and kissed him. Moses told Aaron all the words of the LORD with which he had sent him, and all the signs with which he had charged him. Then Moses and Aaron went and assembled all the elders of the Israelites. Aaron spoke all the words that the LORD had spoken to Moses, and performed the signs in the sight of the people. The people believed; and when they heard that the LORD had given heed to the Israelites and that he had seen their misery, they bowed down and worshiped. (Exod. 4:27-31)

Additional Readings:

Acts 7:35-43
*Israel doubts Moses,
prevails upon Aaron*

Psalm 100
We are God's people

Hymn: God Is Here! ELW 526

God, you see our misery and know our weakness. Open our eyes to see your power and our ears to hear your word of salvation, so that we might bow down and worship you as our Lord and Savior.

Saturday, June 14, 2008
TIME AFTER PENTECOST

Basil the Great, Bishop of Caesarea, 379; Gregory, Bishop of Nyssa, c. 385
Gregory of Nazianzus, Bishop of Constantinople, c. 389;
Macrina, teacher, c. 379

Mark 7:1-13
Moses' witness spurned by religious leaders

Then [Jesus] said to the [Pharisees and scribes], "You have a fine way of rejecting the commandment of God in order to keep your tradition! For Moses said, 'Honor your father and your mother'; and, 'Whoever speaks evil of father or mother must surely die.' But you say that if anyone tells father or mother, 'Whatever support you might have had from me is Corban' (that is, an offering to God)— then you no longer permit doing anything for a father or mother, thus making void the word of God through your tradition that you have handed on. And you do many things like this." (Mark 7:9-13)

Additional Readings:

Exodus 6:28—7:13   Psalm 100
Moses and Aaron before   *We are God's people*
Pharaoh

Hymn: Salvation unto Us Has Come, ELW 590

Lord, your ways are true and your commandments are life-giving. Forgive us when we distort your clear word to sanction our selfishness. Help us to live according to your will and walk according to your commands.

Sunday, June 15, 2008

Time after Pentecost

Matthew 9:35—10:8 [9-23]
The sending of the Twelve

These twelve [disciples] Jesus sent out with the following instructions: "Go nowhere among the Gentiles, and enter no town of the Samaritans, but go rather to the lost sheep of the house of Israel. As you go, proclaim the good news, 'The kingdom of heaven has come near.' Cure the sick, raise the dead, cleanse the lepers, cast out demons. You received without payment; give without payment." (Matt. 10:5-8)

Additional Readings:

Exodus 19:2-8a	Psalm 100	Romans 5:1-8
The covenant with Israel at Sinai	*We are God's people*	*While we were sinners, Christ died for us*

Hymn: The Son of God, Our Christ, ELW 584

God of compassion, you have opened the way for us and brought us to yourself. Pour your love into our hearts, that, overflowing with joy, we may freely share the blessings of your realm and faithfully proclaim the good news of your Son, Jesus Christ, our Savior and Lord.

Monday, June 16, 2008
TIME AFTER PENTECOST

Psalm 105:1-11, 37-45
God saves the chosen people

So he brought his people out with joy,
   his chosen ones with singing.
He gave them the lands of the nations,
   and they took possession of the wealth of the peoples,
that they might keep his statutes
   and observe his laws.
Praise the LORD! (Ps. 105:43-45)

Additional Readings:

Joshua 1:1-11
God calls Joshua

1 Thessalonians 3:1-5
Timothy is sent to Thessalonica

Hymn: Sing with All the Saints in Glory, ELW 426

Your blessings are great and our lives overflow with your abundance. All that we have and are is a gift from your gracious hand. May our lives be filled with joy as we sing your praises!

2 Thessalonians 2:13—3:5
The life of those chosen by God

But we must always give thanks to God for you, brothers and sisters beloved by the Lord, because God chose you as the first fruits for salvation through sanctification by the Spirit and through belief in the truth. For this purpose he called you through our proclamation of the good news, so that you may obtain the glory of our Lord Jesus Christ. So then, brothers and sisters, stand firm and hold fast to the traditions that you were taught by us, either by word of mouth or by our letter. (2 Thess. 2:13-15)

Additional Readings:
1 Samuel 3:1-9   Psalm 105:1-11, 37-45
God calls Samuel   *God saves the chosen people*

Hymn: Lord Jesus Christ, Be Present Now, ELW 527

The good news of salvation rings out through the ages. Thank you, Lord, for witnesses of old who have faithfully proclaimed the gospel. Help us hold fast to your eternal word and be faithful witnesses in this time and place.

Wednesday, June 18, 2008
Time after Pentecost

Proverbs 4:10-27
Choosing the way of wisdom

Hear, my child, and accept my words,
    that the years of your life may be many.
I have taught you the way of wisdom;
    I have led you in the paths of uprightness.
When you walk, your step will not be hampered;
    and if you run, you will not stumble.
Keep hold of instruction; do not let go;
    guard her, for she is your life. (Prov. 4:10-13)

Additional Readings:

Luke 6:12-19
Jesus chooses the apostles

Psalm 105:1-11, 37-45
God saves the chosen people

Hymn: Beloved, God's Chosen, ELW 648

All wisdom comes from you, O Lord. Forgive us when we turn to worldly understanding and knowledge rather than your wise counsel to guide our lives. Help us to walk in the paths of your righteousness.

Thursday, June 19, 2008

TIME AFTER PENTECOST

Psalm 69:7-10 [11-15] 16-18

Draw near to me

Answer me, O LORD, for your steadfast love is good;
  according to your abundant mercy, turn to me.
Do not hide your face from your servant,
  for I am in distress—make haste to answer me.
Draw near to me, redeem me,
  set me free because of my enemies. (Ps. 69:16-18)

Additional Readings:

Jeremiah 18:12-17
Israel's stubborn idolatry

Hebrews 2:5-9
Exaltation through abasement

Hymn: What Wondrous Love Is This, ELW 666

Where are you, Lord? I call out to you but my cry echoes back to me empty. I know that you love me, and I know that you are there. Hear my prayer and answer me according to your mercy.

Friday, June 20, 2008
TIME AFTER PENTECOST

Jeremiah 18:18-23
A plot against Jeremiah

Give heed to me, O LORD,
  and listen to what my adversaries say!
Is evil a recompense for good?
  Yet they have dug a pit for my life.
Remember how I stood before you
  to speak good for them,
  to turn away your wrath from them.
Yet you, O LORD, know
  all their plotting to kill me.
Do not forgive their iniquity,
  do not blot out their sin from your sight.
Let them be tripped up before you;
  deal with them while you are angry. (Jer. 18:19-20, 23)

Additional Readings:

Acts 5:17-26
The apostles are persecuted

Psalm 69:7-10 [11-15] 16-18
Draw near to me

Hymn: Forgive Our Sins As We Forgive, ELW 605

Deceit and falsehood surround us, Lord. Sometimes even people we trust betray our trust and misuse our love. Forgive us when we harm others with our words or deeds. When we are harmed, let us turn to you for justice.

Saturday, June 21, 2008
Time after Pentecost

Onesimos Nesib, translator, evangelist, 1931

Luke 11:53—12:3
What is secret will become known

When he went outside, the scribes and the Pharisees began to be very hostile toward him and to cross-examine him about many things, lying in wait for him, to catch him in something he might say.

Meanwhile, when the crowd gathered by the thousands, so that they trampled on one another, he began to speak first to his disciples, "Beware of the yeast of the Pharisees, that is, their hypocrisy. Nothing is covered up that will not be uncovered, and nothing secret that will not become known. Therefore whatever you have said in the dark will be heard in the light, and what you have whispered behind closed doors will be proclaimed from the housetops." (Luke 11:53—12:3)

Additional Readings:

Jeremiah 20:1-6
Jeremiah persecuted by Pashhur

Psalm 69:7-10 [11-15] 16-18
Draw near to me

Hymn: Praise the One Who Breaks the Darkness, ELW 843

God, before you our lives are laid bare and nothing is hidden. You know all and see all. Forgive our hypocrisy and falsehood. Help us to speak words that build up instead of tear down.

Sunday, June 22, 2008
TIME AFTER PENTECOST

Matthew 10:24-39
The cost of discipleship

Whoever loves father or mother more than me is not worthy
of me; and whoever loves son or daughter more than me is not
worthy of me; and whoever does not take up the cross and follow
me is not worthy of me. Those who find their life will lose it, and
those who lose their life for my sake will find it. (Matt. 10:37-39)

Additional Readings:

Jeremiah 20:7-13	Psalm 69:7-10 [11-15]	Romans 6:1b-11
The prophet must speak	16-18	*Buried and raised with*
	Draw near to me	*Christ in baptism*

Hymn: Take Up Your Cross, the Savior Said, ELW 667

Teach us, good Lord God, to serve you as you deserve, to give and
not to count the cost, to fight and not to heed the wounds, to toil and not
to seek for rest, to labor and not to ask for reward, except that of knowing
that we do your will, through Jesus Christ, our Savior and Lord.

Monday, June 23, 2008
Time after Pentecost

Psalm 6
Prayer for deliverance

O Lord, do not rebuke me in your anger,
　　or discipline me in your wrath.
Be gracious to me, O Lord, for I am languishing;
　　O Lord, heal me, for my bones are shaking with terror.
My soul also is struck with terror,
　　while you, O Lord—how long?
Turn, O Lord, save my life;
　　deliver me for the sake of your steadfast love.
For in death there is no remembrance of you;
　　in Sheol who can give you praise? (Ps. 6:1-5)

Additional Readings:

Micah 7:1-7
The corruption of the people

Revelation 2:1-7
Remember from what you have fallen

Hymn: O God, Our Help in Ages Past, ELW 632

O God of all the living, when bodies fail and spirits falter we ask that you turn to us with your healing power. Remember us according to your love, and deliver us from all dangers that threaten body or soul.

Tuesday, June 24, 2008
JOHN THE BAPTIST

Luke 1:57-67 (68-80)
The birth and naming of John

On the eighth day [Elizabeth and her neighbors and relatives] came to circumcise the child, and they were going to name him Zechariah after his father. But his mother said, "No; he is to be called John." They said to her, "None of your relatives has this name." Then they began motioning to his father to find out what name he wanted to give him. He asked for a writing tablet and wrote, "His name is John." And all of them were amazed. Immediately his mouth was opened and his tongue freed, and he began to speak, praising God. (Luke 1:59-64)

Additional Readings:

Malachi 3:1-4
My messenger, a refiner and purifier

Psalm 141
My eyes are turned to God

Acts 13:13-26
The gospel for the descendents of Abraham

Hymn: Blessed Be the God of Israel, ELW 250

Almighty God, by your gracious providence your servant John the Baptist was born to Elizabeth and Zechariah. Grant to your people the wisdom to see your purpose and the openness to hear your will, that the light of Christ may increase in us, through Jesus Christ, our Savior and Lord, who lives and reigns with you and the Holy Spirit, one God, now and forever.

Wednesday, June 25, 2008
TIME AFTER PENTECOST

Presentation of the Augsburg Confession, 1530
Philipp Melanchthon, renewer of the church, 1560

Matthew 10:5-23
Jesus speaks about persecution

"See, I am sending you out like sheep into the midst of wolves; so be wise as serpents and innocent as doves. Beware of them, for they will hand you over to councils and flog you in their synagogues; and you will be dragged before governors and kings because of me, as a testimony to them and the Gentiles. When they hand you over, do not worry about how you are to speak or what you are to say; for what you are to say will be given to you at that time; for it is not you who speak, but the Spirit of your Father speaking through you." (Matt. 10:16-20)

Additional Readings:

Jeremiah 38:1-13
Jeremiah imprisoned and released

Psalm 6
Prayer for deliverance

Hymn: O God, My Faithful God, ELW 806

Lord, your Son suffered and died for our sake. Be with us when we are persecuted because of our faith. Give us courage to bear witness to the gospel, knowing that you are at work in us.

Thursday, June 26, 2008
TIME AFTER PENTECOST

Psalm 89:1-4, 15-18
I sing of your love

I will sing of your steadfast love, O LORD, forever;
  with my mouth I will proclaim your faithfulness
      to all generations.
I declare that your steadfast love is established forever;
  your faithfulness is as firm as the heavens.
You said, "I have made a covenant with my chosen one,
  I have sworn to my servant David:
'I will establish your descendants forever,
  and build your throne for all generations.'" (Ps. 89:1-4)

Additional Readings:

Jeremiah 25:1-7   Galatians 5:2-6
Israel provokes God's anger   *The nature of Christian freedom*

Hymn: Golden Breaks the Dawn, ELW 852

O Lord, your love is steadfast and your faithfulness is firm. Thank you that we can count on the covenant that you have made with us through your Son, Jesus Christ. May our lives proclaim your praise this day.

Friday, June 27, 2008
Time after Pentecost

Cyril, Bishop of Alexandria, 444

Galatians 5:7-12
Beware of false teachers

You were running well; who prevented you from obeying the truth? Such persuasion does not come from the one who calls you. A little yeast leavens the whole batch of dough. I am confident about you in the Lord that you will not think otherwise. But whoever it is that is confusing you will pay the penalty. But my friends, why am I still being persecuted if I am still preaching circumcision? In that case the offense of the cross has been removed. I wish those who unsettle you would castrate themselves! (Gal. 5:7-12)

Additional Readings:

Jeremiah 25:8-14   Psalm 89:1-4, 15-18
Captivity of Israel foretold   *I sing of your love*

Hymn: Strengthen for Service, Lord, ELW 497

Whereas many preach of glory, you, Lord, point us to the cross. Help us to run the race of faith focused on your grace and mercy, won for us through the death of your Son, Jesus Christ, our Lord.

Saturday, June 28, 2008
TIME AFTER PENTECOST

Irenaeus, Bishop of Lyons, c. 202

Jeremiah 28:1-4
Hananiah prophesies falsely

In that same year, at the beginning of the reign of King Zedekiah of Judah, in the fifth month of the fourth year, the prophet Hananiah son of Azzur, from Gibeon, spoke to me in the house of the LORD, in the presence of the priests and all the people, saying, "Thus says the LORD of hosts, the God of Israel: I have broken the yoke of the king of Babylon. Within two years I will bring back to this place all the vessels of the LORD's house, which King Nebuchadnezzar of Babylon took away from this place and carried to Babylon. I will also bring back to this place King Jeconiah son of Jehoiakim of Judah, and all the exiles from Judah who went to Babylon, says the LORD, for I will break the yoke of the king of Babylon." (Jer. 28:1-4)

Additional Readings:

Luke 17:1-4
Causing little ones to stumble

Psalm 89:1-4, 15-18
I sing of your love

Hymn: God of Grace and God of Glory, ELW 705

Many voices claim to speak for you, Lord. *Give us a discerning spirit, that we might know what truly comes from you. Keep us true to your word made known to us in the scriptures and in your Son, Jesus Christ.*

Sunday, June 29, 2008

Time after Pentecost

Peter and Paul, Apostles

Matthew 10:40-42

Welcome Christ in those Christ sends

"Whoever welcomes you welcomes me, and whoever welcomes
me welcomes the one who sent me. Whoever welcomes a
prophet in the name of a prophet will receive a prophet's reward;
and whoever welcomes a righteous person in the name of a
righteous person will receive the reward of the righteous; and
whoever gives even a cup of cold water to one of these little ones
in the name of a disciple—truly I tell you, none of these will lose
their reward." (Matt. 10:40-42)

Additional Readings:

Jeremiah 28:5-9	Psalm 89:1-4, 15-18	Romans 6:12-23
Test of a true prophet	*I sing of your love*	*No longer under law but under grace*

Hymn: O Christ, Your Heart, Compassionate, ELW 722

*O God, you direct our lives by your grace, and your words of justice
and mercy reshape the world. Mold us into a people who welcome your
word and serve one another through Jesus Christ, our Savior and Lord.*

Monday, June 30, 2008
PETER AND PAUL, APOSTLES

(transferred from June 29)

John 21:15-19
Jesus says to Peter: Tend my sheep

When they had finished breakfast, Jesus said to Simon Peter, "Simon son of John, do you love me more than these?" He said to him, "Yes, Lord; you know that I love you." Jesus said to him, "Feed my lambs." A second time he said to him, "Simon son of John, do you love me?" He said to him, "Yes, Lord; you know that I love you." Jesus said to him, "Tend my sheep." He said to him the third time, "Simon son of John, do you love me?" Peter felt hurt because he said to him the third time, "Do you love me?" And he said to him, "Lord, you know everything; you know that I love you." Jesus said to him, "Feed my sheep." (John 21:15-17)

Additional Readings:

Acts 12:1-11	Psalm 87:1-3, 5-6	2 Timothy 4:6-8, 17-18
Peter released from prison	*Glorious things are spoken of you*	*The good fight of faith*

Hymn: Lord, You Give the Great Commission, ELW 579

Almighty God, we praise you that your blessed apostles Peter and Paul glorified you by their martyrdoms. Grant that your church throughout the world may always be instructed by their teaching and example, be knit together in unity by your Spirit, and ever stand firm upon the one foundation who is Jesus Christ our Lord, for he lives and reigns with you and the Holy Spirit, one God, now and forever.

~ Prayer list for July

Tuesday, July 1, 2008
TIME AFTER PENTECOST

Catherine Winkworth, 1878; John Mason Neale, 1866; hymn translators

1 John 4:1-6
Testing the spirits

Beloved, do not believe every spirit, but test the spirits to see whether they are from God; for many false prophets have gone out into the world. By this you know the Spirit of God: every spirit that confesses that Jesus Christ has come in the flesh is from God, and every spirit that does not confess Jesus is not from God. And this is the spirit of the antichrist, of which you have heard that it is coming; and now it is already in the world. (1 John 4:1-3)

Additional Readings:

1 Kings 21:17-29   Psalm 119:161-168
Elijah confronts Ahab   *Loving God's law*

Hymn: Let Us Ever Walk with Jesus, ELW 802

Source of love and faithfulness, you lead us in ways we can trust. When competing voices urge us to follow, help us sort the genuine from the false. In the name of our truth and life: Jesus Christ our Savior.

Matthew 11:20-24
Jesus prophesies against the cities

Then he began to reproach the cities in which most of his deeds of power had been done, because they did not repent. "Woe to you, Chorazin! Woe to you, Bethsaida! For if the deeds of power done in you had been done in Tyre and Sidon, they would have repented long ago in sackcloth and ashes. But I tell you, on the day of judgment it will be more tolerable for Tyre and Sidon than for you. And you, Capernaum,
  will you be exalted to heaven?
    No, you will be brought down to Hades.
For if the deeds of power done in you had been done in Sodom, it would have remained until this day. But I tell you that on the day of judgment it will be more tolerable for the land of Sodom than for you." (Matt. 11:20-24)

Additional Readings:

Jeremiah 18:1-11
Jeremiah at the potter's wheel

Psalm 119:161-168
Loving God's law

Hymn: Mine Eyes Have Seen the Glory, ELW 890

O God, the turn of galaxies and the dance of molecules show your wonderworking power; our very life and breath are extraordinary gifts. Open our hearts to recognize your deeds, that we may turn again to you and respond with praise; through Jesus Christ our Lord.

Thursday, July 3, 2008
THOMAS, APOSTLE

John 14:1-7
Jesus, the way, the truth, the life

Thomas said to [Jesus], "Lord, we do not know where you are going. How can we know the way?" Jesus said to him, "I am the way, and the truth, and the life. No one comes to the Father except through me. If you know me, you will know my Father also. From now on you do know him and have seen him." (John 14:5-7)

Additional Readings:

Judges 6:36-40
God affirms Gideon's calling

Psalm 136:1-4, 23-26
God's mercy endures forever

Ephesians 4:11-16
The body of Christ has various gifts

Hymn: Come, My Way, My Truth, My Life, ELW 816

Ever-living God, *you strengthened your apostle Thomas with firm and certain faith in the resurrection of your Son. Grant that we too may confess our faith in Jesus Christ, our Lord and our God, who lives and reigns with you and the Holy Spirit, one God, now and forever.*

Friday, July 4, 2008
TIME AFTER PENTECOST

Psalm 145:8-14
God is full of compassion

The LORD is gracious and merciful,
   slow to anger and abounding in steadfast love.
The LORD is good to all,
   and his compassion is over all that he has made.
(Ps. 145:8-9)

Additional Readings:

Zechariah 2:6-13
*Exiles are the apple of
God's eye*

Romans 7:7-20
Sin and the law kill us

Hymn: Thine the Amen, ELW 826

*O everlasting author of liberty and life: throughout our struggles
you keep us as the apple of your eye. From all oppression, free us; when
we fall, lift us; in the name of Christ, in whom we discover mercy,
goodness, and amazing grace.*

Saturday, July 5, 2008
TIME AFTER PENTECOST

Luke 10:21-24
Jesus rejoices in the Holy Spirit

At that same hour Jesus rejoiced in the Holy Spirit and said, "I thank you, Father, Lord of heaven and earth, because you have hidden these things from the wise and the intelligent and have revealed them to infants; yes, Father, for such was your gracious will. All things have been handed over to me by my Father; and no one knows who the Son is except the Father, or who the Father is except the Son and anyone to whom the Son chooses to reveal him."

Then turning to the disciples, Jesus said to them privately, "Blessed are the eyes that see what you see! For I tell you that many prophets and kings desired to see what you see, but did not see it, and to hear what you hear, but did not hear it." (Luke 10:21-24)

Additional Readings:

Zechariah 4:1-7   Psalm 145:8-14
By my Spirit, says God   *God is full of compassion*

Hymn: O God of Mercy, God of Light, ELW 714

Father of mystery and grace, you draw us near and bless the simple with insight. Pour out upon us your Holy Spirit, that we may rejoice in what nations and prophets longed to see: Jesus Christ your Son.

Sunday, July 6, 2008
TIME AFTER PENTECOST

Jan Hus, martyr, 1415

Matthew 11:16-19, 25-30
The yoke of discipleship

"Come to me, all you that are weary and are carrying heavy burdens, and I will give you rest. Take my yoke upon you, and learn from me; for I am gentle and humble in heart, and you will find rest for your souls. For my yoke is easy, and my burden is light." (Matt. 11:28-30)

Additional Readings:

Zechariah 9:9-12	Psalm 145:8-14	Romans 7:15-25a
The king comes in peace	*God is full of compassion*	*The struggle within the self*

Hymn: Softly and Tenderly Jesus Is Calling, ELW 608

You are great, O God, and greatly to be praised. You have made us for yourself, and our hearts are restless until they rest in you. Grant that we may believe in you, call upon you, know you, and serve you through your Son, Jesus Christ, our Savior and Lord.

Monday, July 7, 2008
Time after Pentecost

Psalm 131
I rest like a weaned child on God

O Lord, my heart is not lifted up,
  my eyes are not raised too high;
I do not occupy myself with things
  too great and too marvelous for me.
But I have calmed and quieted my soul,
  like a weaned child with its mother;
  my soul is like the weaned child that is with me.
O Israel, hope in the Lord
  from this time on and forevermore. (Ps. 131:1-3)

Additional Readings:

Jeremiah 27:1-11, 16-22   Romans 1:18-25
Jeremiah wears the evil   *The guilt of humankind*
yoke

Hymn: Come Down, O Love Divine, ELW 804

Sleeping like babies, we rest content in you, O God, nourished on the bread of heaven and the cup of salvation. Amid foolishness, violence, and sin, grant us calm, quiet, and hope. In the name of Christ, our true food and drink.

Jeremiah 28:10-17
Hananiah breaks Jeremiah's yoke

Sometime after the prophet Hananiah had broken the yoke from the neck of the prophet Jeremiah, the word of the LORD came to Jeremiah: Go, tell Hananiah, Thus says the LORD: You have broken wooden bars only to forge iron bars in place of them! For thus says the LORD of hosts, the God of Israel: I have put an iron yoke on the neck of all these nations so that they may serve King Nebuchadnezzar of Babylon, and they shall indeed serve him; I have even given him the wild animals. And the prophet Jeremiah said to the prophet Hananiah, "Listen, Hananiah, the LORD has not sent you, and you made this people trust in a lie. Therefore thus says the LORD: I am going to send you off the face of the earth. Within this year you will be dead, because you have spoken rebellion against the LORD."

In that same year, in the seventh month, the prophet Hananiah died. (Jer. 28:12-17)

Additional Readings:

Romans 3:1-8
The faithfulness of God

Psalm 131
I rest like a weaned child on God

Hymn: Bring Peace to Earth Again, ELW 700

Judge of all nations and ground of truth: at times the yokes on our shoulders are heavier than we can bear. Comfort and strengthen us in the name of the one who, sharing our burden, brought salvation to all: Jesus Christ our Lord.

Wednesday, July 9, 2008
Time after Pentecost

Jeremiah 13:1-11
Jeremiah's loincloth

Then the word of the LORD came to me: Thus says the LORD: Just so I will ruin the pride of Judah and the great pride of Jerusalem. This evil people, who refuse to hear my words, who stubbornly follow their own will and have gone after other gods to serve them and worship them, shall be like this loincloth, which is good for nothing. For as the loincloth clings to one's loins, so I made the whole house of Israel and the whole house of Judah cling to me, says the LORD, in order that they might be for me a people, a name, a praise, and a glory. But they would not listen. (Jer. 13:8-11)

Additional Readings:

John 13:1-17
Jesus washes the disciples' feet

Psalm 131
I rest like a weaned child on God

Hymn: Abide with Me, ELW 629

Merciful Creator, in our care for what is tender and vulnerable in our lives, we sense your steadfast care for us. Fill us with reverence rather than shame, that we may glorify you in our bodies, for the sake of the Word made flesh, Jesus Christ.

Thursday, July 10, 2008
Time after Pentecost

Psalm 65:[1-8] 9-13
Your paths overflow with plenty

You visit the earth and water it,
  you greatly enrich it;
the river of God is full of water;
  you provide the people with grain,
  for so you have prepared it.
You water its furrows abundantly,
  settling its ridges,
softening it with showers,
  and blessing its growth.
You crown the year with your bounty;
  your wagon tracks overflow with richness.
The pastures of the wilderness overflow,
  the hills gird themselves with joy,
the meadows clothe themselves with flocks,
  the valleys deck themselves with grain,
  they shout and sing together for joy. (Ps. 65:9-13)

Additional Readings:

Isaiah 48:1-5
What God declared long ago

Romans 2:12-16
God judges the secret thoughts

Hymn: Praise and Thanksgiving, ELW 689

Joyful Giver, watermelon and sunflower spring up in abundance; tomatoes and corn and squash vines give you praise. May fields and gardens remind us of the glorious power you have hidden in the merest seeds; through the word-sower, Jesus Christ our Lord.

Friday, July 11, 2008
Time after Pentecost

Benedict of Nursia, Abbot of Monte Cassino, c. 540

Romans 15:14-21
Sanctified by the Holy Spirit

I myself feel confident about you, my brothers and sisters, that you yourselves are full of goodness, filled with all knowledge, and able to instruct one another. Nevertheless on some points I have written to you rather boldly by way of reminder, because of the grace given me by God to be a minister of Christ Jesus to the Gentiles in the priestly service of the gospel of God, so that the offering of the Gentiles may be acceptable, sanctified by the Holy Spirit. In Christ Jesus, then, I have reason to boast of my work for God. (Rom. 15:14-17)

Additional Readings:

Isaiah 48:6-11
You will hear new, hidden things

Psalm 65:[1-8] 9-13
Your paths overflow with plenty

Hymn: What Is This Place, ELW 524

As you cause seed to sprout, O God, bringing forth life, so you call unknown things into being and gather a new people around your word. Make us holy in the work of welcoming and instructing one another, our priestly service of the gospel of Christ.

Saturday, July 12, 2008
Time after Pentecost

Nathan Söderblom, Bishop of Uppsala, 1931

Isaiah 52:1-6
Sold, redeemed without money

For thus says the Lord: You were sold for nothing, and you shall be redeemed without money. For thus says the Lord God: Long ago, my people went down into Egypt to reside there as aliens; the Assyrian, too, has oppressed them without cause. Now therefore what am I doing here, says the Lord, seeing that my people are taken away without cause? Their rulers howl, says the Lord, and continually, all day long, my name is despised. Therefore my people shall know my name; therefore in that day they shall know that it is I who speak; here am I. (Isa. 52:3-6)

Additional Readings:

John 12:44-50
I have come as light into the world

Psalm 65:[1-8] 9-13
Your paths overflow with plenty

Hymn: O God of Every Nation, ELW 713

God, our redeemer and our refuge: long ago you spoke to your people and blessed them with your name. In times of sojourn and exile, grant that we may hear your voice; through Christ our Savior, whose words are light and life.

Sunday, July 13, 2008
TIME AFTER PENTECOST

Matthew 13:1-9, 18-23
The parable of the sower and the seed

And he told them many things in parables, saying: "Listen! A sower went out to sow. And as he sowed, some seeds fell on the path, and the birds came and ate them up. Other seeds fell on rocky ground, where they did not have much soil, and they sprang up quickly, since they had no depth of soil. But when the sun rose, they were scorched; and since they had no root, they withered away. Other seeds fell among thorns, and the thorns grew up and choked them. Other seeds fell on good soil and brought forth grain, some a hundredfold, some sixty, some thirty. Let anyone with ears listen!" (Matt. 13:3-9)

Additional Readings:

Isaiah 55:10-13
The growth of the word

Psalm 65:[1-8] 9-13
Your paths overflow with plenty

Romans 8:1-11
Living according to the Spirit

Hymn: Lord, Let My Heart Be Good Soil, ELW 512

Almighty God, we thank you for planting in us the seed of your word. By your Holy Spirit help us to receive it with joy, live according to it, and grow in faith and hope and love, through Jesus Christ, our Savior and Lord.

Monday, July 14, 2008
Time after Pentecost

Psalm 92
The righteous as a tree

The righteous flourish like the palm tree,
   and grow like a cedar in Lebanon.
They are planted in the house of the LORD;
   they flourish in the courts of our God.
In old age they still produce fruit;
   they are always green and full of sap,
showing that the LORD is upright;
   he is my rock, and there is no unrighteousness in him.
(Ps. 92:12-15)

Additional Readings:

Leviticus 26:3-20   1 Thessalonians 4:1-8
A rich and a poor harvest   A life pleasing to God

Hymn: My Hope Is Built on Nothing Less, ELW 596/597

As trees of the forest sink down roots toward hidden streams, so stretch us to seek our refreshment in you, O God, that we may grow all the days of our life and bear fruit. This we ask through the one victorious on a tree, Christ our Lord.

Ephesians 4:17—5:2
The old life and the new

Let no evil talk come out of your mouths, but only what is useful for building up, as there is need, so that your words may give grace to those who hear. And do not grieve the Holy Spirit of God, with which you were marked with a seal for the day of redemption. Put away from you all bitterness and wrath and anger and wrangling and slander, together with all malice, and be kind to one another, tenderhearted, forgiving one another, as God in Christ has forgiven you. (Eph. 4:29-32)

Additional Readings:

Deuteronomy 28:1-14   Psalm 92
The blessings of obedience   *The righteous as a tree*

Hymn: God, When Human Bonds Are Broken, ELW 603

God of the new creation, when conflicts arise that tempt us to tear one another down, teach us to argue in ways that build up; for you have sealed us with the Holy Spirit and marked us with the cross of Christ forever.

Wednesday, July 16, 2008
Time after Pentecost

Proverbs 11:23-30
The fruit of righteousness

Whoever diligently seeks good seeks favor,
   but evil comes to the one who searches for it.
Those who trust in their riches will wither,
   but the righteous will flourish like green leaves.
Those who trouble their households will inherit wind,
   and the fool will be servant to the wise.
The fruit of the righteous is a tree of life,
   but violence takes lives away. (Prov. 11:27-30)

Additional Readings:

Matthew 13:10-17
The purpose of parable

Psalm 92
The righteous as a tree

Hymn: Be Thou My Vision, ELW 793

Holy One, you speak in words that spark our imagination and cause us to reflect. Send forth your Spirit, that we may ponder them and form our lives according to your will. In the name of Christ, our Wisdom and Word.

Thursday, July 17, 2008
TIME AFTER PENTECOST

Bartolomé de Las Casas, missionary to the Indies, 1566

Psalm 86:11-17
Teach me your ways

Teach me your way, O LORD,
  that I may walk in your truth;
  give me an undivided heart to revere your name.
I give thanks to you, O Lord my God, with my whole heart,
  and I will glorify your name forever.
For great is your steadfast love toward me;
  you have delivered my soul from the depths of Sheol.
(Ps. 86:11-13)

Additional Readings:

Isaiah 41:21-29
The futility of idols

Hebrews 2:1-9
Warning to pay attention

Hymn: O Master, Let Me Walk with You, ELW 818

Lord our God, you alone have power to rescue our souls from death. In a world filled with idols, help us to fix our trust in you, that we may serve you with gladness and singleness of heart; through Christ our Savior.

Friday, July 18, 2008
Time after Pentecost

Hebrews 6:13-20
The certainty of God's promises

When God made a promise to Abraham, because he had no one greater by whom to swear, he swore by himself, saying, "I will surely bless you and multiply you." And thus Abraham, having patiently endured, obtained the promise. (Heb. 6:13-15)

Additional Readings:

Isaiah 44:9-17
Those who make idols are nothing

Psalm 86:11-17
Teach me your ways

Hymn: The God of Abraham Praise, ELW 831

God, who numbers the stars and the sands of the seashore: to Abraham and Sarah, childless in old age, you promised offspring. Encourage us to seize the hope set before us as a sure and steadfast anchor; in Christ, whose promise endures forever.

Matthew 7:15-20
A tree and its fruit

"Beware of false prophets, who come to you in sheep's clothing but inwardly are ravenous wolves. You will know them by their fruits. Are grapes gathered from thorns, or figs from thistles? In the same way, every good tree bears good fruit, but the bad tree bears bad fruit. A good tree cannot bear bad fruit, nor can a bad tree bear good fruit. Every tree that does not bear good fruit is cut down and thrown into the fire. Thus you will know them by their fruits." (Matt. 7:15-20)

Additional Readings:

Isaiah 44:18-20
Idols do not know or comprehend

Psalm 86:11-17
Teach me your ways

Hymn: If God My Lord Be for Me, ELW 788

O Creator of thistle and grape, of fig and thorn: as we watch plants that grow and listen to people around us, looks and sounds may deceive. Give us patience in judgment until the truth hidden within is revealed by their fruits; in the name of Christ.

Sunday, July 20, 2008
Time after Pentecost

Matthew 13:24-30, 36-43
The parable of the weeds

He put before them another parable: "The kingdom of heaven
may be compared to someone who sowed good seed in his field;
but while everybody was asleep, an enemy came and sowed
weeds among the wheat, and then went away. So when the plants
came up and bore grain, then the weeds appeared as well. And
the slaves of the householder came and said to him, 'Master,
did you not sow good seed in your field? Where, then, did these
weeds come from?' He answered, 'An enemy has done this.' The
slaves said to him, 'Then do you want us to go and gather them?'
But he replied, 'No; for in gathering the weeds you would uproot
the wheat along with them. Let both of them grow together until
the harvest; and at harvest time I will tell the reapers, Collect the
weeds first and bind them in bundles to be burned, but gather
the wheat into my barn.'" (Matt. 13:24-30)

Additional Readings:

Isaiah 44:6-8	Psalm 86:11-17	Romans 8:12-25
There is no other God	*Teach me your ways*	*The revealing of the children of God*

Hymn: Come, Ye Thankful People, Come, ELW 693

*Faithful God, most merciful judge, you care for your children with
firmness and compassion. By your Spirit nurture us who live in your
kingdom, that we may be rooted in the way of your Son, Jesus Christ,
our Savior and Lord.*

Psalm 75
God's judgment

We give thanks to you, O God;
   we give thanks; your name is near.
People tell of your wondrous deeds.
At the set time that I appoint
   I will judge with equity.
When the earth totters, with all its inhabitants,
   it is I who keep its pillars steady. (Ps. 75:1-3)

Additional Readings:

Nahum 1:1-13
The wrath and mercy of God

Revelation 14:12-20
The harvest at the end of time

Hymn: How Great Thou Art, ELW 856

God Most High, slow to anger but great in power: your judgments are strong and sure. Amid terror and chaos, refine our focus and steady our hearts with the assurance of Christ's unfailing love; in whose name we dare to pray.

Tuesday, July 22, 2008
Mary Magdalene, Apostle

John 20:1-2, 11-18
Mary Magdalene meets Jesus in the garden

Jesus said to [Mary Magdalene], "Woman, why are you weeping? Whom are you looking for?" Supposing him to be the gardener, she said to him, "Sir, if you have carried him away, tell me where you have laid him, and I will take him away." Jesus said to her, "Mary!" She turned and said to him in Hebrew, "Rabbouni!" (which means Teacher). Jesus said to her, "Do not hold on to me, because I have not yet ascended to the Father. But go to my brothers and say to them, 'I am ascending to my Father and your Father, to my God and your God.'" Mary Magdalene went and announced to the disciples, "I have seen the Lord"; and she told them that he had said these things to her. (John 20:15-18)

Additional Readings:

Ruth 1:6-18	Psalm 73:23-28	Acts 13:26-33a
Ruth stays with Naomi	*I will speak of all God's works*	*The raising of Jesus fulfills God's promise*

Hymn: Hallelujah! Jesus Lives! ELW 380

Almighty God, your Son first entrusted the apostle Mary Magdalene with the joyful news of his resurrection. Following the example of her witness, may we proclaim Christ as our living Lord and one day see him in glory, for he lives and reigns with you and the Holy Spirit, one God, now and forever.

Wednesday, July 23, 2008
TIME AFTER PENTECOST

Birgitta of Sweden, renewer of the church, 1373

Daniel 12:1-13
The righteous will shine

"At that time Michael, the great prince, the protector of your people, shall arise. There shall be a time of anguish, such as has never occurred since nations first came into existence. But at that time your people shall be delivered, everyone who is found written in the book. Many of those who sleep in the dust of the earth shall awake, some to everlasting life, and some to shame and everlasting contempt. Those who are wise shall shine like the brightness of the sky, and those who lead many to righteousness, like the stars forever and ever. But you, Daniel, keep the words secret and the book sealed until the time of the end. Many shall be running back and forth, and evil shall increase." (Dan. 12:1-4)

Additional Readings:

Matthew 12:15-21   Psalm 75
God's chosen servant   *God's judgment*

Hymn: I'm So Glad Jesus Lifted Me, ELW 860

Lord of all eternity, in our times of anguish, rouse us from despair and fear by the bright vision of resurrection into glory. Inscribe us in your book and deliver us from evil, through the mercy of Jesus Christ, our mediator and Morning Star.

Psalm 119:129-136
Light and understanding

Your decrees are wonderful;
  therefore my soul keeps them.
The unfolding of your words gives light;
  it imparts understanding to the simple.
With open mouth I pant,
  because I long for your commandments.
Turn to me and be gracious to me,
  as is your custom toward those who love your name.
Keep my steps steady according to your promise,
  and never let iniquity have dominion over me.
(Ps. 119:129-133)

Additional Readings:

1 Kings 1:28-37
Solomon designated as king

1 Corinthians 4:14-20
Reign of God depends not on talk but power

Hymn: Let All Things Now Living, ELW 881

God our covenant-partner, your word gives shape and meaning to our lives. Sharpen our desire for holy Scripture. Let every encounter increase our love for you and enrich our understanding; through Jesus of Nazareth, incarnate Word.

Friday, July 25, 2008
JAMES, APOSTLE

Mark 10:35-45
Whoever wishes to be great must serve

James and John, the sons of Zebedee, came forward to him and said to him, "Teacher, we want you to do for us whatever we ask of you." And he said to them, "What is it you want me to do for you?" And they said to him, "Grant us to sit, one at your right hand and one at your left, in your glory." But Jesus said to them, "You do not know what you are asking. Are you able to drink the cup that I drink, or be baptized with the baptism that I am baptized with?" They replied, "We are able." Then Jesus said to them, "The cup that I drink you will drink; and with the baptism with which I am baptized, you will be baptized; but to sit at my right hand or at my left is not mine to grant, but it is for those for whom it has been prepared." (Mark 10:35-40)

Additional Readings:

1 Kings 19:9-18	Psalm 7:1-10	Acts 11:27—12:3a
Elijah hears God in the midst of silence	*God, my shield and defense*	*James is killed by Herod*

Hymn: Will You Let Me Be Your Servant, ELW 659

Gracious God, we remember before you today your servant and apostle James, the first among the twelve to be martyred for the name of Jesus Christ. Pour out on the leaders of your church that spirit of self-denying service which is the true mark of authority among your people, through Jesus Christ our servant, who lives and reigns with you and the Holy Spirit, one God, now and forever.

Saturday, July 26, 2008
TIME AFTER PENTECOST

1 Kings 2:1-4
David's instructions to Solomon

When David's time to die drew near, he charged his son
Solomon, saying: "I am about to go the way of all the earth.
Be strong, be courageous, and keep the charge of the LORD
your God, walking in his ways and keeping his statutes, his
commandments, his ordinances, and his testimonies, as it is
written in the law of Moses, so that you may prosper in all that
you do and wherever you turn. Then the LORD will establish his
word that he spoke concerning me: 'If your heirs take heed to
their way, to walk before me in faithfulness with all their heart
and with all their soul, there shall not fail you a successor on the
throne of Israel.'" (1 Kings 2:1-4)

Additional Readings:

Matthew 12:38-42
*Something greater than
Solomon is here*

Psalm 119:129-136
Light and understanding

Hymn: Lord of All Nations, Grant Me Grace, ELW 716

*Blessed are you, O Ancient of Days, for the inheritance received
through your chosen people from generation to generation until now.
Help us honor the precious gift of your law by walking before you in
faithfulness; through Jesus, heir of the promise.*

Sunday, July 27, 2008
TIME AFTER PENTECOST

Matthew 13:31-33, 44-52
Parables of the reign of heaven

[Jesus] told them another parable: "The kingdom of heaven is like yeast that a woman took and mixed in with three measures of flour until all of it was leavened.

"The kingdom of heaven is like treasure hidden in a field, which someone found and hid; then in his joy he goes and sells all that he has and buys that field.

"Again, the kingdom of heaven is like a merchant in search of fine pearls; on finding one pearl of great value, he went and sold all that he had and bought it." (Matt. 13:33, 44-46)

Additional Readings:

1 Kings 3:5-12
Solomon's prayer for wisdom

Psalm 119:129-136
Light and understanding

Romans 8:26-39
Nothing can separate us from God's love

Hymn: Jesus, Priceless Treasure, ELW 775

Beloved and sovereign God, through the death and resurrection of your Son you bring us into your kingdom of justice and mercy. By your Spirit, give us your wisdom, that we may treasure the life that comes from Jesus Christ, our Savior and Lord.

Monday, July 28, 2008
Time after Pentecost

Johann Sebastian Bach, 1750; Heinrich Schütz, 1672;
George Frederick Handel, 1759; musicians

Psalm 119:121-128
Give me understanding

I am your servant; give me understanding,
   so that I may know your decrees.
It is time for the LORD to act,
   for your law has been broken.
Truly I love your commandments
   more than gold, more than fine gold.
Truly I direct my steps by all your precepts;
   I hate every false way. (Ps. 119:125-128)

Additional Readings:

1 Kings 3:16-28   James 3:13-18
Solomon's wisdom in   *Two kinds of wisdom*
judgment

Hymn: Come with Us, O Blessed Jesus, ELW 501

Almighty and ever-living God, the words of your law sing in our hearts and direct our steps in joyful paths. Give us this music always, for you have become our strength, our song, and our salvation: Jesus Christ our Lord.

Tuesday, July 29, 2008

TIME AFTER PENTECOST

Mary, Martha, and Lazarus of Bethany
Olaf, King of Norway, martyr, 1030

Ephesians 6:10-18

The allegory of the armor of God

Finally, be strong in the Lord and in the strength of his power. Put on the whole armor of God, so that you may be able to stand against the wiles of the devil. For our struggle is not against enemies of blood and flesh, but against the rulers, against the authorities, against the cosmic powers of this present darkness, against the spiritual forces of evil in the heavenly places. Therefore take up the whole armor of God, so that you may be able to withstand on that evil day, and having done everything, to stand firm. (Eph. 6:10-13)

Additional Readings:

1 Kings 4:29-34	Psalm 119:121-128
God gave Solomon wisdom	*Give me understanding*

Hymn: Lord of Our Life, ELW 766

Protect us, O God; for in you we take refuge. May we use discretion with the power of our knowledge; that in the conflict against ignorance and fear we may be wise as serpents and innocent as doves, obedient to Jesus Christ.

Wednesday, July 30, 2008
TIME AFTER PENTECOST

Proverbs 1:1-7, 20-33
The call of wisdom

Wisdom cries out in the street;
 in the squares she raises her voice.
At the busiest corner she cries out;
 at the entrance of the city gates she speaks:
"How long, O simple ones, will you love being simple?
How long will scoffers delight in their scoffing
 and fools hate knowledge?
Give heed to my reproof;
I will pour out my thoughts to you;
 I will make my words known to you. (Prov. 1:20-23)

Additional Readings:

Mark 4:30-34   Psalm 119:121-128
Jesus' use of parables   *Give me understanding*

Hymn: We Eat the Bread of Teaching, ELW 518

Mothering God, you call to us in hope that we might listen and respond. Above the clamor at the busiest corners of our souls, raise your voice, that we too may enter the gates of understanding; in the name of Wisdom's prophet, Rabbi Jesus.

Thursday, July 31, 2008
TIME AFTER PENTECOST

Psalm 145:8-9, 14-21
You open wide your hand

The LORD upholds all who are falling,
   and raises up all who are bowed down.
The eyes of all look to you,
   and you give them their food in due season.
You open your hand,
   satisfying the desire of every living thing.
(Ps. 145:14-16)

Additional Readings:

Proverbs 10:1-5
*The righteous will not go
hungry*

Philippians 4:10-15
*Being well fed and yet
hungry*

Hymn: You Satisfy the Hungry Heart, ELW 484

Gracious Provider, in compassion you give us daily bread. Coax open our fingers, that our outspread hands may be signs of your own. We ask this through the one whose generous hands, having blessed and broken and given bread, opened widest of all for us upon the cross.

Prayer list for August

Friday, August 1, 2008
Time after Pentecost

Isaiah 51:17-23
Drink no more from the bowl of wrath

Therefore hear this, you who are wounded,
    who are drunk, but not with wine:
Thus says your Sovereign, the LORD,
    your God who pleads the cause of his people:
See, I have taken from your hand the cup of staggering;
you shall drink no more
    from the bowl of my wrath.
And I will put it into the hand of your tormentors,
    who have said to you,
    "Bow down, that we may walk on you";
and you have made your back like the ground
    and like the street for them to walk on. (Isa. 51:21-23)

Additional Readings:

Romans 9:6-13
True descendants of Abraham

Psalm 145:8-9, 14-21
You open wide your hand

Hymn: All Are Welcome, ELW 641

Sovereign Lord, the downtrodden look to you for justice. Stir us up to join your work, to help you plead the cause of the oppressed in this world. This we ask through your Son, our Lord Jesus Christ.

Isaiah 44:1-5
God's blessing on Israel

But now hear, O Jacob my servant,
  Israel whom I have chosen!
Thus says the LORD who made you,
  who formed you in the womb and will help you:
Do not fear, O Jacob my servant,
  Jeshurun whom I have chosen.
For I will pour water on the thirsty land,
  and streams on the dry ground;
I will pour my spirit upon your descendants,
  and my blessing on your offspring.
They shall spring up like a green tamarisk,
  like willows by flowing streams.
This one will say, "I am the LORD's,"
  another will be called by the name of Jacob,
yet another will write on the hand, "The LORD's,"
  and adopt the name of Israel. (Isa. 44:1-5)

Additional Readings:

Matthew 7:7-11   Psalm 145:8-9, 14-21
Bread and stones   *You open wide your hand*

Hymn: How Sweet the Name of Jesus Sounds, ELW 620

Creator God, you bless us by pouring out water and your spirit on us, your adopted children. Grant us grace to respond with joy, gratefully serving you and our neighbor. We pray through your Son, our Lord Jesus Christ.

Sunday, August 3, 2008
TIME AFTER PENTECOST

Matthew 14:13-21
Jesus feeds 5000

Then [Jesus] ordered the crowds to sit down on the grass. Taking the five loaves and the two fish, he looked up to heaven, and blessed and broke the loaves, and gave them to the disciples, and the disciples gave them to the crowds. And all ate and were filled; and they took up what was left over of the broken pieces, twelve baskets full. And those who ate were about five thousand men, besides women and children. (Matt. 14:19-21)

Additional Readings:

Isaiah 55:1-5
Eat and drink what truly satisfies

Psalm 145:8-9, 14-21
You open wide your hand

Romans 9:1-5
The glory of God's people in Israel

Hymn: O Bread of Life from Heaven, ELW 480

Glorious God, your generosity waters the world with goodness, and you cover creation with abundance. Awaken in us a hunger for the food that satisfies both body and spirit, and with this food fill all the starving world; through your Son, Jesus Christ, our Savior and Lord.

Monday, August 4, 2008
TIME AFTER PENTECOST

Psalm 78:1-8, 17-29
God fed the people with manna

Yet [the LORD] commanded the skies above,
  and opened the doors of heaven;
he rained down on them manna to eat,
  and gave them the grain of heaven.
Mortals ate of the bread of angels;
  he sent them food in abundance. (Ps. 78:23-25)

Additional Readings:

Deuteronomy 8:1-10
God will feed the people

Romans 1:8-15
A harvest among the Gentiles

Hymn: Break Now the Bread of Life, ELW 515

Generous God, you feed your hungry people with the bread of the angels. Let that food strengthen us to praise your name and call others to feast at your table. This we ask through your Son, Jesus Christ our Lord.

Tuesday, August 5, 2008
TIME AFTER PENTECOST

Acts 2:37-47
The believers breaking bread

Awe came upon everyone, because many wonders and signs were being done by the apostles. All who believed were together and had all things in common; they would sell their possessions and goods and distribute the proceeds to all, as any had need. Day by day, as they spent much time together in the temple, they broke bread at home and ate their food with glad and generous hearts, praising God and having the goodwill of all the people. And day by day the Lord added to their number those who were being saved. (Acts 2:43-47)

Additional Readings:

Deuteronomy 26:1-15
A tithe from God's harvest

Psalm 78:1-8, 17-29
God fed the people with manna

Hymn: Draw Us in the Spirit's Tether, ELW 470

Loving God, your Holy Spirit led the first believers to generosity and peace. Grant that we too may be renewed by your Spirit, that we may praise you with glad and generous hearts. We pray through Jesus Christ our Lord.

Wednesday, August 6, 2008
TIME AFTER PENTECOST

Exodus 16:2-15, 31-35
God feeds the people manna

The whole congregation of the Israelites complained against Moses and Aaron in the wilderness. The Israelites said to them, "If only we had died by the hand of the LORD in the land of Egypt, when we sat by the fleshpots and ate our fill of bread; for you have brought us out into this wilderness to kill this whole assembly with hunger."

Then the LORD said to Moses, "I am going to rain bread from heaven for you, and each day the people shall go out and gather enough for that day. In that way I will test them, whether they will follow my instruction or not." (Exod. 16:2-4)

Additional Readings:

Matthew 15:32-39
Jesus feeds 4000

Psalm 78:1-8, 17-29
God fed the people with manna

Hymn: Glorious Things of You Are Spoken, ELW 647

Blessed are you, saving God, for you answer our ingratitude with unheard-of generosity. Forgive our selfishness, and teach us gratitude for all your gifts. This we ask through your greatest gift, your Son, our Lord Jesus Christ.

Thursday, August 7, 2008
TIME AFTER PENTECOST

Psalm 85:8-13
I will listen to God

Let me hear what God the LORD will speak,
   for he will speak peace to his people,
   to his faithful, to those who turn to him in their hearts.
Surely his salvation is at hand for those who fear him,
   that his glory may dwell in our land.
Steadfast love and faithfulness will meet;
   righteousness and peace will kiss each other.
Faithfulness will spring up from the ground,
   and righteousness will look down from the sky.
The LORD will give what is good,
   and our land will yield its increase.
Righteousness will go before him,
   and will make a path for his steps. (Ps. 85:8-13)

Additional Readings:

1 Kings 18:1-16
God promises relief from drought

Acts 17:10-15
The good news is shared

Hymn: Lord, Speak to Us, That We May Speak, ELW 676

O Lord, we yearn to hear your word of peace! Open our hearts, that we may not only hear but understand that word, and grant us courage to act upon it. We pray through your Son, Jesus Christ.

Friday, August 8, 2008
Time after Pentecost

Dominic, founder of the Order of Preachers (Dominicans), 1221

Acts 18:24-28
A new disciple preaches

Now there came to Ephesus a Jew named Apollos, a native of Alexandria. He was an eloquent man, well-versed in the scriptures. He had been instructed in the Way of the Lord; and he spoke with burning enthusiasm and taught accurately the things concerning Jesus, though he knew only the baptism of John. He began to speak boldly in the synagogue; but when Priscilla and Aquila heard him, they took him aside and explained the Way of God to him more accurately. And when he wished to cross over to Achaia, the believers encouraged him and wrote to the disciples to welcome him. On his arrival he greatly helped those who through grace had become believers, for he powerfully refuted the Jews in public, showing by the scriptures that the Messiah is Jesus. (Acts 18:24-28)

Additional Readings:

1 Kings 18:17-19, 30-40   Psalm 85:8-13
God's flooded altar burns   *I will listen to God*

Hymn: In Christ Called to Baptize, ELW 575

Lord, you blessed Apollos with eloquence, knowledge, and the humility to accept correction. Bless us also with such gifts, that we too may speak boldly and accurately about your Son, our Lord Jesus Christ, through whom we pray.

Saturday, August 9, 2008
TIME AFTER PENTECOST

1 Kings 18:41-46
From drought to heavy rain

Elijah said to Ahab, "Go up, eat and drink; for there is a sound of rushing rain." So Ahab went up to eat and to drink. Elijah went up to the top of Carmel; there he bowed himself down upon the earth and put his face between his knees. He said to his servant, "Go up now, look toward the sea." He went up and looked, and said, "There is nothing." Then he said, "Go again seven times." At the seventh time he said, "Look, a little cloud no bigger than a person's hand is rising out of the sea." Then he said, "Go say to Ahab, 'Harness your chariot and go down before the rain stops you.'" In a little while the heavens grew black with clouds and wind; there was a heavy rain. Ahab rode off and went to Jezreel. But the hand of the LORD was on Elijah; he girded up his loins and ran in front of Ahab to the entrance of Jezreel.
(1 Kings 18:41-46)

Additional Readings:

Matthew 16:1-4   Psalm 85:8-13
The sign of Jonah   *I will listen to God*

Hymn: Crashing Waters at Creation, ELW 455

Holy One, you sent Elijah to call the rulers of the people back to you. Rest your hand on us as well, that we too may speak your truth to rulers. This we ask through Christ our Lord.

Sunday, August 10, 2008

Time after Pentecost

Lawrence, deacon, martyr, 258

Matthew 14:22-33
Jesus walking on the sea

Immediately [Jesus] made the disciples get into the boat and go on ahead to the other side, while he dismissed the crowds. And after he had dismissed the crowds, he went up the mountain by himself to pray. When evening came, he was there alone, but by this time the boat, battered by the waves, was far from the land, for the wind was against them. And early in the morning he came walking toward them on the sea. But when the disciples saw him walking on the sea, they were terrified, saying, "It is a ghost!" And they cried out in fear. But immediately Jesus spoke to them and said, "Take heart, it is I; do not be afraid." (Matt. 14:22-27)

Additional Readings:

1 Kings 19:9-18
Elijah on Mount Horeb

Psalm 85:8-13
I will listen to God

Romans 10:5-15
The word of faith

Hymn: Calm to the Waves, ELW 794

O God our defender, storms rage around and within us and cause us to be afraid. Rescue your people from despair, deliver your sons and daughters from fear, and preserve us all in the faith of your Son, Jesus Christ, our Savior and Lord.

Monday, August 11, 2008
TIME AFTER PENTECOST

Clare, Abbess of San Damiano, 1253

Psalm 18:1-19
God saves from the waters

[The LORD] reached down from on high, he took me;
   he drew me out of mighty waters.
He delivered me from my strong enemy,
   and from those who hated me;
   for they were too mighty for me.
They confronted me in the day of my calamity;
   but the LORD was my support.
He brought me out into a broad place;
   he delivered me, because he delighted in me.
(Ps. 18:16-19)

Additional Readings:

Genesis 7:11—8:5
God saves Noah from the flood

2 Peter 2:4-10
God judges and rescues

Hymn: Eternal Father, Strong to Save, ELW 756

Saving God, you deliver us because you delight in us, though we cannot understand why. Teach us to accept your gracious love and help us respond with grateful service. We pray through your Son, Love Incarnate, Jesus Christ.

Tuesday, August 12, 2008
TIME AFTER PENTECOST

Genesis 19:1-29
God saves Lot

Abraham went early in the morning to the place where he had stood before the LORD; and he looked down toward Sodom and Gomorrah and toward all the land of the Plain and saw the smoke of the land going up like the smoke of a furnace.

So it was that, when God destroyed the cities of the Plain, God remembered Abraham, and sent Lot out of the midst of the overthrow, when he overthrew the cities in which Lot had settled. (Gen. 19:27-29)

Additional Readings:
Romans 9:14-29   Psalm 18:1-19
God's wrath, God's mercy   *God saves from the waters*

Hymn: In All Our Grief, ELW 615

Again and again, Holy One, you save your people even as the smoke goes up all around us. Grant us grace to trust in you and listen to your messengers as Lot did. This we ask through Christ our Lord.

Wednesday, August 13, 2008
TIME AFTER PENTECOST

Florence Nightingale, 1910; Clara Maass, 1901; renewers of society

Matthew 8:23-27
Jesus stills the storm

And when he got into the boat, his disciples followed him. A windstorm arose on the sea, so great that the boat was being swamped by the waves; but he was asleep. And they went and woke him up, saying, "Lord, save us! We are perishing!" And he said to them, "Why are you afraid, you of little faith?" Then he got up and rebuked the winds and the sea; and there was a dead calm. They were amazed, saying, "What sort of man is this, that even the winds and the sea obey him?" (Matt. 8:23-27)

Additional Readings:

Job 36:24-33; 37:14-24
The waters of God's creation

Psalm 18:1-19
God saves from the waters

Hymn: Jesus, Savior, Pilot Me, ELW 755

Saving God, with you the waters of chaos become the waters of salvation. Answer our pleas for help with words of power, that our faith and trust may continue to grow. We pray through Jesus Christ our Lord.

Thursday, August 14, 2008
TIME AFTER PENTECOST

Maximilian Kolbe, 1941; Kaj Munk, 1944, martyrs

Psalm 67
Let all the peoples praise God

May God be gracious to us and bless us
   and make his face to shine upon us,
that your way may be known upon earth,
   your saving power among all nations.
Let the peoples praise you, O God;
   let all the peoples praise you.
Let the nations be glad and sing for joy,
   for you judge the peoples with equity
   and guide the nations upon earth.
Let the peoples praise you, O God;
   let all the peoples praise you. (Ps. 67:1-5)

Additional Readings:

Isaiah 45:20-25
All the ends of the earth shall be saved

Revelation 15:1-4
All nations will worship God

Hymn: Praise to the Lord, the Almighty, ELW 858

Loving God, you are gracious to us and you do bless us! May we sing continually for joy, for you have made your way known to us, most especially in your Son, our Lord Jesus Christ, through whom we pray.

Luke 1:46-55
Mary's thanksgiving

And Mary said,
   "My soul magnifies the Lord,
      and my spirit rejoices in God my Savior,
for he has looked with favor on the lowliness of his servant.
      Surely, from now on all generations will call me blessed;
for the Mighty One has done great things for me,
      and holy is his name." (Luke 1:46-49)

Additional Readings:

Isaiah 61:7-11	Psalm 34:1-9	Galatians 4:4-7
God will cause righteousness to spring up	*O magnify the Lord with me*	*We are no longer slaves, but children*

Hymn: Signs and Wonders, ELW 672

Almighty God, in choosing the virgin Mary to be the mother of your Son, you made known your gracious regard for the poor, the lowly, and the despised. Grant us grace to receive your word in humility, and so to be made one with your Son, Jesus Christ our Savior and Lord, who lives and reigns with you and the Holy Spirit, one God, now and forever.

Isaiah 56:1-5
A covenant for all who obey

Thus says the LORD:
Maintain justice, and do what is right,
for soon my salvation will come,
    and my deliverance be revealed.
Happy is the mortal who does this,
    the one who holds it fast,
who keeps the sabbath, not profaning it,
    and refrains from doing any evil.
Do not let the foreigner joined to the LORD say,
    "The LORD will surely separate me from his people";
and do not let the eunuch say,
    "I am just a dry tree." (Isa. 56:1-3)

Additional Readings:

Matthew 14:34-36
Jesus heals the sick

Psalm 67
Let all the peoples praise God

Hymn: Let Justice Flow like Streams, ELW 717

Saving God, we look for your promised deliverance. Grant us wisdom to choose what is right, for by so doing we will find happiness with you and your beloved people. This we ask through your Son, Jesus Christ, our Lord.

Sunday, August 17, 2008
TIME AFTER PENTECOST

Matthew 15:[10-20] 21-28
The Canaanite woman's daughter is healed

[The Canaanite woman] came and knelt before [Jesus], saying, "Lord, help me." He answered, "It is not fair to take the children's food and throw it to the dogs." She said, "Yes, Lord, yet even the dogs eat the crumbs that fall from their masters' table." Then Jesus answered her, "Woman, great is your faith! Let it be done for you as you wish." And her daughter was healed instantly. (Matt. 15:25-28)

Additional Readings:

Isaiah 56:1, 6-8	Psalm 67	Romans 11:1-2a, 29-32
A house of prayer for all people	*Let all the peoples praise God*	*God's mercy to all, Jew and Gentile*

Hymn: We Come to You for Healing, Lord, ELW 617

God of all peoples, your arms reach out to embrace all those who call upon you. Teach us as disciples of your Son to love the world with compassion and constancy, that your name may be known throughout the earth, through Jesus Christ, our Savior and Lord.

Psalm 87
Foreigners praise God in Zion

On the holy mount stands the city he founded;
  the Lord loves the gates of Zion
  more than all the dwellings of Jacob.
Glorious things are spoken of you,
  O city of God.
Among those who know me I mention Rahab and Babylon;
  Philistia too, and Tyre, with Ethiopia—
  "This one was born there," they say.
And of Zion it shall be said,
  "This one and that one were born in it";
  for the Most High himself will establish it. (Ps. 87:1-5)

Additional Readings:

2 Kings 5:1-14
The foreigner Naaman is healed

Acts 15:1-21
The believing Jews accept the Gentiles

Hymn: Come, We That Love the Lord, ELW 625

Lord Most High, you make your holy city the admiration and hope of all. Let us come into your gates and join together with all peoples in praising you with works of justice. We pray through your Son, Jesus Christ.

Romans 11:13-29
God saves Jews and Gentiles

So that you may not claim to be wiser than you are, brothers and sisters, I want you to understand this mystery: a hardening has come upon part of Israel, until the full number of the Gentiles has come in. And so all Israel will be saved; as it is written,

"Out of Zion will come the Deliverer;
   he will banish ungodliness from Jacob."
"And this is my covenant with them,
   when I take away their sins."

As regards the gospel they are enemies of God for your sake; but as regards election they are beloved, for the sake of their ancestors; for the gifts and the calling of God are irrevocable. (Rom. 11:25-29)

Additional Readings:

Isaiah 43:8-13
Let all the nations gather

Psalm 87
Foreigners praise God in Zion

Hymn: Alleluia! Sing to Jesus, ELW 392

Saving God, your gifts are irrevocable; your calling is forever. Grant us grace to act in accordance with your great mercy to all your beloved people, O God, and serve our neighbor with love and justice. This we ask through Jesus Christ our Lord.

Wednesday, August 20, 2008
Time after Pentecost

Bernard, Abbot of Clairvaux, 1153

Matthew 8:1-13
Jesus heals many people

When [Jesus] entered Capernaum, a centurion came to him, appealing to him and saying, "Lord, my servant is lying at home paralyzed, in terrible distress." And he said to him, "I will come and cure him." The centurion answered, "Lord, I am not worthy to have you come under my roof; but only speak the word, and my servant will be healed. For I also am a man under authority, with soldiers under me; and I say to one, 'Go,' and he goes, and to another, 'Come,' and he comes, and to my slave, 'Do this,' and the slave does it." When Jesus heard him, he was amazed and said to those who followed him, "Truly I tell you, in no one in Israel have I found such faith." (Matt. 8:5-10)

Additional Readings:

Isaiah 66:18-23
All nations shall come to worship

Psalm 87
Foreigners praise God in Zion

Hymn: Jesus, the Very Thought of You, ELW 754

Healing God, even Jesus was amazed at the faith of the centurion, an enemy of his people. Open our hearts, Lord, to honor the faith of those we consider enemies as well. We pray through your Son, Jesus Christ.

Thursday, August 21, 2008
TIME AFTER PENTECOST

Psalm 138
Your love endures forever

All the kings of the earth shall praise you, O LORD,
    for they have heard the words of your mouth.
They shall sing of the ways of the LORD,
    for great is the glory of the LORD.
For though the LORD is high, he regards the lowly;
    but the haughty he perceives from far away.
Though I walk in the midst of trouble,
    you preserve me against the wrath of my enemies;
you stretch out your hand,
    and your right hand delivers me.
The LORD will fulfill his purpose for me;
    your steadfast love, O LORD, endures forever.
    Do not forsake the work of your hands. (Ps. 138:4-8)

Additional Readings:

Ezekiel 28:11-19   1 Corinthians 6:1-11
Disobedience and the loss of Eden   *When believers disagree*

Hymn: Holy God, Holy and Glorious, ELW 637

Lord, your steadfast love endures forever! We rejoice that we have heard your word, and we sing your praises through your Son, Jesus Christ, who lives and reigns in unity with you and the Holy Spirit, now and for ever.

Ezekiel 31:15-18
Israel like the cedars of Lebanon

Thus says the Lord God: On the day it went down to Sheol I closed the deep over it and covered it; I restrained its rivers, and its mighty waters were checked. I clothed Lebanon in gloom for it, and all the trees of the field fainted because of it. I made the nations quake at the sound of its fall, when I cast it down to Sheol with those who go down to the Pit; and all the trees of Eden, the choice and best of Lebanon, all that were well watered, were consoled in the world below. They also went down to Sheol with it, to those killed by the sword, along with its allies, those who lived in its shade among the nations.

Which among the trees of Eden was like you in glory and in greatness? Now you shall be brought down with the trees of Eden to the world below; you shall lie among the uncircumcised, with those who are killed by the sword. This is Pharaoh and all his horde, says the Lord God. (Ezek. 31:15-18)

Additional Readings:

2 Corinthians 10:12-18
Let those who boast, boast in the Lord

Psalm 138
Your love endures forever

Hymn: Light Dawns on a Weary World, ELW 726

O Lord God, in your wrath against the unjust you make the nations quake! Grant that we may always take the side of the oppressed, for this is your will and way. We pray through your Son, our Lord Jesus Christ.

Saturday, August 23, 2008
TIME AFTER PENTECOST

Ezekiel 36:33-38
A desolate land becomes like Eden

Thus says the Lord GOD: On the day that I cleanse you from all your iniquities, I will cause the towns to be inhabited, and the waste places shall be rebuilt. The land that was desolate shall be tilled, instead of being the desolation that it was in the sight of all who passed by. And they will say, "This land that was desolate has become like the garden of Eden; and the waste and desolate and ruined towns are now inhabited and fortified." Then the nations that are left all around you shall know that I, the LORD, have rebuilt the ruined places, and replanted that which was desolate; I, the LORD, have spoken, and I will do it. (Ezek. 36:33-36)

Additional Readings:

Matthew 16:5-12
Bread as a sign of other things

Psalm 138
Your love endures forever

Hymn: Come, Ye Disconsolate, ELW 607

O Lord God, you promised to cleanse the people from their iniquities and restore the desolate land. Grant us grace to trust in you, as you cleanse and restore our own hearts, through your Son Jesus Christ.

Sunday, August 24, 2008
TIME AFTER PENTECOST

Bartholomew, Apostle

Matthew 16:13-20
The profession of Peter's faith

[Jesus] said to the [disciples], "But who do you say that I am?" Simon Peter answered, "You are the Messiah, the Son of the living God." And Jesus answered him, "Blessed are you, Simon son of Jonah! For flesh and blood has not revealed this to you, but my Father in heaven. And I tell you, you are Peter, and on this rock I will build my church, and the gates of Hades will not prevail against it. I will give you the keys of the kingdom of heaven, and whatever you bind on earth will be bound in heaven, and whatever you loose on earth will be loosed in heaven." (Matt. 16:15-19)

Additional Readings:

Isaiah 51:1-6	Psalm 138	Romans 12:1-8
God's enduring salvation	*Your love endures forever*	*One body in Christ, with gifts that differ*

Hymn: Built on a Rock, ELW 652

O God, with all your faithful followers of every age, we praise you, the rock of our life. Be our strong foundation and form us into the body of your Son, that we may gladly minister to all the world, through Jesus Christ, our Savior and Lord.

Monday, August 25, 2008

BARTHOLOMEW, APOSTLE

(transferred from August 24)

John 1:43-51
Jesus says: Follow me

When Jesus saw Nathanael coming toward him, he said of him, "Here is truly an Israelite in whom there is no deceit!" Nathanael asked him, "Where did you get to know me?" Jesus answered, "I saw you under the fig tree before Philip called you." Nathanael replied, "Rabbi, you are the Son of God! You are the King of Israel!" Jesus answered, "Do you believe because I told you that I saw you under the fig tree? You will see greater things than these." And he said to him, "Very truly, I tell you, you will see heaven opened and the angels of God ascending and descending upon the Son of Man." (John 1:47-51)

Additional Readings:

Exodus 19:1-6	Psalm 12	1 Corinthians 12:27-31a
Israel is God's priestly kingdom	*A plea for help in evil times*	*The body of Christ*

Hymn: Beautiful Savior, ELW 838

Almighty and everlasting God, you gave to your apostle Bartholomew grace truly to believe and courageously to preach your word. Grant that your church may proclaim the good news to the ends of the earth, through Jesus Christ, our Savior and Lord, who lives and reigns with you and the Holy Spirit, one God, now and forever.

Psalm 18:1-3, 20-32
God the rock

I love you, O Lord, my strength.
The Lord is my rock, my fortress, and my deliverer,
  my God, my rock in whom I take refuge,
  my shield, and the horn of my salvation, my stronghold.
I call upon the Lord, who is worthy to be praised,
  so I shall be saved from my enemies. (Ps. 18:1-3)

Additional Readings:

Deuteronomy 32:18-20, 28-39
Praise the rock that is God

Romans 11:33-36
The riches, wisdom, and knowledge of God

Hymn: On Eagle's Wings, ELW 787

Blessed are you, O Lord, our rock, our fortress, our deliverer. In trouble, may we run to you for refuge, and in peace, may we sing your praise. We pray through your Son, our Lord Jesus Christ.

Wednesday, August 27, 2008

TIME AFTER PENTECOST

Isaiah 28:14-22
God lays a cornerstone in Zion

Therefore hear the word of the LORD, you scoffers
   who rule this people in Jerusalem.
Because you have said, "We have made a covenant with death,
   and with Sheol we have an agreement;
when the overwhelming scourge passes through
   it will not come to us;
for we have made lies our refuge,
   and in falsehood we have taken shelter";
therefore thus says the Lord GOD,
See, I am laying in Zion a foundation stone,
   a tested stone,
a precious cornerstone, a sure foundation:
   "One who trusts will not panic." (Isa. 28:14-16)

Additional Readings:

Matthew 26:6-13
A woman anoints Jesus

Psalm 18:1-3, 20-32
God the rock

Hymn: Christ Is Made the Sure Foundation, ELW 645

Lord God, your cornerstone still stands firm. Help us to build our lives on that sure foundation of trust in you, that all nations will come to know your truth. We pray through Jesus Christ our Lord.

Thursday, August 28, 2008
Time after Pentecost

Augustine, Bishop of Hippo, 430
Moses the Black, monk, martyr, c. 400

Psalm 26:1-8
Your love is before my eyes

Vindicate me, O LORD,
 for I have walked in my integrity,
 and I have trusted in the LORD without wavering.
Prove me, O LORD, and try me;
 test my heart and mind.
For your steadfast love is before my eyes,
 and I walk in faithfulness to you. (Ps. 26:1-3)

Additional Readings:

Jeremiah 14:13-18
Denunciation of lying prophets

Ephesians 5:1-6
Do not be deceived by empty words

Hymn: We Praise You, O God, ELW 870

Eternal God, your steadfast love is always before our eyes. Grant us grace to walk in faithfulness to you, in integrity, without wavering; and let your Son Jesus Christ always be our model and our guide.

Friday, August 29, 2008
TIME AFTER PENTECOST

2 Thessalonians 2:7-12
Refusal to love the truth

For the mystery of lawlessness is already at work, but only until the one who now restrains it is removed. And then the lawless one will be revealed, whom the Lord Jesus will destroy with the breath of his mouth, annihilating him by the manifestation of his coming. The coming of the lawless one is apparent in the working of Satan, who uses all power, signs, lying wonders, and every kind of wicked deception for those who are perishing, because they refused to love the truth and so be saved. For this reason God sends them a powerful delusion, leading them to believe what is false, so that all who have not believed the truth but took pleasure in unrighteousness will be condemned. (2 Thess. 2:7-12)

Additional Readings:

Jeremiah 15:1-9   Psalm 26:1-8
The consequences of sin   *Your love is before my eyes*

Hymn: Abide, O Dearest Jesus, ELW 539

God of truth, you reveal your ways through your Son, your Spirit, and your scriptures. Help us to stand firm in that truth even against the wiles of the wicked. This we ask through Jesus Christ our Lord.

Jeremiah 15:10-14
Jeremiah's complaint to God

Woe is me, my mother, that you ever bore me, a man of strife and contention to the whole land! I have not lent, nor have I borrowed, yet all of them curse me. The Lord said: Surely I have intervened in your life for good, surely I have imposed enemies on you in a time of trouble and in a time of distress. Can iron and bronze break iron from the north?

Your wealth and your treasures I will give as plunder, without price, for all your sins, throughout all your territory. I will make you serve your enemies in a land that you do not know, for in my anger a fire is kindled that shall burn forever. (Jer. 15:10-14)

Additional Readings:

Matthew 8:14-17
Jesus heals many at Peter's house

Psalm 26:1-8
Your love is before my eyes

Hymn: If You But Trust in God to Guide You, ELW 769

O Lord, we see our troubles but you see what lies behind them. Help us to trust that you intervene in our lives for good, even as we bewail our woes. We pray through your Son, Jesus Christ.

Sunday, August 31, 2008
Time after Pentecost

Matthew 16:21-28
The rebuke to Peter

From that time on, Jesus began to show his disciples that he must go to Jerusalem and undergo great suffering at the hands of the elders and chief priests and scribes, and be killed, and on the third day be raised. And Peter took him aside and began to rebuke him, saying, "God forbid it, Lord! This must never happen to you." But he turned and said to Peter, "Get behind me, Satan! You are a stumbling block to me; for you are setting your mind not on divine things but on human things."
(Matt. 16:21-23)

Additional Readings:

Jeremiah 15:15-21	Psalm 26:1-8	Romans 12:9-21
God fortifies the prophet	*Your love is before my eyes*	*Live in harmony*

Hymn: Take Up Your Cross, the Savior Said, ELW 667

O God, we thank you for your Son who chose the path of suffering for the sake of the world. Humble us by his example, point us to the path of obedience, and give us strength to follow your commands, through Jesus Christ, our Savior and Lord.

~ Prayer list for September

_____

_____

_____

_____

_____

_____

_____

_____

_____

_____

_____

Monday, September 1, 2008
Time after Pentecost

Psalm 17
The righteous shall see God

I call upon you, for you will answer me, O God;
  incline your ear to me, hear my words.
Wondrously show your steadfast love,
  O savior of those who seek refuge
  from their adversaries at your right hand.
Guard me as the apple of the eye;
  hide me in the shadow of your wings,
from the wicked who despoil me,
  my deadly enemies who surround me. (Ps. 17:6-9)

Additional Readings:

2 Samuel 11:2-26
David sins

Revelation 3:1-6
Wake up to your faithlessness

Hymn: What Wondrous Love Is This, ELW 666

We trust in your steadfast love, O God, and count on your abiding presence. Continue to strengthen our faith, especially in times of difficulty, so that we might live more deeply with you and become a blessing to others.

Tuesday, September 2, 2008
Time after Pentecost

Nikolai Frederik Severin Grundtvig, bishop, renewer of the church, 1872

Revelation 3:7-13
Facing the hour of trial

"And to the angel of the church in Philadelphia write:
  These are the words of the holy one, the true one,
    who has the key of David,
    who opens and no one will shut,
        who shuts and no one opens:
Because you have kept my word of patient endurance, I will keep
you from the hour of trial that is coming on the whole world
to test the inhabitants of the earth. I am coming soon; hold fast
to what you have, so that no one may seize your crown. If you
conquer, I will make you a pillar in the temple of my God; you
will never go out of it. I will write on you the name of my God,
and the name of the city of my God, the new Jerusalem that
comes down from my God out of heaven, and my own new
name." (Rev. 3:7, 10-12)

Additional Readings:

2 Samuel 11:27b—12:15
Nathan rebukes David

Psalm 17
The righteous shall see God

Hymn: Just As I Am, without One Plea, ELW 592

*It can be difficult to live faithfully, dear Lord, especially in hours of
trial. Strengthen us in those times and help us grow in patient endurance,
so that our faith can mature and we can become better witnesses of your
love.*

Wednesday, September 3, 2008
Time after Pentecost

Jeremiah 17:5-18
The vindication of the righteous

Thus says the LORD:
Cursed are those who trust in mere mortals
  and make mere flesh their strength,
  whose hearts turn away from the LORD.
They shall be like a shrub in the desert,
  and shall not see when relief comes.
They shall live in the parched places of the wilderness,
  in an uninhabited salt land.
Blessed are those who trust in the LORD,
  whose trust is the LORD.
They shall be like a tree planted by water,
  sending out its roots by the stream.
It shall not fear when heat comes,
  and its leaves shall stay green;
in the year of drought it is not anxious,
  and it does not cease to bear fruit. (Jer. 17:5-8)

Additional Readings:

Matthew 12:22-32
Jesus comes to cast out Satan

Psalm 17
The righteous shall see God

Hymn: O Blessed Spring, ELW 447

Our precious Lord, we thank you for the life and nurturance you provide for your children. Help us deepen our spiritual roots in you so that we can share your life with others.

Thursday, September 4, 2008
Time after Pentecost

Psalm 119:33–40
The path of your commandments

Teach me, O Lord, the way of your statutes,
   and I will observe it to the end.
Give me understanding, that I may keep your law
   and observe it with my whole heart.
Lead me in the path of your commandments,
   for I delight in it.
Turn my heart to your decrees,
   and not to selfish gain. (Ps. 119:33-36)

Additional Readings:
Ezekiel 24:1-14
God judges unrepentant Israel

2 Corinthians 12:11-21
Sinners warned but unrepentant

Hymn: O God of Light, ELW 507

Your statutes are a gift of life for us, O Lord. We thank you for the form they give to our lives, and we ask that you give us the grace to understand your commandments and to live them whole-heartedly.

Friday, September 5, 2008
TIME AFTER PENTECOST

Romans 10:15b-21
God reaches out to erring Israel

As it is written, "How beautiful are the feet of those who bring good news!" But not all have obeyed the good news; for Isaiah says, "Lord, who has believed our message?" So faith comes from what is heard, and what is heard comes through the word of Christ. (Rom. 10:15b-17)

Additional Readings:
Ezekiel 24:15-27
God opens the prophet's mouth

Psalm 119:33-40
The path of your commandments

Hymn: Spread, Oh, Spread, Almighty Word, ELW 663

We know that your word is communicated every moment in so many ways, Almighty God, and yet in our busyness we often neglect hearing it. Come to our aid; let us hear and speak your word more truly.

Saturday, September 6, 2008
Time after Pentecost

Ezekiel 33:1-6
The prophet's vocation

The word of the LORD came to me: O Mortal, speak to your people and say to them, If I bring the sword upon a land, and the people of the land take one of their number as their sentinel; and if the sentinel sees the sword coming upon the land and blows the trumpet and warns the people; then if any who hear the sound of the trumpet do not take warning, and the sword comes and takes them away, their blood shall be upon their own heads. They heard the sound of the trumpet and did not take warning; their blood shall be upon themselves. But if they had taken warning, they would have saved their lives. But if the sentinel sees the sword coming and does not blow the trumpet, so that the people are not warned, and the sword comes and takes any of them, they are taken away in their iniquity, but their blood I will require at the sentinel's hand. (Ezek. 33:1-6)

Additional Readings:

Matthew 23:29-36
The martyrdom of the prophets

Psalm 119:33-40
The path of your commandments

Hymn: Lo! He Comes with Clouds Descending, ELW 435

Our gracious God, you have called each of us to particular vocations that build up your people and work your will for the creation. Open the ears of our souls so we might hear clearly your call for each of us.

Sunday, September 7, 2008
TIME AFTER PENTECOST

Matthew 18:15-20
Reconciliation in the community of faith

"If another member of the church sins against you, go and point out the fault when the two of you are alone. If the member listens to you, you have regained that one. But if you are not listened to, take one or two others along with you, so that every word may be confirmed by the evidence of two or three witnesses. If the member refuses to listen to them, tell it to the church; and if the offender refuses to listen even to the church, let such a one be to you as a Gentile and a tax collector. (Matt. 18:15-17)

Additional Readings:

Ezekiel 33:7-11
The prophet's responsibility

Psalm 119:33-40
The path of your commandments

Romans 13:8-14
Live honorably as in the day

Hymn: Forgive Our Sins As We Forgive, ELW 605

O Lord God, enliven and preserve your church with your perpetual mercy. Without your help, we mortals will fail; remove far from us everything that is harmful, and lead us toward all that gives life and salvation, through Jesus Christ, our Savior and Lord.

Monday, September 8, 2008
Time after Pentecost

Psalm 119:65-72
The law humbles me

You have dealt well with your servant,
   O Lord, according to your word.
Teach me good judgment and knowledge,
   for I believe in your commandments.
Before I was humbled I went astray,
   but now I keep your word. (Ps. 119:65-67)

Additional Readings:

Leviticus 4:27-31; 5:14-16
*Atoning for sin in the
community*

1 Peter 2:11-17
Live as servants of God

Hymn: O Word of God Incarnate, ELW 514

*We are grateful, beloved God, for the gift of humility that helps us
live in the truth of our lives and in relationship with you. Teach us to
stay rooted in your commandments so that we might live more fully
with you.*

Tuesday, September 9, 2008
Time after Pentecost

Peter Claver, priest, missionary to Colombia, 1654

Romans 13:1-7
Obeying authority

Let every person be subject to the governing authorities; for there is no authority except from God, and those authorities that exist have been instituted by God. Therefore whoever resists authority resists what God has appointed, and those who resist will incur judgment. For rulers are not a terror to good conduct, but to bad. Do you wish to have no fear of the authority? Then do what is good, and you will receive its approval; for it is God's servant for your good. But if you do what is wrong, you should be afraid, for the authority does not bear the sword in vain! It is the servant of God to execute wrath on the wrongdoer. (Rom. 13:1-4)

Additional Readings:

Deuteronomy 17:2-13
Punishment for sin in community

Psalm 119:65-72
The law humbles me

Hymn: Let the Whole Creation Cry, ELW 876

We commend our governing authorities to you, dear Lord, as they work for the care of others. Help us humbly respect their responsibilities and efforts and find ways to support their work that benefits your people.

Wednesday, September 10, 2008
Time after Pentecost

Matthew 21:18-22
Jesus teaches about praying in faith

In the morning, when he returned to the city, he was hungry.
And seeing a fig tree by the side of the road, he went to it and
found nothing at all on it but leaves. Then he said to it, "May no
fruit ever come from you again!" And the fig tree withered at
once. When the disciples saw it, they were amazed, saying, "How
did the fig tree wither at once?" Jesus answered them, "Truly I
tell you, if you have faith and do not doubt, not only will you
do what has been done to the fig tree, but even if you say to this
mountain, 'Be lifted up and thrown into the sea,' it will be done.
Whatever you ask for in prayer with faith, you will receive."
(Matt. 21:18-22)

Additional Readings:

Leviticus 16:1-5, 20-28
*The scapegoat cleanses the
community*

Psalm 119:65-72
The law humbles me

Hymn: Lord, Teach Us How to Pray Aright, ELW 745

*You have promised us, gracious God, that extraordinary things
can happen when we pray. Infuse us with that trust in you, even in our
hesitancy; and help us become people of greater faith.*

Thursday, September 11, 2008
Time after Pentecost

Psalm 103:[1-7] 8-13
God's compassion and mercy

The LORD is merciful and gracious,
    slow to anger and abounding in steadfast love.
He will not always accuse,
    nor will he keep his anger forever.
He does not deal with us according to our sins,
    nor repay us according to our iniquities.
For as the heavens are high above the earth,
    so great is his steadfast love toward those who fear him;
as far as the east is from the west,
    so far he removes our transgressions from us.
(Ps. 103:8-12)

Additional Readings:

Genesis 37:12-36
Joseph's brothers sin against him

1 John 3:11-16
Love one another

Hymn: Praise, My Soul, the God of Heaven, ELW 864

We count on the words of the psalmist, loving Lord, and believe in your steadfast love. Your love is the very source of our lives. Help us live in your love as we listen to, care for, and serve those around us.

Friday, September 12, 2008
Time after Pentecost

Genesis 41:53—42:17
Joseph acts harshly against his brothers

But Joseph said to his brothers, "It is just as I have said to you; you are spies! Here is how you shall be tested: as Pharaoh lives, you shall not leave this place unless your youngest brother comes here! Let one of you go and bring your brother, while the rest of you remain in prison, in order that your words may be tested, whether there is truth in you; or else, as Pharaoh lives, surely you are spies." And he put them all together in prison for three days. (Gen. 42:14-17)

Additional Readings:

Acts 7:9-16
Joseph's family is fed in Egypt

Psalm 103:[1-7] 8-13
God's compassion and mercy

Hymn: Lord of Glory, You Have Bought Us, ELW 707

In the midst of testing, O God, we often resent the challenges and yet, like Joseph's final reconciliation with his family, you mercifully see us through the difficulties and into your compassionate embrace.

Saturday, September 13, 2008
Time after Pentecost

John Chrysostom, Bishop of Constantinople, 407

Matthew 6:7-15
Forgiving one another

Pray then in this way:
Our Father in heaven,
  hallowed be your name.
  Your kingdom come.
  Your will be done,
    on earth as it is in heaven.
  Give us this day our daily bread.
  And forgive us our debts,
    as we also have forgiven our debtors.
  And do not bring us to the time of trial,
    but rescue us from the evil one. (Matt. 6:9-13)

Additional Readings:

Genesis 45:1-20
Joseph forgives his brothers

Psalm 103:[1-7] 8-13
God's compassion and mercy

Hymn: Our Father, God in Heaven Above, ELW 746/747

How easy it is to let self-righteousness and pain drive us from loving relationships, O God. Bless us with courage to forgive those who hurt us, the wisdom to see our own failings, and humility to seek forgiveness from others.

Sunday, September 14, 2008
Time after Pentecost

Holy Cross Day

Matthew 18:21-35
A parable of forgiveness

Then Peter came and said to him, "Lord, if another member of the church sins against me, how often should I forgive? As many as seven times?" Jesus said to him, "Not seven times, but, I tell you, seventy-seven times." (Matt. 18:21-22)

Additional Readings:

Genesis 50:15-21
Joseph reconciles with his brothers

Psalm 103:[1-7] 8-13
God's compassion and mercy

Romans 14:1-12
When brothers and sisters judge each other

Hymn: Listen, God Is Calling, ELW 513

O Lord God, merciful judge, you are the inexhaustible fountain of forgiveness. Replace our hearts of stone with hearts that love and adore you, that we may delight in doing your will, through Jesus Christ, our Savior and Lord.

Monday, September 15, 2008
HOLY CROSS DAY

(transferred from September 14)

John 3:13-17
The Son of Man will be lifted up

[Jesus said:] "No one has ascended into heaven except the one who descended from heaven, the Son of Man. And just as Moses lifted up the serpent in the wilderness, so must the Son of Man be lifted up, that whoever believes in him may have eternal life.

"For God so loved the world that he gave his only Son, so that everyone who believes in him may not perish but may have eternal life.

"Indeed, God did not send the Son into the world to condemn the world, but in order that the world might be saved through him." (John 3:13-17)

Additional Readings:

Numbers 21:4b-9	Psalm 98:1-4	1 Corinthians 1:18-24
A bronze serpent in the wilderness	*The LORD has done marvelous things*	*The cross is the power of God*

Hymn: When I Survey the Wondrous Cross, ELW 803

Almighty God, your Son Jesus Christ was lifted high upon the cross so that he might draw the whole world to himself. To those who look upon the cross, grant your wisdom, healing, and eternal life, through Jesus Christ, our Savior and Lord, who lives and reigns with you and the Holy Spirit, one God, now and forever.

Tuesday, September 16, 2008
TIME AFTER PENTECOST

Cyprian, Bishop of Carthage, martyr, c. 258

Psalm 133
How good it is to live in unity

How very good and pleasant it is
  when kindred live together in unity!
It is like the precious oil on the head,
  running down upon the beard,
on the beard of Aaron,
  running down over the collar of his robes.
It is like the dew of Hermon,
  which falls on the mountains of Zion.
For there the LORD ordained his blessing,
  life forevermore. (Ps. 133:1-3)

Additional Readings:

Genesis 49:29—50:14
*Honoring Jacob's burial
wishes*

Romans 14:13—15:2
Building each other up

Hymn: Behold, How Pleasant, ELW 649

*Our Lord, you have blessed us with precious times of loving unity
through people whose lives intersect our own. Help us to live in ways
that build up healthy and caring relationships.*

Wednesday, September 17, 2008
TIME AFTER PENTECOST

Hildegard, Abbess of Bingen, 1179

Genesis 50:22-26
Joseph dies

So Joseph remained in Egypt, he and his father's household; and Joseph lived one hundred ten years. Joseph saw Ephraim's children of the third generation; the children of Machir son of Manasseh were also born on Joseph's knees.

Then Joseph said to his brothers, "I am about to die; but God will surely come to you, and bring you up out of this land to the land that he swore to Abraham, to Isaac, and to Jacob." So Joseph made the Israelites swear, saying, "When God comes to you, you shall carry up my bones from here." And Joseph died, being one hundred ten years old; he was embalmed and placed in a coffin in Egypt. (Gen. 50:22-26)

Additional Readings:

Mark 11:20-25
Forgiveness for those who forgive

Psalm 133
How good it is to live in unity

Hymn: Children of the Heavenly Father, ELW 781

We are thankful, dear Lord, for the ancient stories like those of Joseph that have been passed on over the millennia. Let them teach us about your faithfulness and inspire us to live more faithfully with you.

Thursday, September 18, 2008

TIME AFTER PENTECOST

Dag Hammarskjöld, renewer of society, 1961

Psalm 145:1-8
God is slow to anger

I will extol you, my God and King,
   and bless your name forever and ever.
Every day I will bless you,
   and praise your name forever and ever.
Great is the Lord, and greatly to be praised;
   his greatness is unsearchable.
The Lord is gracious and merciful,
   slow to anger and abounding in steadfast love.
(Ps. 145:1-3, 8)

Additional Readings:

Nahum 1:1, 14—2:2
*God's wrath toward
Nineveh*

2 Corinthians 13:1-4
Dissent among believers

Hymn: Before You, Lord, We Bow, ELW 893

*You are indeed a great and amazing Lord, O God. Hear our
praise of you and our gratitude for all you are in the life of the world.
Thank you for your gracious mercy and steadfast love.*

Friday, September 19, 2008
TIME AFTER PENTECOST

2 Corinthians 13:5-10
Correction that builds up

But we pray to God that you may not do anything wrong—not that we may appear to have met the test, but that you may do what is right, though we may seem to have failed. For we cannot do anything against the truth, but only for the truth. For we rejoice when we are weak and you are strong. This is what we pray for, that you may become perfect. So I write these things while I am away from you, so that when I come, I may not have to be severe in using the authority that the Lord has given me for building up and not for tearing down. (2 Cor. 13:7-10)

Additional Readings:

Nahum 2:3-13   Psalm 145:1-8
Nineveh under siege   *God is slow to anger*

Hymn: Holy Spirit, Ever Dwelling, ELW 582

Loving Lord, you provide us with dear and faithful saints who can correct us when we lose our way. Help us hear their wisdom and be willing to make the necessary changes in our lives that will enable us to live more faithfully.

Saturday, September 20, 2008

Time after Pentecost

Zephaniah 2:13-15
Judgment on Nineveh

And he will stretch out his hand against the north,
  and destroy Assyria;
and he will make Nineveh a desolation,
  a dry waste like the desert.
Herds shall lie down in it, every wild animal;
the desert owl and the screech owl
  shall lodge on its capitals;
the owl shall hoot at the window,
  the raven croak on the threshold;
  for its cedar work will be laid bare.
Is this the exultant city that lived secure, that said to itself,
  "I am, and there is no one else"?
What a desolation it has become,
  a lair for wild animals!
Everyone who passes by it
  hisses and shakes the fist. (Zeph. 2:13-15)

Additional Readings:

Matthew 19:23-30
The last will be first

Psalm 145:1-8
God is slow to anger

Hymn: There's a Wideness in God's Mercy, ELW 587/588

How easy it is, our God, to act like the people of Nineveh, impressed with our own power and success, and gaining it at the expense of others. We acknowledge how desolate that is and seek to live in deeper faithfulness.

Sunday, September 21, 2008
TIME AFTER PENTECOST

Matthew, Apostle and Evangelist

Matthew 20:1-16
The parable of the vineyard workers

"But [the landowner] replied to one of [the laborers], 'Friend, I am doing you no wrong; did you not agree with me for the usual daily wage? Take what belongs to you and go; I choose to give to this last the same as I give to you. Am I not allowed to do what I choose with what belongs to me? Or are you envious because I am generous?' So the last will be first, and the first will be last." (Matt. 20:13-16)

Additional Readings:

Jonah 3:10—4:11	Psalm 145:1-8	Philippians 1:21-30
God's concern for Nineveh	*God is slow to anger*	*Standing firm in the gospel*

Hymn: Praise and Thanksgiving, ELW 689

Almighty and eternal God, you show perpetual lovingkindness to us your servants. Because we cannot rely on our own abilities, grant us your merciful judgment, and train us to embody the generosity of your Son, Jesus Christ, our Savior and Lord.

Monday, September 22, 2008

Matthew, Apostle and Evangelist

(transferred from September 21)

Matthew 9:9-13
Jesus calls to Matthew: Follow me

As Jesus was walking along, he saw a man called Matthew sitting at the tax booth; and he said to him, "Follow me." And he got up and followed him.

And as he sat at dinner in the house, many tax collectors and sinners came and were sitting with him and his disciples. When the Pharisees saw this, they said to his disciples, "Why does your teacher eat with tax collectors and sinners?" But when he heard this, he said, "Those who are well have no need of a physician, but those who are sick. Go and learn what this means, 'I desire mercy, not sacrifice.' For I have come to call not the righteous but sinners." (Matt. 9:9-13)

Additional Readings:

Ezekiel 2:8—3:11	Psalm 119:33-40	Ephesians 2:4-10
A prophet to the house of Israel	*Give me understanding*	*By grace you have been saved*

Hymn: Where Cross the Crowded Ways of Life, ELW 719

Almighty God, your Son our Savior called a despised tax collector to become one of his apostles. Help us, like Matthew, to respond to the transforming call of Jesus Christ, who lives and reigns with you and the Holy Spirit, one God, now and forever.

Psalm 106:1-12
God's mercy

Both we and our ancestors have sinned;
  we have committed iniquity, have done wickedly.
Our ancestors, when they were in Egypt,
  did not consider your wonderful works;
they did not remember the abundance of your steadfast love,
  but rebelled against the Most High at the Red Sea.
Yet he saved them for his name's sake,
  so that he might make known his mighty power.
(Ps. 106:6-8)

Additional Readings:

Genesis 28:10-17
God blesses the runaway Jacob

Romans 16:17-20
A warning about troublemakers

Hymn: Praise and Thanks and Adoration, ELW 783

We confess, almighty God, the many ways we fall short each day and fail to live in the love with which you created us. We resist your path, we hurt others, we deceive ourselves. Be merciful with us, O Lord.

Wednesday, September 24, 2008
Time after Pentecost

Matthew 18:1-5
True greatness

At that time the disciples came to Jesus and asked, "Who is the greatest in the kingdom of heaven?" He called a child, whom he put among them, and said, "Truly I tell you, unless you change and become like children, you will never enter the kingdom of heaven. Whoever becomes humble like this child is the greatest in the kingdom of heaven. Whoever welcomes one such child in my name welcomes me." (Matt. 18:1-5)

Additional Readings:

Isaiah 41:1-13
God will be with the last

Psalm 106:1-12
God's mercy

Hymn: Cradling Children in His Arm, ELW 444

To live in the humility and simplicity of a child is a difficult task, dear Lord, yet we know that is your call to us. Help us shed our self-importance and discover ways to live in the world like one of your children.

Thursday, September 25, 2008
TIME AFTER PENTECOST

Psalm 25:1-9
God's compassion and love

Make me to know your ways, O LORD;
 teach me your paths.
Lead me in your truth, and teach me,
 for you are the God of my salvation;
 for you I wait all day long.
Be mindful of your mercy, O LORD, and of your steadfast love,
 for they have been from of old.
Do not remember the sins of my youth or my transgressions;
 according to your steadfast love remember me,
 for your goodness' sake, O LORD! (Ps. 25:4-7)

Additional Readings:

Ezekiel 12:17-28
God's judgment is timely

James 4:11-16
*We do not know what
tomorrow will bring*

Hymn: My Shepherd, You Supply My Need, ELW 782

*We want to know your ways, O Lord, and live to proclaim your
truth and love. Guide us on your path and teach us your way; be merciful
to us as we seek to live more fully with you.*

Ezekiel 18:5-18
Those who repent shall live

If a man is righteous and does what is lawful and right—if
he does not eat upon the mountains or lift up his eyes to the
idols of the house of Israel, does not defile his neighbor's wife
or approach a woman during her menstrual period, does not
oppress anyone, but restores to the debtor his pledge, commits
no robbery, gives his bread to the hungry and covers the naked
with a garment, does not take advance or accrued interest,
withholds his hand from iniquity, executes true justice between
contending parties, follows my statutes, and is careful to observe
my ordinances, acting faithfully—such a one is righteous; he
shall surely live, says the Lord God. (Ezek. 18:5-9)

Additional Readings:

Acts 13:32-41
*Through Jesus forgiveness
is proclaimed*

Psalm 25:1-9
God's compassion and love

Hymn: Almighty God, Your Word Is Cast, ELW 516

*Our beloved God, you have given us your statutes to help us live
better and longer. We thank you for your guidance as we seek to live
well with others. Help us receive your teaching willingly and to live in
your ways.*

Saturday, September 27, 2008
TIME AFTER PENTECOST

Ezekiel 18:19-24
A child does not suffer for a parent's sin

Yet you say, "Why should not the son suffer for the iniquity of the father?" When the son has done what is lawful and right, and has been careful to observe all my statutes, he shall surely live. The person who sins shall die. A child shall not suffer for the iniquity of a parent, nor a parent suffer for the iniquity of a child; the righteousness of the righteous shall be his own, and the wickedness of the wicked shall be his own. (Ezek. 18:19-20)

Additional Readings:

Mark 11:27-33
Jesus' authority is questioned

Psalm 25:1-9
God's compassion and love

Hymn: The Numberless Gifts of God's Mercies, ELW 683

Ezekiel's words are both freeing and frightful, dear Lord. We are grateful not to be held responsible for another's iniquity; we accept responsibility for our own and their consequences. Mercifully forgive our failings.

Matthew 21:23-32
A parable of doing God's will

"What do you think? A man had two sons; he went to the first and said, 'Son, go and work in the vineyard today.' He answered, 'I will not'; but later he changed his mind and went. The father went to the second and said the same; and he answered, 'I go, sir'; but he did not go. Which of the two did the will of his father?" They said, "The first." Jesus said to them, "Truly I tell you, the tax collectors and the prostitutes are going into the kingdom of God ahead of you. For John came to you in the way of righteousness and you did not believe him, but the tax collectors and the prostitutes believed him; and even after you saw it, you did not change your minds and believe him." (Matt. 21:28-32)

Additional Readings:

Ezekiel 18:1-4, 25-32	Psalm 25:1-9	Philippians 2:1-13
The fairness of God's way	*God's compassion and love*	*Christ humbled to the point of death*

Hymn: Take My Life, That I May Be, ELW 685

God of love, Giver of life, you know our frailties and failings. Give us your grace to overcome them, keep us from those things that harm us, and guide us in the way of salvation, through Jesus Christ, our Savior and Lord.

Monday, September 29, 2008
MICHAEL AND ALL ANGELS

Revelation 12:7-12
Michael defeats Satan in a cosmic battle

And war broke out in heaven; Michael and his angels fought against the dragon. The dragon and his angels fought back, but they were defeated, and there was no longer any place for them in heaven. The great dragon was thrown down, that ancient serpent, who is called the Devil and Satan, the deceiver of the whole world—he was thrown down to the earth, and his angels were thrown down with him. (Rev. 12:7-9)

Additional Readings:

Daniel 10:10-14; 12:1-3
Michael shall arise

Psalm 103:1-5, 20-22
Bless the LORD, you angels

Luke 10:17-20
Jesus gives his followers authority

Hymn: Come, Let Us Join Our Cheerful Songs, ELW 847

Everlasting God, you have wonderfully established the ministries of angels and mortals. Mercifully grant that as Michael and the angels contend against the cosmic forces of evil, so by your direction they may help and defend us here on earth, through your Son, Jesus Christ our Lord, who lives and reigns with you and the Holy Spirit, one God whom we worship and praise with angels and archangels and all the company of heaven, now and forever.

Tuesday, September 30, 2008

Time after Pentecost

Jerome, translator, teacher, 420

Psalm 28
Prayer to do God's will

Blessed be the Lord,
   for he has heard the sound of my pleadings.
The Lord is my strength and my shield;
   in him my heart trusts;
so I am helped, and my heart exults,
   and with my song I give thanks to him.
The Lord is the strength of his people;
   he is the saving refuge of his anointed.
O save your people, and bless your heritage;
   be their shepherd, and carry them forever. (Ps. 28:6-9)

Additional Readings:

Judges 16:1-22
Samson asked about his strength

Philippians 1:15-21
Christ is proclaimed regardless of the motive

Hymn: A Mighty Fortress Is Our God, ELW 503/504/505

You are indeed our strength, almighty God, and the breath of our very lives. Your faithfulness to us is trustworthy and we delight in you. May our life in you be a blessing to all those around us.

∾ Prayer list for October

_____

_____

_____

_____

_____

_____

_____

_____

_____

_____

_____

Wednesday, October 1, 2008

Time after Pentecost

Judges 16:23-31

Samson prays to do God's will

Then Samson called to the Lord and said, "Lord God, remember me and strengthen me only this once, O God, so that with this one act of revenge I may pay back the Philistines for my two eyes." And Samson grasped the two middle pillars on which the house rested, and he leaned his weight against them, his right hand on the one and his left hand on the other. Then Samson said, "Let me die with the Philistines." He strained with all his might; and the house fell on the lords and all the people who were in it. So those he killed at his death were more than those he had killed during his life. Then his brothers and all his family came down and took him and brought him up and buried him between Zorah and Eshtaol in the tomb of his father Manoah. He had judged Israel twenty years. (Judg. 16:28-31)

Additional Readings:

Matthew 9:2-8
Jesus' authority to forgive and heal

Psalm 28
Prayer to do God's will

Hymn: Lead On, O King Eternal! ELW 805

O God our strength, with your help we can face any obstacle that comes our way. Remember us according to the multitude of your mercies, that we might not be overcome in our adversities but find rest in your everlasting arms.

Thursday, October 2, 2008
TIME AFTER PENTECOST

Psalm 80:7-15
Look down from heaven, O God

Restore us, O God of hosts;
   let your face shine, that we may be saved.
You brought a vine out of Egypt;
   you drove out the nations and planted it.
You cleared the ground for it;
   it took deep root and filled the land.
Turn again, O God of hosts;
   look down from heaven, and see;
have regard for this vine,
   the stock that your right hand planted.
(Ps. 80:7-9, 14-15)

Additional Readings:

Jeremiah 2:14-22
The choice vine becomes degenerate

Colossians 2:16-23
Hold fast to Christ, the head

Hymn: Like the Murmur of the Dove's Song, ELW 403

God of field and farm, you till the soil, plant the seeds, and harvest the fruits of your Spirit in the lives of all your people. Strengthen all whose work is to harvest the crops in this season, that an abundance of the fruits of the earth will feed all who hunger.

Friday, October 3, 2008
Time after Pentecost

Philippians 2:14-18; 3:1-4a
Boast only in Jesus Christ

Do all things without murmuring and arguing, so that you may be blameless and innocent, children of God without blemish in the midst of a crooked and perverse generation, in which you shine like stars in the world. It is by your holding fast to the word of life that I can boast on the day of Christ that I did not run in vain or labor in vain. But even if I am being poured out as a libation over the sacrifice and the offering of your faith, I am glad and rejoice with all of you—and in the same way you also must be glad and rejoice with me. (Phil. 2:14-18)

Additional Readings:

Jeremiah 2:23-37
Israel shall be shamed

Psalm 80:7-15
Look down from heaven, O God

Hymn: O Savior, Precious Savior, ELW 820

Light of the world, in you there is no darkness at all and by your grace you cause us to reflect your love through lives of service. Let your light shine in every shadowy corner of our hearts, so your presence may be known in all the world.

Saturday, October 4, 2008

TIME AFTER PENTECOST

Francis of Assisi, renewer of the church, 1226
Theodor Fliedner, renewer of society, 1864

Jeremiah 6:1-10
Gleaning a remnant from the vine

Thus says the LORD of hosts:
Glean thoroughly as a vine
  the remnant of Israel;
like a grape-gatherer, pass your hand again
  over its branches.
To whom shall I speak and give warning,
  that they may hear?
See, their ears are closed,
  they cannot listen.
The word of the LORD is to them an object of scorn;
  they take no pleasure in it. (Jer. 6:9-10)

Additional Readings:

John 7:40-52 | Psalm 80:7-15
Some accept, others reject | *Look down from heaven,*
Jesus Christ | *O God*

Hymn: Dearest Jesus, at Your Word, ELW 520

God of gleaning and gathering, you feed us by your word and nourish us with your holy sacraments. Prepare our hearts to be receptive to your grace, and make our lives fertile soil in which your word can take root and grow.

293

Sunday, October 5, 2008
TIME AFTER PENTECOST

Matthew 21:33-46
The parable of the vineyard owner's son

Jesus said to them, "Have you never read in the scriptures:
  'The stone that the builders rejected
    has become the cornerstone;
  this was the Lord's doing,
    and it is amazing in our eyes'?
Therefore I tell you, the kingdom of God will be taken away
from you and given to a people that produces the fruits of the
kingdom. The one who falls on this stone will be broken to
pieces; and it will crush anyone on whom it falls."

　　When the chief priests and the Pharisees heard his parables,
they realized that he was speaking about them. They wanted to
arrest him, but they feared the crowds, because they regarded
him as a prophet. (Matt. 21:42-46)

Additional Readings:

Isaiah 5:1-7	Psalm 80:7-15	Philippians 3:4b-14
The song of the vineyard	*Look down from heaven, O God*	*Nothing surpasses knowing Christ*

Hymn: God Loved the World, ELW 323

*Beloved God, from you come all things that are good. Lead us by the
inspiration of your Spirit to know those things that are right, and by
your merciful guidance, help us to do them, through Jesus Christ, our
Savior and Lord.*

Monday, October 6, 2008
Time after Pentecost

William Tyndale, translator, martyr, 1536

Psalm 144
Prayer for blessing

Blessed be the LORD, my rock,
   who trains my hands for war, and my fingers for battle;
my rock and my fortress,
   my stronghold and my deliverer,
my shield, in whom I take refuge,
   who subdues the peoples under me.
O LORD, what are human beings that you regard them,
   or mortals that you think of them?
They are like a breath;
   their days are like a passing shadow. (Ps. 144:1-4)

Additional Readings:

Ezekiel 19:10-14   1 Peter 2:4-10
A lament for Israel the vine   *Christ the cornerstone*

Hymn: Lord, Enthroned in Heavenly Splendor, ELW 475

Rock of our salvation, your presence shields us when everything around and within us is chaos. Deliver us from despair, and strengthen us always to look to you as our mighty fortress and strong deliverer.

Tuesday, October 7, 2008
TIME AFTER PENTECOST

Henry Melchior Muhlenberg, pastor in North America, 1787

2 Corinthians 5:17-21
God reconciles us through Christ

So if anyone is in Christ, there is a new creation: everything old has passed away; see, everything has become new! All this is from God, who reconciled us to himself through Christ, and has given us the ministry of reconciliation; that is, in Christ God was reconciling the world to himself, not counting their trespasses against them, and entrusting the message of reconciliation to us. So we are ambassadors for Christ, since God is making his appeal through us; we entreat you on behalf of Christ, be reconciled to God. For our sake he made him to be sin who knew no sin, so that in him we might become the righteousness of God. (2 Cor. 5:17-21)

Additional Readings:

Isaiah 27:1-6
God will save Israel the vine

Psalm 144
Prayer for blessing

Hymn: Love Divine, All Loves Excelling, ELW 631

Reconciling God, you yearn for us to be in a good relationship with you. Restore to us the joy of your salvation, rekindle in us the fire of your love, and make all things new for us as we walk in your ways.

John 11:45-57
Critics plan to silence Jesus

Now the Passover of the Jews was near, and many went up from the country to Jerusalem before the Passover to purify themselves. They were looking for Jesus and were asking one another as they stood in the temple, "What do you think? Surely he will not come to the festival, will he?" Now the chief priests and the Pharisees had given orders that anyone who knew where Jesus was should let them know, so that they might arrest him. (John 11:55-57)

Additional Readings:

Song of Solomon 8:5-14
A love song for the vineyard

Psalm 144
Prayer for blessing

Hymn: Oh, Love, How Deep, ELW 322

Gracious God, your love is without condition and you provide us with the gift of salvation despite our attempts to earn it or deserve it. Help our restless souls to find their rest in you, that we may take joy in your boundless grace.

Psalm 23
You spread a table before me

The LORD is my shepherd, I shall not want.
   He makes me lie down in green pastures;
he leads me beside still waters;
   he restores my soul.
He leads me in right paths for his name's sake.
Even though I walk through the darkest valley,
   I fear no evil; for you are with me;
   your rod and your staff—they comfort me.
You prepare a table before me
   in the presence of my enemies;
you anoint my head with oil;
   my cup overflows.
Surely goodness and mercy shall follow me
   all the days of my life,
and I shall dwell in the house of the LORD
   my whole life long. (Ps. 23:1-6)

Additional Readings:

Isaiah 22:1-8a
A futile cry to the mountains for help

1 Peter 5:1-5, 12-14
Stand fast, the chief shepherd is coming

Hymn: Savior, like a Shepherd Lead Us, ELW 789

Good Shepherd of our souls, you guide us through the deepest valleys and the darkest nights of the soul. Gently lead us to those who struggle in sickness or sorrow, that your merciful presence may be made known to all.

Friday, October 10, 2008
TIME AFTER PENTECOST

James 4:4-10
Humble yourselves before God

Submit yourselves therefore to God. Resist the devil, and he will flee from you. Draw near to God, and he will draw near to you. Cleanse your hands, you sinners, and purify your hearts, you double-minded. Lament and mourn and weep. Let your laughter be turned into mourning and your joy into dejection. Humble yourselves before the Lord, and he will exalt you. (James 4:7-10)

Additional Readings:

Isaiah 22:8b-14
False joy instead of repentance

Psalm 23
You spread a table before me

Hymn: Lord, Whose Love in Humble Service, ELW 712

God of forgiveness, *even though our hearts wander and we go our own ways, you take us back into your loving arms. Strengthen us in our struggle against sin, that we might not be overcome by it but remain strong in following you.*

Isaiah 24:17-23
God judges the earth from Mount Zion

On that day the Lord will punish
   the host of heaven in heaven,
   and on earth the kings of the earth.
They will be gathered together
   like prisoners in a pit;
they will be shut up in a prison,
   and after many days they will be punished.
Then the moon will be abashed,
   and the sun ashamed;
for the Lord of hosts will reign
   on Mount Zion and in Jerusalem,
and before his elders he will manifest his glory.
(Isa. 24:21-23)

Additional Readings:

Mark 2:18-22
No fasting when the bridegroom is present

Psalm 23
You spread a table before me

Hymn: Oh, Happy Day When We Shall Stand, ELW 441

God of all, you hate nothing you have created and you love all that you have made. Help us to care for the world and its resources, that the earth, sea, sky, and every living creature would reflect your glory and praise.

Sunday, October 12, 2008
Time after Pentecost

Matthew 22:1-14
The parable of the unwelcome guest

"But when the king came in to see the guests, he noticed a man there who was not wearing a wedding robe, and he said to him, 'Friend, how did you get in here without a wedding robe?' And he was speechless. Then the king said to the attendants, 'Bind him hand and foot, and throw him into the outer darkness, where there will be weeping and gnashing of teeth.' For many are called, but few are chosen." (Matt. 22:11-14)

Additional Readings:

Isaiah 25:1-9	Psalm 23	Philippians 4:1-9
The feast of victory	*You spread a table before me*	*Rejoice in the Lord always*

Hymn: As We Gather at Your Table, ELW 522

Lord of the feast, you have prepared a table before all peoples and poured out your life with abundance. Call us again to your banquet. Strengthen us by what is honorable, just, and pure, and transform us into a people of righteousness and peace, through Jesus Christ, our Savior and Lord.

Monday, October 13, 2008

Time after Pentecost

Day of Thanksgiving (Canada)

Psalm 34
Taste and see

O taste and see that the LORD is good;
  happy are those who take refuge in him.
O fear the LORD, you his holy ones,
  for those who fear him have no want.
The young lions suffer want and hunger,
  but those who seek the LORD lack no good thing.
(Ps. 34:8-10)

Additional Readings:

Exodus 19:7-20
God meets Moses on the mountain

Jude 17-25
Prepare for the Lord's coming

Hymn: Taste and See, ELW 493

Abundant God, your goodness has no limits and your grace is without end. Grant us an ever-increasing awareness of your faithfulness, and open our hearts to provide for all who suffer from hunger or any kind of need, through Jesus Christ our Lord.

Tuesday, October 14, 2008
Time after Pentecost

Amos 9:5-15
Sweet wine from the mountains

The time is surely coming, says the LORD,
   when the one who plows shall overtake the one who reaps,
   and the treader of grapes the one who sows the seed;
the mountains shall drip sweet wine,
   and all the hills shall flow with it.
I will restore the fortunes of my people Israel,
   and they shall rebuild the ruined cities and inhabit them;
they shall plant vineyards and drink their wine,
   and they shall make gardens and eat their fruit.
I will plant them upon their land,
   and they shall never again be plucked up
   out of the land that I have given them,
says the LORD your God. (Amos 9:13-15)

Additional Readings:

Philippians 3:13—4:1   Psalm 34
Hold fast to Christ   *Taste and see*

Hymn: Build Us Up, Lord, ELW 670

God of mercy, your love restores us when we are empty and your grace rebuilds what we have ruined. Give us your compassion to see in every human need the opportunity to bring relief and tangible signs of your presence, in Jesus' name.

Wednesday, October 15, 2008

Time after Pentecost

Teresa of Avila, teacher, renewer of the church, 1582

Song of Solomon 7:10 — 8:4

Love like rich fruit

I am my beloved's,
   and his desire is for me.
Come, my beloved,
   let us go forth into the fields,
   and lodge in the villages;
let us go out early to the vineyards,
   and see whether the vines have budded,
whether the grape blossoms have opened
   and the pomegranates are in bloom.
There I will give you my love.
The mandrakes give forth fragrance,
   and over our doors are all choice fruits,
new as well as old,
   which I have laid up for you, O my beloved.
(Song of Sol. 7:10-13)

Additional Readings:

John 6:25-35   Psalm 34
God will feed the believer   *Taste and see*

Hymn: Beloved, God's Chosen, ELW 648

Lover of our souls, your irresistible grace daily draws us into deeper communion with you. Make us lovers of the world that you have made and have so loved by sending us your Son, our Savior Jesus Christ.

Psalm 96:1-9 [10-13]
God's glory among the nations

O sing to the LORD a new song;
  sing to the LORD, all the earth.
Sing to the LORD, bless his name;
  tell of his salvation from day to day.
Declare his glory among the nations,
  his marvelous works among all the peoples.
For great is the LORD, and greatly to be praised;
  he is to be revered above all gods. (Ps. 96:1-4)

Additional Readings:

Judges 17:1-6   3 John 9-12
Before Israel had a king   *Imitate what is good*

Hymn: Earth and All Stars! ELW 731

God of new songs and new voices, you inspire melody and verse, color and art, words and literature. Bless the work of all musicians, artists, and authors, that our eyes, ears, and every sense would be awakened to new visions of your grace.

Friday, October 17, 2008

Time after Pentecost

Ignatius, Bishop of Antioch, martyr, c. 115

1 Peter 5:1-5

Exemplary leadership

Now as an elder myself and a witness of the sufferings of Christ, as well as one who shares in the glory to be revealed, I exhort the elders among you to tend the flock of God that is in your charge, exercising the oversight, not under compulsion but willingly, as God would have you do it—not for sordid gain but eagerly. Do not lord it over those in your charge, but be examples to the flock. And when the chief shepherd appears, you will win the crown of glory that never fades away. In the same way, you who are younger must accept the authority of the elders. And all of you must clothe yourselves with humility in your dealings with one another, for

"God opposes the proud,
    but gives grace to the humble." (1 Pet. 5:1-5)

Additional Readings:

Deuteronomy 17:14-20
The limitations of royal authority

Psalm 96:1-9 [10-13]
God's glory among the nations

Hymn: We Are an Offering, ELW 692

Gentle God, you call forth people from among us to be leaders in your church. Bless our bishops, pastors, diaconal ministers, and associates in ministry, that they would find joy in their service and strength for their many tasks, through Jesus Christ our Lord.

Saturday, October 18, 2008
LUKE, EVANGELIST

Luke 1:1-4; 24:44-53
Luke witnesses to the ministry of Jesus

Since many have undertaken to set down an orderly account of the events that have been fulfilled among us, just as they were handed on to us by those who from the beginning were eyewitnesses and servants of the word, I too decided, after investigating everything carefully from the very first, to write an orderly account for you, most excellent Theophilus, so that you may know the truth concerning the things about which you have been instructed. (Luke 1:1-4)

Additional Readings:

Isaiah 43:8-13	Psalm 124	2 Timothy 4:5-11
You are my witnesses	*Our help is in God*	*The good fight of faith*

Hymn: I Love to Tell the Story, ELW 661

Almighty God, you inspired your servant Luke to reveal in his gospel the love and healing power of your Son. Give your church the same love and power to heal, and to proclaim your salvation to the nations, to the glory of your name, through Jesus Christ, your Son, our healer, who lives and reigns with you and the Holy Spirit, one God, now and forever.

Sunday, October 19, 2008

Time after Pentecost

Matthew 22:15-22

A teaching about the emperor and God

But Jesus, aware of [the Pharisees'] malice, said, "Why are you putting me to the test, you hypocrites? Show me the coin used for the tax." And they brought him a denarius. Then he said to them, "Whose head is this, and whose title?" They answered, "The emperor's." Then he said to them, "Give therefore to the emperor the things that are the emperor's, and to God the things that are God's." When they heard this, they were amazed; and they left him and went away. (Matt. 22:18-22)

Additional Readings:

Isaiah 45:1-7
An earthly ruler works God's will

Psalm 96:1-9 [10-13]
God's glory among the nations

1 Thessalonians 1:1-10
Thanksgiving for the church at Thessalonica

Hymn: As Saints of Old, ELW 695

Sovereign God, raise your throne in our hearts. Created by you, let us live in your image; created for you, let us act for your glory; redeemed by you, let us give you what is yours, through Jesus Christ, our Savior and Lord.

Monday, October 20, 2008
Time after Pentecost

Psalm 98
God reigns over the nations

O sing to the LORD a new song,
   for he has done marvelous things.
His right hand and his holy arm
   have gotten him victory.
The LORD has made known his victory;
   he has revealed his vindication in the sight of the nations.
He has remembered his steadfast love and faithfulness
   to the house of Israel.
All the ends of the earth have seen
   the victory of our God. (Ps. 98:1-3)

Additional Readings:

Daniel 3:1-18
*Three disobey
Nebuchadnezzar*

Revelation 18:1-10, 19-20
The fall of Babylon

Hymn: Oh, Sing to the Lord, ELW 822

The light of your face shines upon us, O God, and your faithful presence illumines our every path. Guide our steps in your ways of justice and peace, that our world and every child of earth may be restored and reconciled in you.

Tuesday, October 21, 2008
Time after Pentecost

Daniel 3:19-30
God saves three men in the furnace

Nebuchadnezzar then approached the door of the furnace of blazing fire and said, "Shadrach, Meshach, and Abednego, servants of the Most High God, come out! Come here!" . . . And the satraps, the prefects, the governors, and the king's counselors gathered together and saw that the fire had not had any power over the bodies of those men; the hair of their heads was not singed, their tunics were not harmed, and not even the smell of fire came from them. Nebuchadnezzar said, "Blessed be the God of Shadrach, Meshach, and Abednego, who has sent his angel and delivered his servants who trusted in him. They disobeyed the king's command and yielded up their bodies rather than serve and worship any god except their own God. Therefore I make a decree: Any people, nation, or language that utters blasphemy against the God of Shadrach, Meshach, and Abednego shall be torn limb from limb, and their houses laid in ruins; for there is no other god who is able to deliver in this way." (Dan. 3:26-29)

Additional Readings:

Revelation 18:21-24
Babylon will be found no more

Psalm 98
God reigns over the nations

Hymn: Evening and Morning, ELW 761

God of wind and flame, you promise to surround us with your presence through all of life's trials. Enable us to sense your nearness even when it seems that we have drifted away from you.

Wednesday, October 22, 2008
Time after Pentecost

Matthew 17:22-27
Jesus pays the temple tax

When they reached Capernaum, the collectors of the temple tax came to Peter and said, "Does your teacher not pay the temple tax?" He said, "Yes, he does." And when he came home, Jesus spoke of it first, asking, "What do you think, Simon? From whom do kings of the earth take toll or tribute? From their children or from others?" When Peter said, "From others," Jesus said to him, "Then the children are free. However, so that we do not give offense to them, go to the sea and cast a hook; take the first fish that comes up; and when you open its mouth, you will find a coin; take that and give it to them for you and me." (Matt. 17:24-27)

Additional Readings:

Daniel 6:1-28   Psalm 98
Daniel disobeys King   *God reigns over the nations*
Darius

Hymn: Oh, Praise the Gracious Power, ELW 651

God whose giving knows no ending, your grace and love for us overflows in Jesus Christ. Teach us to share out of our abundance, that your church would be strengthened in mission by the resources of our time, talents, and treasure.

Thursday, October 23, 2008

Time after Pentecost

James of Jerusalem, martyr, c. 62

Psalm 1
Their delight is in the law

Happy are those
  who do not follow the advice of the wicked,
or take the path that sinners tread,
  or sit in the seat of scoffers;
but their delight is in the law of the LORD,
  and on his law they meditate day and night.
They are like trees
  planted by streams of water,
which yield their fruit in its season,
  and their leaves do not wither.
In all that they do, they prosper. (Ps. 1:1-3)

Additional Readings:

Numbers 5:5-10
Restitution for wronged neighbors

Titus 1:5-16
Troublemakers deny God

Hymn: Oh, That the Lord Would Guide My Ways, ELW 772

O God, in whose presence our souls take delight, by your hand you feed us with your word and sacraments. Refresh us daily as we find you in scripture and prayer, that the seed of faith may take root and bear much fruit in us.

Friday, October 24, 2008
TIME AFTER PENTECOST

Titus 2:7-8, 11-15
A life devoted to good works

For the grace of God has appeared, bringing salvation to all, training us to renounce impiety and worldly passions, and in the present age to live lives that are self-controlled, upright, and godly, while we wait for the blessed hope and the manifestation of the glory of our great God and Savior, Jesus Christ. He it is who gave himself for us that he might redeem us from all iniquity and purify for himself a people of his own who are zealous for good deeds. (Titus 2:11-14)

Additional Readings:

Deuteronomy 9:25—10:5   Psalm 1
The second set of   *Their delight is in the law*
commandments

Hymn: Salvation unto Us Has Come, ELW 590

Hope of the world, you reveal your glory to all and withhold your grace from no one. Invigorate us in your all-consuming love for the world, that our lives would reflect the generosity of your mercy for the whole creation.

Saturday, October 25, 2008
Time after Pentecost

John 5:39-47
Moses judges the disobedient

[Jesus said:] "I have come in my Father's name, and you do not accept me; if another comes in his own name, you will accept him. How can you believe when you accept glory from one another and do not seek the glory that comes from the one who alone is God? Do not think that I will accuse you before the Father; your accuser is Moses, on whom you have set your hope. If you believed Moses, you would believe me, for he wrote about me. But if you do not believe what he wrote, how will you believe what I say?" (John 5:43-47)

Additional Readings:

Proverbs 24:23-34   Psalm 1
Rise above retribution   *Their delight is in the law*

Hymn: We All Believe in One True God, ELW 411

You have the words of eternal life, O God. Renew us this day with the assurance that nothing in all creation can ever separate us from your love, in Jesus Christ our Lord.

Sunday, October 26, 2008

TIME AFTER PENTECOST

Reformation Sunday

*Philipp Nicolai, 1608; Johann Heermann, 1647;
Paul Gerhardt, 1676; hymnwriters*

Matthew 22:34-46

Loving God and neighbor

When the Pharisees heard that [Jesus] had silenced the
Sadducees, they gathered together, and one of them, a
lawyer, asked him a question to test him. "Teacher, which
commandment in the law is the greatest?" He said to him, " 'You
shall love the Lord your God with all your heart, and with all
your soul, and with all your mind.' This is the greatest and first
commandment. And a second is like it: 'You shall love your
neighbor as yourself.' On these two commandments hang all the
law and the prophets." (Matt. 22:34-40)

Additional Readings:

Leviticus 19:1-2, 15-18	Psalm 1	1 Thessalonians 2:1-8
Acts of justice	*Their delight is in the law*	*The apostle's concern*

Hymn: O Holy Spirit, Enter In, ELW 786

*O Lord God, you are the holy lawgiver, you are the salvation of your
people. By your Spirit renew us in your covenant of love, and train us
to care tenderly for all our neighbors, through Jesus Christ, our Savior
and Lord.*

Psalm 119:41-48
I will keep God's law

Let your steadfast love come to me, O LORD,
    your salvation according to your promise.
Then I shall have an answer for those who taunt me,
    for I trust in your word.
Do not take the word of truth utterly out of my mouth,
    for my hope is in your ordinances.
I will keep your law continually,
    forever and ever. (Ps. 119:41-44)

Additional Readings:

Deuteronomy 6:1-9, 20-25   James 2:8-13
The great commandment   *Fulfilling the royal law*

Hymn: O Jesus, I Have Promised, ELW 810

Great is your faithfulness, O God of steadfast love. Deepen our trust
*in your promise of grace, that we would be emboldened to live out your
gospel of justice and joy in the world around us.*

Tuesday, October 28, 2008
Simon and Jude, Apostles

John 14:21-27
Those who love Jesus will keep his word

"They who have my commandments and keep them are those who love me; and those who love me will be loved by my Father, and I will love them and reveal myself to them." Judas (not Iscariot) said to him, "Lord, how is it that you will reveal yourself to us, and not to the world?" Jesus answered him, "Those who love me will keep my word, and my Father will love them, and we will come to them and make our home with them. Whoever does not love me does not keep my words; and the word that you hear is not mine, but is from the Father who sent me." (John 14:21-24)

Additional Readings:

Jeremiah 26:[1-6] 7-16	Psalm 11	1 John 4:1-6
Jeremiah promises the judgment of God	*Take refuge in God*	*Do not believe every spirit of this world*

Hymn: Here, O Lord, Your Servants Gather, ELW 530

O God, we thank you for the glorious company of the apostles, and especially on this day for Simon and Jude. We pray that, as they were faithful and zealous in your mission, so we may with ardent devotion make known the love and mercy of our Savior Jesus Christ, who lives and reigns with you and the Holy Spirit, one God, now and forever.

Wednesday, October 29, 2008
Time after Pentecost

Matthew 19:16-22
Keeping the commandments

Then someone came to him and said, "Teacher, what good deed must I do to have eternal life?" And he said to him, "Why do you ask me about what is good? There is only one who is good. If you wish to enter into life, keep the commandments." He said to him, "Which ones?" And Jesus said, "You shall not murder; You shall not commit adultery; You shall not steal; You shall not bear false witness; Honor your father and mother; also, You shall love your neighbor as yourself." The young man said to him, "I have kept all these; what do I still lack?" Jesus said to him, "If you wish to be perfect, go, sell your possessions, and give the money to the poor, and you will have treasure in heaven; then come, follow me." When the young man heard this word, he went away grieving, for he had many possessions. (Matt. 19:16-22)

Additional Readings:

Proverbs 16:1-20   Psalm 119:41-48
It is good to obey   *I will keep God's law*

Hymn: You Are the Way, ELW 758

God of goodness and life, you are the source of our salvation, and without your grace we are nothing. Strengthen us to respond to your love in gratitude and holy living, to the honor and glory of your name, through Christ our Lord.

Psalm 43
Send out your light and truth

Vindicate me, O God, and defend my cause
   against an ungodly people;
from those who are deceitful and unjust
   deliver me!
For you are the God in whom I take refuge;
   why have you cast me off?
Why must I walk about mournfully
   because of the oppression of the enemy?
O send out your light and your truth;
   let them lead me;
let them bring me to your holy hill
   and to your dwelling.
Then I will go to the altar of God,
   to God my exceeding joy;
and I will praise you with the harp,
   O God, my God. (Ps. 43:1-4)

Additional Readings:

1 Samuel 2:27-36	Romans 2:17-29
Hope for a better	*Real circumcision a matter*
priesthood	*of the heart*

Hymn: Christ, Be Our Light, ELW 715

You are our refuge and strength, O God, and our secure shelter in the storms of life. Free us from our fears, deliver us from all evil, and grant us joy as we live in the freedom of your gospel, through Jesus Christ our Lord.

Friday, October 31, 2008
Reformation Day

John 8:31-36
The truth will set you free

Then Jesus said to the Jews who had believed in him, "If you continue in my word, you are truly my disciples; and you will know the truth, and the truth will make you free." They answered him, "We are descendants of Abraham and have never been slaves to anyone. What do you mean by saying, 'You will be made free'?"

Jesus answered them, "Very truly, I tell you, everyone who commits sin is a slave to sin. The slave does not have a permanent place in the household; the son has a place there forever. So if the Son makes you free, you will be free indeed." (John 8:31-36)

Additional Readings:

Jeremiah 31:31-34	Psalm 46	Romans 3:19-28
I will write my law in their hearts	*The God of Jacob is our stronghold*	*Justified by God's grace as a gift*

Hymn: That Priceless Grace, ELW 591

Almighty God, gracious Lord, we thank you that your Holy Spirit renews the church in every age. Pour out your Holy Spirit on your faithful people. Keep them steadfast in your word, protect and comfort them in times of trial, defend them against all enemies of the gospel, and bestow on the church your saving peace, through Jesus Christ, our Savior and Lord, who lives and reigns with you and the Holy Spirit, one God, now and forever.

∾ Prayer list for November

_____

_____

_____

_____

_____

_____

_____

_____

_____

_____

_____

_____

Saturday, November 1, 2008
ALL SAINTS DAY

Matthew 5:1-12
Blessed are the poor in spirit

"Blessed are those who are persecuted for righteousness' sake, for theirs is the kingdom of heaven.

"Blessed are you when people revile you and persecute you and utter all kinds of evil against you falsely on my account. Rejoice and be glad, for your reward is great in heaven, for in the same way they persecuted the prophets who were before you." (Matt. 5:10-12)

Additional Readings:

Revelation 7:9-17
The multitude of heaven worship the Lamb

Psalm 34:1-10, 22
Fear the LORD, you saints

1 John 3:1-3
We are God's children

Hymn: Blest Are They, ELW 728

Almighty God, you have knit your people together in one communion in the mystical body of your Son, Jesus Christ our Lord. Grant us grace to follow your blessed saints in lives of faith and commitment, and to know the inexpressible joys you have prepared for those who love you, through Jesus Christ, our Savior and Lord, who lives and reigns with you and the Holy Spirit, one God, now and forever.

Sunday, November 2, 2008
TIME AFTER PENTECOST

All Saints Sunday

Matthew 23:1-12
Humble yourselves

Then Jesus said to the crowds and to his disciples, " . . . call no one your father on earth, for you have one Father—the one in heaven. Nor are you to be called instructors, for you have one instructor, the Messiah. The greatest among you will be your servant. All who exalt themselves will be humbled, and all who humble themselves will be exalted." (Matt. 23:1, 9-12)

Additional Readings:

Micah 3:5-12	Psalm 43	1 Thessalonians 2:9-13
Judgment upon corrupt leaders	*Send out your light and truth*	*The apostle's teaching*

Hymn: Rise, O Church, like Christ Arisen, ELW 548

O God, generous and supreme, your loving Son lived among us, instructing us in the ways of humility and justice. Continue to ease our burdens, and train us to serve alongside of him, Jesus Christ, our Savior and Lord.

Psalm 5
God blesses the righteous

Give ear to my words, O LORD;
  give heed to my sighing.
Listen to the sound of my cry,
  my King and my God,
  for to you I pray.
O LORD, in the morning you hear my voice;
  in the morning I plead my case to you, and watch.
Lead me, O LORD, in your righteousness
  because of my enemies;
  make your way straight before me. (Ps. 5:1-3, 8)

Additional Readings:

Jeremiah 5:18-31   1 Thessalonians 2:13-20
Prophets and priests who   *Words to the church*
mislead

Hymn: Golden Breaks the Dawn, ELW 852

God our defender, open us to confidence by loving us deeply. Hear our cry and answer us with the gift of your Holy Spirit. Where we are wrong, forgive us; where we are fearful, strengthen us through Jesus Christ our Lord.

Lamentations 2:13-17
When prophets see false visions

What can I say for you, to what compare you,
  O daughter Jerusalem?
To what can I liken you, that I may comfort you,
  O virgin daughter Zion? . . .
Your prophets have seen for you
  false and deceptive visions;
they have not exposed your iniquity
  to restore your fortunes,
but have seen oracles for you
  that are false and misleading.
All who pass along the way
  clap their hands at you;
they hiss and wag their heads
  at daughter Jerusalem;
"Is this the city that was called
  the perfection of beauty,
  the joy of all the earth?" (Lam. 2:13-15)

Additional Readings:

Acts 13:1-12   Psalm 5
Paul and Barnabas   *God blesses the righteous*
confront a false prophet

Hymn: Jerusalem, My Happy Home, ELW 628

What shall we do, Lord, if we have lost our way? To whom can we flee but you? Deliver us from error, set us on your paths, and lead us to life through Jesus Christ our Lord.

Proverbs 16:21-33
The wise heart and persuasive lips

The wise of heart is called perceptive,
   and pleasant speech increases persuasiveness.
Wisdom is a fountain of life to one who has it,
   but folly is the punishment of fools.
The mind of the wise makes their speech judicious,
   and adds persuasiveness to their lips. (Prov. 16:21-23)

Additional Readings:

Matthew 15:1-9
Lips that misrepresent the heart

Psalm 5
God blesses the righteous

Hymn: Holy God, Holy and Glorious, ELW 637

O holy Wisdom! Fill our hearts with yourself, and open our mouths
to sing your praise. Cleanse us from within, and then we shall be strong
to witness to your life and love in Jesus' name.

Psalm 70
You are my helper and deliverer

Be pleased, O God, to deliver me.
  O Lord, make haste to help me!
Let those be put to shame and confusion
  who seek my life.
Let those be turned back and brought to dishonor
  who desire to hurt me.
Let those who say, "Aha, Aha!"
  turn back because of their shame.
Let all who seek you
  rejoice and be glad in you.
Let those who love your salvation
  say evermore, "God is great!"
But I am poor and needy;
  hasten to me, O God!
You are my help and my deliverer;
  O Lord, do not delay! (Ps. 70:1-5)

Additional Readings:

Amos 1:1—2:5
*God judges Israel's
neighbors*

Revelation 8:6—9:12
*The trumpet of God's
judgment*

Hymn: Immortal, Invisible, God Only Wise, ELW 834

*When chaos swirls around us, God, be the still center of our souls.
Empty us of pride and arrogance so that in our poverty we may know
you are our hope and help, through Jesus Christ our Lord.*

Friday, November 7, 2008
Time after Pentecost

*John Christian Frederick Heyer, 1873; Bartholomaeus Ziegenbalg, 1719;
Ludwig Nommensen, 1918; missionaries*

Amos 3:1-12
Israel's guilt and punishment

Proclaim to the strongholds in Ashdod,
   and to the strongholds in the land of Egypt,
and say, "Assemble yourselves on Mount Samaria,
   and see what great tumults are within it,
   and what oppressions are in its midst."
They do not know how to do right, says the LORD,
   those who store up violence and robbery in their
      strongholds.
Therefore thus says the Lord GOD:
An adversary shall surround the land,
   and strip you of your defense;
   and your strongholds shall be plundered.
(Amos 3:9-11)

Additional Readings:

Revelation 9:13-21
*Unrepentant humankind
persists in sin*

Psalm 70
*You are my helper and
deliverer*

Hymn: My Life Flows On in Endless Song, ELW 763

*O God, when headlines and eyewitness news overwhelm us, teach us to
turn to you. Teach us also to look in the mirror, to seek your forgiveness,
and to know your renewing love in Jesus Christ our Lord.*

Matthew 24:1-14
Jesus foretells the end

When [Jesus] was sitting on the Mount of Olives, the disciples came to him privately, saying, "Tell us, when will this be, and what will be the sign of your coming and of the end of the age?" Jesus answered them, "Beware that no one leads you astray. For many will come in my name, saying, 'I am the Messiah!' and they will lead many astray. And you will hear of wars and rumors of wars; see that you are not alarmed; for this must take place, but the end is not yet." (Matt. 24:3-6)

Additional Readings:

Amos 4:6-13
Israel, prepare to meet your God

Psalm 70
You are my helper and deliverer

Hymn: Lord Christ, When First You Came to Earth, ELW 727

Is there time, God? Will we finish our tasks, reach our goals? Our times are in your hands. Help us to place our lives in you so that we may know our security in your Messiah, Jesus.

Sunday, November 9, 2008

Time after Pentecost

Matthew 25:1-13
Wise and foolish bridesmaids

"Then the kingdom of heaven will be like this. Ten bridesmaids took their lamps and went to meet the bridegroom. Five of them were foolish, and five were wise. When the foolish took their lamps, they took no oil with them; but the wise took flasks of oil with their lamps." (Matt. 25:1-4)

Additional Readings:

Amos 5:18-24
Let justice roll down like waters

Psalm 70
You are my helper and deliverer

1 Thessalonians 4:13-18
The promise of the resurrection

Hymn: Rejoice, Rejoice, Believers, ELW 244

O God of justice and love, you illumine our way through life with the words of your Son. Give us the light we need, awaken us to the needs of others, through Jesus Christ, our Savior and Lord.

Monday, November 10, 2008
TIME AFTER PENTECOST

Psalm 63
God is a rich feast

My soul is satisfied as with a rich feast,
   and my mouth praises you with joyful lips
when I think of you on my bed,
   and meditate on you in the watches of the night;
for you have been my help,
   and in the shadow of your wings I sing for joy.
My soul clings to you;
   your right hand upholds me. (Ps. 63:5-8)

Additional Readings:

Amos 8:7-14
A famine of hearing God's word

1 Corinthians 14:20-25
They will not listen to me

Hymn: Thy Holy Wings, ELW 613

O God, you are the rest for our souls. Help us to live in you, to meditate upon your words, to sing your praises, and to hear and believe the good news you have promised through Jesus Christ our Lord.

Tuesday, November 11, 2008
Time after Pentecost

Martin, Bishop of Tours, 397
Søren Aabye Kierkegaard, teacher, 1855

1 Thessalonians 3:6-13
Stand firm in the faith

Now may our God and Father himself and our Lord Jesus direct our way to you. And may the Lord make you increase and abound in love for one another and for all, just as we abound in love for you. And may he so strengthen your hearts in holiness that you may be blameless before our God and Father at the coming of our Lord Jesus with all his saints. (1 Thess. 3:11-13)

Additional Readings:

Joel 1:1-14
Call to repentance

Psalm 63
God is a rich feast

Hymn: Blest Be the Tie That Binds, ELW 656

O God, we commend to you all from whom we are separated: distant family and friends, opponents and enemies, and all the blessed dead. Fill the distances between us with hope, and bring us to your great reunion through Jesus Christ our Lord.

Wednesday, November 12, 2008
TIME AFTER PENTECOST

Matthew 24:29-35
My words will not pass away

"From the fig tree learn its lesson: as soon as its branch becomes tender and puts forth its leaves, you know that summer is near. So also, when you see all these things, you know that he is near, at the very gates. Truly I tell you, this generation will not pass away until all these things have taken place. Heaven and earth will pass away, but my words will not pass away." (Matt. 24:32-35)

Additional Readings:

Joel 3:9-21
Promise of a glorious future

Psalm 63
God is a rich feast

Hymn: My Lord, What a Morning, ELW 438

You promise us, O God, that your words will not pass away. Let your word so work inside us that we may eagerly await your coming and greet you at the gate, through Jesus Christ our Lord.

Psalm 90:1-8 [9-11] 12
Number your days

Lord, you have been our dwelling place
    in all generations.
Before the mountains were brought forth,
    or ever you had formed the earth and the world,
    from everlasting to everlasting you are God.
You turn us back to dust,
    and say, "Turn back, you mortals."
For a thousand years in your sight
    are like yesterday when it is past,
    or like a watch in the night. (Ps. 90:1-4)

Additional Readings:

Ezekiel 6:1-14
Judgment on idolatrous Israel

Revelation 16:1-7
God's judgments are true and just

Hymn: How Small Our Span of Life, ELW 636

Our very existence—even the universe—is a mote of dust worn away from the mountains of eternity. But you, Lord God, have given us a home forever. Help us to number our days in you, through Jesus Christ our Lord.

Ezekiel 7:1-9
The end is upon us

The word of the LORD came to me: You, O mortal,
thus says the Lord GOD to the land of Israel:
  An end! The end has come
    upon the four corners of the land.
  Now the end is upon you,
    I will let loose my anger upon you;
  I will judge you according to your ways,
    I will punish you for all your abominations.
  My eye will not spare you, I will have no pity.
    I will punish you for your ways,
    while your abominations are among you.
Then you shall know that I am the LORD. (Ezek. 7:1-4)

Additional Readings:

Revelation 16:8-21	Psalm 90:1-8 [9-11] 12
The judged curse God	*Number your days*

Hymn: My God, How Wonderful Thou Art, ELW 863

If you turn your back on us, O God, we have no hope. Spare and save the people whom you have loved, we pray! We dare to ask it for the sake of Jesus.

Matthew 12:43-45
From bad to worse

"When the unclean spirit has gone out of a person, it wanders through waterless regions looking for a resting place, but it finds none. Then it says, 'I will return to my house from which I came.' When it comes, it finds it empty, swept, and put in order. Then it goes and brings along seven other spirits more evil than itself, and they enter and live there; and the last state of that person is worse than the first. So will it be also with this evil generation." (Matt. 12:43-45)

Additional Readings:

Ezekiel 7:10-27
You shall know that the Lord is God

Psalm 90:1-8 [9-11] 12
Number your days

Hymn: Goodness Is Stronger than Evil, ELW 721

The housework is never done! The demons of disorder plague us! But you, O Lord, are our mop and broom. Order our lives in Christ, and make us healthy and whole.

Sunday, November 16, 2008

TIME AFTER PENTECOST

Matthew 25:14-30

Slaves entrusted with talents

"Then the [slave] who had received the one talent also came forward, saying, 'Master, I knew that you were a harsh man, reaping where you did not sow, and gathering where you did not scatter seed; so I was afraid, and I went and hid your talent in the ground. Here you have what is yours.' But his master replied, 'You wicked and lazy slave! You knew, did you, that I reap where I did not sow, and gather where I did not scatter? Then you ought to have invested my money with the bankers, and on my return I would have received what was my own with interest. So take the talent from him, and give it to the one with the ten talents.'" (Matt. 25:24-28)

Additional Readings:

Zephaniah 1:7, 12-18
The day of the Lord

Psalm 90:1-8 [9-11] 12
Number your days

1 Thessalonians 5:1-11
Be alert for the day of the Lord

Hymn: God, Whose Giving Knows No Ending, ELW 678

Righteous God, our merciful master, you own the earth and all its peoples, and you give us all that we have. Inspire us to serve you with justice and wisdom, and prepare us for the joy of the day of your coming, through Jesus Christ, our Savior and Lord.

Monday, November 17, 2008

TIME AFTER PENTECOST

Elizabeth of Hungary, renewer of society, 1231

Psalm 9:1-14
God's reward for the righteous

I will give thanks to the LORD with my whole heart;
  I will tell of all your wonderful deeds.
I will be glad and exult in you;
  I will sing praise to your name, O Most High.
When my enemies turned back,
  they stumbled and perished before you.
For you have maintained my just cause;
  you have sat on the throne giving righteous judgment.
(Ps. 9:1-4)

Additional Readings:

Zechariah 1:7-17
God's judgment and mercy

Romans 2:1-11
The righteous judgment of God

Hymn: Praise to the Lord, the Almighty, ELW 858

Our hearts overflow with gratitude to you, O Lord, for all your care and protection. Help us to sing your praises and to know that our only hope for your righteous judgment is through your forgiving grace in Jesus Christ our Lord.

Zechariah 2:1-5; 5:1-4
Visions of mercy and judgment

I looked up and saw a man with a measuring line in his hand.
Then I asked, "Where are you going?" He answered me, "To
measure Jerusalem, to see what is its width and what is its
length." Then the angel who talked with me came forward, and
another angel came forward to meet him, and said to him, "Run,
say to that young man: Jerusalem shall be inhabited like villages
without walls, because of the multitude of people and animals
in it. For I will be a wall of fire all around it, says the Lord, and I
will be the glory within it." (Zech. 2:1-5)

Additional Readings:

1 Thessalonians 5:12-18
The Christian life

Psalm 9:1-14
God's reward for the righteous

Hymn: Alleluia, Song of Gladness, ELW 318

*Sometimes, O God, we worry about the dimensions of our lives, the
sphere of our influence, the length of our reach. Help us to see that the
fire of your love encircles us and makes us great in you, through Jesus
our Lord.*

Matthew 24:45-51
Parable of the unfaithful slave

Who then is the faithful and wise slave, whom his master has put in charge of his household, to give the other slaves their allowance of food at the proper time? Blessed is that slave whom his master will find at work when he arrives. Truly I tell you, he will put that one in charge of all his possessions. (Matt. 24:45-47)

Additional Readings:

Job 16:1-21
A lament about unjust punishment

Psalm 9:1-14
God's reward for the righteous

Hymn: Lord Jesus, You Shall Be My Song, ELW 808

Extravagant Creator, you honor us with holy responsibilities, asking us to assist you in upholding the world. Make us faithful and wise stewards of your wealth by giving us your gift of generosity, through Jesus Christ our Lord.

Thursday, November 20, 2008
Time after Pentecost

Psalm 95:1-7a
We are the people of God's pasture

O come, let us sing to the Lord;
　let us make a joyful noise to the rock of our salvation!
Let us come into his presence with thanksgiving;
　let us make a joyful noise to him with songs of praise!
For the Lord is a great God,
　and a great King above all gods.
In his hand are the depths of the earth;
　the heights of the mountains are his also.
The sea is his, for he made it,
　and the dry land, which his hands have formed.
(Ps. 95:1-5)

Additional Readings:

1 Kings 22:13-23
Israel like sheep without a shepherd

Revelation 14:1-11
Fear God and give God glory

Hymn: O Christ, What Can It Mean for Us, ELW 431

All creation sings your praise, O God. From atoms to galaxies, all space and all time are yours. Hold us, also, in your strong and gentle hands—we, your creatures, loved by you in Jesus Christ our Lord.

Revelation 22:1-9
Worship God alone

Then the angel showed me the river of the water of life, bright as crystal, flowing from the throne of God and of the Lamb through the middle of the street of the city. On either side of the river is the tree of life with its twelve kinds of fruit, producing its fruit each month; and the leaves of the tree are for the healing of the nations. Nothing accursed will be found there any more. But the throne of God and of the Lamb will be in it, and his servants will worship him; they will see his face, and his name will be on their foreheads. And there will be no more night; they need no light of lamp or sun, for the Lord God will be their light, and they will reign forever and ever. (Rev. 22:1-5)

Additional Readings:

1 Chronicles 17:1-15
David, shepherd and king of Israel

Psalm 95:1-7a
We are the people of God's pasture

Hymn: Crown Him with Many Crowns, ELW 855

Keep your dream alive in us, O God, and lead us toward our home with you in paradise. Open our eyes to see the future in the victorious Lamb—crucified, risen and reigning—our hope and our assurance, Jesus Christ our Lord.

Saturday, November 22, 2008

Time after Pentecost

Matthew 12:46-50
The true kindred of Jesus

While he was still speaking to the crowds, his mother and
his brothers were standing outside, wanting to speak to him.
Someone told him, "Look, your mother and your brothers are
standing outside, wanting to speak to you." But to the one who
had told him this, Jesus replied, "Who is my mother, and who are
my brothers?" And pointing to his disciples, he said, "Here are
my mother and my brothers! For whoever does the will of my
Father in heaven is my brother and sister and mother."
(Matt. 12:46-50)

Additional Readings:

Isaiah 44:21-28
*Cyrus, a shepherd for the
Lord*

Psalm 95:1-7a
*We are the people of God's
pasture*

Hymn: What God Ordains Is Good Indeed, ELW 776

*We dare to call you our parent, O God, because Jesus is our
brother. Let his image formed within us lead us to do your will and bear
his family likeness in the world. We ask it in his name.*

Sunday, November 23, 2008
CHRIST THE KING

Clement, Bishop of Rome, c. 100
Miguel Agustín Pro, martyr, 1927

Matthew 25:31-46
The separation of sheep and goats

"Then the king will say to those at his left hand, 'You that are accursed, depart from me into the eternal fire prepared for the devil and his angels; for I was hungry and you gave me no food, I was thirsty and you gave me nothing to drink, I was a stranger and you did not welcome me, naked and you did not give me clothing, sick and in prison and you did not visit me.' Then they also will answer, 'Lord, when was it that we saw you hungry or thirsty or a stranger or naked or sick or in prison, and did not take care of you?" Then he will answer them, 'Truly I tell you, just as you did not do it to one of the least of these, you did not do it to me.' " (Matt. 25:41-45)

Additional Readings:

Ezekiel 34:11-16, 20-24	Psalm 95:1-7a	Ephesians 1:15-23
God will shepherd Israel	*We are the people of God's pasture*	*The reign of Christ*

Hymn: Soon and Very Soon, ELW 439

O God of power and might, your Son shows us the way of service, and in him we inherit the riches of your grace. Give us the wisdom to know what is right and the strength to serve the world you have made, through Jesus Christ, our Savior and Lord, who lives and reigns with you and the Holy Spirit, one God, now and forever.

Monday, November 24, 2008
Time after Pentecost

Justus Falckner, 1723; Jehu Jones, 1852, William Passavant, 1894; pastors in North America

Psalm 7
God the righteous judge

O let the evil of the wicked come to an end,
   but establish the righteous,
you who test the minds and hearts,
   O righteous God.
God is my shield,
   who saves the upright in heart.
God is a righteous judge,
   and a God who has indignation every day.
(Ps. 7:9-11)

Additional Readings:

Esther 2:1-18
Lowly Esther becomes queen

2 Timothy 2:8-13
Those who endure with Christ reign with him

Hymn: Rejoice, Ye Pure in Heart! ELW 873/874

Your fierce indignation, O righteous Judge, can slay us in an instant. We have no hope except in him who called us into his flock, offered himself for us, and rose from the dead to give us life—Jesus Christ our Lord.

Tuesday, November 25, 2008
Time after Pentecost

Isaac Watts, hymnwriter, 1748

Esther 8:3-17
Queen Esther saves her people

Then Esther spoke again to the king; she fell at his feet, weeping and pleading with him to avert the evil design of Haman the Agagite and the plot that he had devised against the Jews. The king held out the golden scepter to Esther, and Esther rose and stood before the king. She said, "If it pleases the king, and if I have won his favor, and if the thing seems right before the king, and I have his approval, let an order be written to revoke the letters devised by Haman son of Hammedatha the Agagite, which he wrote giving orders to destroy the Jews who are in all the provinces of the king. For how can I bear to see the calamity that is coming on my people? Or how can I bear to see the destruction of my kindred?" (Esther 8:3-6)

Additional Readings:
Revelation 19:1-9   Psalm 7
Praise of God's judgments   *God the righteous judge*

Hymn: The Trumpets Sound, the Angels Sing, ELW 531

Open our eyes, Lord God, to see all those in need. And open our eyes to see ourselves as their defenders and advocates. Then give us courage to speak out on their behalf. We ask this in the name of Christ our King.

John 5:19-40
The judgment of the Son

"Very truly, I tell you, the hour is coming, and is now here, when the dead will hear the voice of the Son of God, and those who hear will live. For just as the Father has life in himself, so he has granted the Son also to have life in himself; and he has given him authority to execute judgment, because he is the Son of Man. Do not be astonished at this; for the hour is coming when all who are in their graves will hear his voice and will come out—those who have done good, to the resurrection of life, and those who have done evil, to the resurrection of condemnation. (John 5:25-29)

Additional Readings:

Ezekiel 33:7-20   Psalm 7
The righteous will live   *God the righteous judge*

Hymn: You Are Mine, ELW 581

You are the Lord of resurrection, and you can call us from the grave. Let your powerful word lift us to life today, and on the last day raise us from the dead, through Jesus Christ our Lord.

Thursday, November 27, 2008
Time after Pentecost

Day of Thanksgiving (U. S. A.)

Psalm 80:1-7, 17-19
We shall be saved

Give ear, O Shepherd of Israel,
  you who lead Joseph like a flock!
You who are enthroned upon the cherubim, shine forth
  before Ephraim and Benjamin and Manasseh.
Stir up your might,
  and come to save us!
Restore us, O God;
  let your face shine, that we may be saved. (Ps. 80:1-3)

Additional Readings:

Zechariah 13:1-9
*The coming day of God
brings cleansing*

Revelation 14:6-13
Hold fast to the faith

Hymn: The King of Love My Shepherd Is, ELW 502

O Guardian Shepherd, you lead us through dark valleys and save us from all that would harm us. We thank you for your care, and we look to you to open our future to your continuing blessing, through Jesus Christ our Lord.

Friday, November 28, 2008
Time after Pentecost

1 Thessalonians 4:1-18
A life pleasing God to the end

But we do not want you to be uninformed, brothers and sisters, about those who have died, so that you may not grieve as others do who have no hope. For since we believe that Jesus died and rose again, even so, through Jesus, God will bring with him those who have died. For this we declare to you by the word of the Lord, that we who are alive, who are left until the coming of the Lord, will by no means precede those who have died. For the Lord himself, with a cry of command, with the archangel's call and with the sound of God's trumpet, will descend from heaven, and the dead in Christ will rise first. Then we who are alive, who are left, will be caught up in the clouds together with them to meet the Lord in the air; and so we will be with the Lord forever. (1 Thess. 4:13-17)

Additional Readings:

Zechariah 14:1-9
God will come to rule

Psalm 80:1-7, 17-19
We shall be saved

Hymn: Lo! He Comes with Clouds Descending, ELW 435

O God, it is hard to let others cut in line! Help us grow in patience, here and now, that we may place others ahead of ourselves as we await the coming of our Lord Jesus Christ, in whom we pray.

Saturday, November 29, 2008
Time after Pentecost

Micah 2:1-13
God will gather all

I will surely gather all of you, O Jacob,
   I will gather the survivors of Israel;
I will set them together
   like sheep in a fold,
like a flock in its pasture;
   it will resound with people.
The one who breaks out will go up before them;
   they will break through and pass the gate,
   going out by it.
Their king will pass on before them,
   the LORD at their head. (Micah 2:12-13)

Additional Readings:

Matthew 24:15-31   Psalm 80:1-7, 17-19
Be ready for that day   *We shall be saved*

Hymn: All People That on Earth Do Dwell, ELW 883

Gather all your scattered sheep, strong and gentle Shepherd. Seek all who wander and are lost. Include us also in your flock, that we too may find safety within the sheepfold of your love, in Jesus Christ our Lord.

Sunday, November 30, 2008
FIRST SUNDAY OF ADVENT

Andrew, Apostle

Mark 13:24-37
The coming of the Son of Man

"But about that day or hour no one knows, neither the angels in heaven, nor the Son, but only the Father. Beware, keep alert; for you do not know when the time will come. It is like a man going on a journey, when he leaves home and puts his slaves in charge, each with his work, and commands the doorkeeper to be on the watch. Therefore, keep awake—for you do not know when the master of the house will come, in the evening, or at midnight, or at cockcrow, or at dawn, or else he may find you asleep when he comes suddenly. And what I say to you I say to all: Keep awake." (Mark 12:32-37)

Additional Readings:

Isaiah 64:1-9	Psalm 80:1-7, 17-19	1 Corinthians 1:3-9
God will come with power and compassion	*We shall be saved*	*Gifts of grace sustain us*

Hymn: Wake, Awake, for Night Is Flying, ELW 436

Stir up your power, Lord Christ, and come. By your merciful protection awaken us to the threatening dangers of our sins, and keep us blameless until the coming of your new day, for you live and reign with the Father and the Holy Spirit, one God, now and forever.

~ Prayer list for December

_____

_____

_____

_____

_____

_____

_____

_____

_____

_____

_____

_____

Monday, December 1, 2008

ANDREW, APOSTLE

(transferred from November 30)

John 1:35-42
Jesus calls Andrew

One of the two who heard John speak and followed him was Andrew, Simon Peter's brother. He first found his brother Simon and said to him, "We have found the Messiah" (which is translated Anointed). He brought Simon to Jesus, who looked at him and said, "You are Simon son of John. You are to be called Cephas" (which is translated Peter). (John 1:40-42)

Additional Readings:

Ezekiel 3:16-21	Psalm 19:1-6	Romans 10:10-18
A sentinel for the house of Israel	*The heavens declare God's glory*	*Faith comes from the word of Christ*

Hymn: Jesus Calls Us; o'er the Tumult, ELW 696

Almighty God, you gave your apostle Andrew the grace to obey the call of your Son and to bring his brother to Jesus. Give us also, who are called by your holy word, grace to follow Jesus without delay and to bring into his presence those who are near to us, for he lives and reigns with you and the Holy Spirit, one God, now and forever.

Psalm 79
Prayer for deliverance

How long, O LORD? Will you be angry forever?
    Will your jealous wrath burn like fire?
Pour out your anger on the nations
    that do not know you,
and on the kingdoms
    that do not call on your name.
For they have devoured Jacob
    and laid waste his habitation.
Do not remember against us the iniquities of our ancestors;
    let your compassion come speedily to meet us,
    for we are brought very low.
Help us, O God of our salvation,
    for the glory of your name;
deliver us, and forgive our sins,
    for your name's sake. (Ps. 79:5-9)

Additional Readings:

Micah 4:6-13
*A promise of restoration
after exile*

Revelation 18:1-10
*Judgment upon human
pride*

Hymn: Come, Thou Long-Expected Jesus, ELW 254

Merciful God, grant compassion to us, your servants, that we may be pardoned from all our sin and empowered to spread the life-giving message of your love to all nations and people throughout the world.

Wednesday, December 3, 2008
WEEK OF ADVENT 1

Francis Xavier, missionary to Asia, 1552

Micah 5:1-5a
A promise of a shepherd

But you, O Bethlehem of Ephrathah,
   who are one of the little clans of Judah,
from you shall come forth for me
   one who is to rule in Israel,
whose origin is from of old,
   from ancient days.
Therefore he shall give them up until the time
   when she who is in labor has brought forth;
then the rest of his kindred shall return
   to the people of Israel.
And he shall stand and feed his flock in the strength
     of the LORD,
   in the majesty of the name of the LORD his God.
And they shall live secure, for now he shall be great
   to the ends of the earth;
   and he shall be the one of peace. (Micah 5:2-5a)

Additional Readings:

Luke 21:34-38   Psalm 79
Be alert for that day   *Prayer for deliverance*

Hymn: Come Now, O Prince of Peace, ELW 247

Eternal God, deliver your creation from the hands of oppression and violence that ravish the world so that all may live in safety. Feed us with your strength, and guide us towards healing the divisions and injustices of our world so that all may know your peace.

Thursday, December 4, 2008

WEEK OF ADVENT 1

John of Damascus, theologian and hymnwriter, c. 749

Psalm 85:1-2, 8-13

Righteousness and peace

Let me hear what God the LORD will speak,
   for he will speak peace to his people,
   to his faithful, to those who turn to him in their hearts.
Surely his salvation is at hand for those who fear him,
   that his glory may dwell in our land.
Steadfast love and faithfulness will meet;
   righteousness and peace will kiss each other.
Faithfulness will spring up from the ground,
   and righteousness will look down from the sky.
The LORD will give what is good,
   and our land will yield its increase. (Ps. 85:8-12)

Additional Readings:

Hosea 6:1-6   1 Thessalonians 1:2-10
Return to the God of life   *Paul thanks God for the*
and love   *Thessalonians*

Hymn: People, Look East, ELW 248

Creator God, your steadfast love and faithfulness fills the earth with good things. Grant favorable weather that nourishes the earth, and enliven us to be good and faithful stewards of all that you provide.

Friday, December 5, 2008
Week of Advent 1

Jeremiah 1:4-10
God appoints a prophet

Now the word of the Lord came to me saying,
   "Before I formed you in the womb I knew you,
   and before you were born I consecrated you;
   I appointed you a prophet to the nations."
Then I said, "Ah, Lord God! Truly I do not know how to speak,
for I am only a boy." But the Lord said to me,
   "Do not say, 'I am only a boy';
   for you shall go to all to whom I send you,
   and you shall speak whatever I command you,
   Do not be afraid of them,
   for I am with you to deliver you, says the Lord."
(Jer. 1:4-8)

Additional Readings:

Acts 11:19-26
*The new community called
"Christian"*

Psalm 85:1-2, 8-13
Righteousness and peace

Hymn: Here I Am, Lord, ELW 574

*Ever-living God, you know our failings and our weaknesses, yet you
call us to be messengers of your word. Accompany us through this life
and give us the courage to speak your word even when it may be difficult
to bear.*

Saturday, December 6, 2008
Week of Advent 1

Nicholas, Bishop of Myra, c. 342

Ezekiel 36:24-28
A new heart and a new spirit

I will take you from the nations, and gather you from all the countries, and bring you into your own land. I will sprinkle clean water upon you, and you shall be clean from all your uncleannesses, and from all your idols I will cleanse you. A new heart I will give you, and a new spirit I will put within you; and I will remove from your body the heart of stone and give you a heart of flesh. I will put my spirit within you, and make you follow my statutes and be careful to observe my ordinances. Then you shall live in the land that I gave to your ancestors; and you shall be my people, and I will be your God. (Ezek. 36:24-28)

Additional Readings:

Mark 11:27-33
Jesus a prophet like John the Baptist

Psalm 85:1-2, 8-13
Righteousness and peace

Hymn: God, My Lord, My Strength, ELW 795

Renewing God, cleanse our bodies from the evils that harden our hearts, and breathe into us new life so that we may be filled with your Spirit and be transformed to live as your people.

Sunday, December 7, 2008

SECOND SUNDAY OF ADVENT

Ambrose, Bishop of Milan, 397

Mark 1:1-8

John appears from the wilderness

John the baptizer appeared in the wilderness, proclaiming a baptism of repentance for the forgiveness of sins. And people from the whole Judean countryside and all the people of Jerusalem were going out to him, and were baptized by him in the river Jordan, confessing their sins. Now John was clothed with camel's hair, with a leather belt around his waist, and he ate locusts and wild honey. He proclaimed, "The one who is more powerful than I is coming after me; I am not worthy to stoop down and untie the thong of his sandals. I have baptized you with water; but he will baptize you with the Holy Spirit." (Mark 1:4-8)

Additional Readings:

Isaiah 40:1-11	Psalm 85:1-2, 8-13	2 Peter 3:8-15a
God's coming to the exiles	*Righteousness and peace*	*Waiting for the day of God*

Hymn: Hark! A Thrilling Voice Is Sounding! ELW 246

Stir up our hearts, Lord God, to prepare the way of your only Son. By his coming strengthen us to serve you with purified lives; through Jesus Christ, our Savior and Lord, who lives and reigns with you and the Holy Spirit, one God, now and forever.

Psalm 27
God's level path

Teach me your way, O Lord,
  and lead me on a level path
  because of my enemies.
Do not give me up to the will of my adversaries,
  for false witnesses have risen against me,
  and they are breathing out violence.
I believe that I shall see the goodness of the Lord
  in the land of the living.
Wait for the Lord;
  be strong, and let your heart take courage;
  wait for the Lord! (Ps. 27:11-14)

Additional Readings:

Isaiah 26:7-15   Acts 2:37-42
The way of the righteous is level   *Baptism in the name of Jesus*

Hymn: Lead Me, Guide Me, ELW 768

O Lord, you are our light and salvation. Though the road seems long and rough, guide our footsteps so that we may forever walk in your ways. Grant us courage during this time of preparation as we await the celebration of our Savior's birth.

Isaiah 4:2-6
God will wash Israel clean

On that day the branch of the LORD shall be beautiful and glorious, and the fruit of the land shall be the pride and glory of the survivors of Israel. Whoever is left in Zion and remains in Jerusalem will be called holy, everyone who has been recorded for life in Jerusalem, once the Lord has washed away the filth of the daughters of Zion and cleansed the bloodstains of Jerusalem from its midst by a spirit of judgment and by a spirit of burning. Then the LORD will create over the whole site of Mount Zion and over its places of assembly a cloud by day and smoke and the shining of a flaming fire by night. Indeed over all the glory there will be a canopy. It will serve as a pavilion, a shade by day from the heat, and a refuge and a shelter from the storm and rain. (Isa. 4:2-6)

Additional Readings:

Acts 11:1-18   Psalm 27
John and Peter baptize   *God's level path*

Hymn: Lost in the Night, ELW 243

Nurturing God, you cultivate us to be your beautiful and glorious people. Gather us together so that we might be cleansed with water and fire. Then send us forth to proclaim your marvelous deeds throughout the land.

Luke 1:5-17
The messenger in the temple

But the angel said to [Zechariah], "Do not be afraid, Zechariah, for your prayer has been heard. Your wife Elizabeth will bear you a son, and you will name him John. You will have joy and gladness, and many will rejoice at his birth, for he will be great in the sight of the Lord. He must never drink wine or strong drink; even before his birth he will be filled with the Holy Spirit. He will turn many of the people of Israel to the Lord their God. With the spirit and power of Elijah he will go before him, to turn the hearts of parents to their children, and the disobedient to the wisdom of the righteous, to make ready a people prepared for the Lord." (Luke 1:13-17)

Additional Readings:

Malachi 2:10—3:1   Psalm 27
The coming messenger   *God's level path*

Hymn: Comfort, Comfort Now My People, ELW 256

Transforming God, you sent messengers to prepare the way for the coming of your Son into our world. So too, make us messengers, announcing joy and gladness to the weary, the marginalized, and the voiceless.

Thursday, December 11, 2008
WEEK OF ADVENT 2

Psalm 126
God does great things for us

When the LORD restored the fortunes of Zion,
  we were like those who dream.
Then our mouth was filled with laughter,
  and our tongue with shouts of joy;
then it was said among the nations,
  "The LORD has done great things for them."
The LORD has done great things for us,
  and we rejoiced. (Ps. 126:1-3)

Additional Readings:

Habakkuk 2:1-5
A vision concerning the end

Philippians 3:7-11
The righteousness that comes through faith

Hymn: Hark, the Glad Sound! ELW 239

O Lord, you have done great things for us. Open our eyes and ears, and empower our senses of smell, taste, and touch so that we may discover your gracious deeds throughout your whole creation in every time and place.

Philippians 3:12-16
The prize of God's call in Christ

Not that I have already obtained this or have already reached the goal; but I press on to make it my own, because Christ Jesus has made me his own. Beloved, I do not consider that I have made it my own; but this one thing I do: forgetting what lies behind and straining forward to what lies ahead, I press on toward the goal for the prize of the heavenly call of God in Christ Jesus. Let those of us then who are mature be of the same mind; and if you think differently about anything, this too God will reveal to you. Only let us hold fast to what we have attained. (Phil. 3:12-16)

Additional Readings:

Habakkuk 3:2-6	Psalm 126
A prayer for God's glory and mercy	*God does great things for us*

Hymn: My Faith Looks Up to Thee, ELW 759

Almighty God, we stand in awe of you for having redeemed us through the cross of Christ. Enliven our faith to profess you boldly as Lord and fill us with the Holy Spirit that we may discern you will.

Saturday, December 13, 2008
WEEK OF ADVENT 2

Lucy, martyr, 304

Habakkuk 3:13-19
God's devastation, God's deliverance

Though the fig tree does not blossom,
    and no fruit is on the vines;
though the produce of the olive fails
    and the fields yield no food;
though the flock is cut off from the fold
    and there is no herd in the stalls,
yet I will rejoice in the LORD;
    I will exult in the God of my salvation.
GOD, the Lord, is my strength;
    he makes my feet like the feet of a deer,
    and makes me tread upon the heights.
(Hab. 3:17-19)

Additional Readings:

Matthew 21:28-32	Psalm 126
Resistance to God in the	*God does great things*
present generation	*for us*

Hymn: Fling Wide the Door, ELW 259

O Lord, you are our strength. Hold us close to you when we find ourselves in dry and desolate places, so that we may find faith where there is hopelessness. Grant deliverance to those experiencing depression and to all who find themselves in the wilderness.

Sunday, December 14, 2008

THIRD SUNDAY OF ADVENT

John of the Cross, renewer of the church, 1591

John 1:6-8, 19-28
A witness to the light

This is the testimony given by John when the Jews sent priests and Levites from Jerusalem to ask him, "Who are you?" He confessed and did not deny it, but confessed, "I am not the Messiah." And they asked him, "What then? Are you Elijah?" He said, "I am not." "Are you the prophet?" He answered, "No." Then they said to him, "Who are you? Let us have an answer for those who sent us. What do you say about yourself?" He said,

"I am the voice of one crying out in the wilderness,
'Make straight the way of the Lord,'"
as the prophet Isaiah said. (John 1:19-23)

Additional Readings:

Isaiah 61:1-4, 8-11	Psalm 126	1 Thessalonians 5:16-24
Righteousness and praise flourish like a garden	*God does great things for us*	*Kept in faith until the coming of Christ*

Hymn: There's a Voice in the Wilderness, ELW 255

Stir up the wills of your faithful people, Lord God, and open our ears to the words of your prophets, that anointed by your Spirit, we may testify to your light; through Jesus Christ, our Savior and Lord, who lives and reigns with you and the Holy Spirit, one God, now and forever.

Monday, December 15, 2008
Week of Advent 3

Psalm 125
Prayer for blessing

Those who trust in the LORD are like Mount Zion,
   which cannot be moved, but abides forever.
As the mountains surround Jerusalem,
   so the LORD surrounds his people,
   from this time on and forevermore.
For the scepter of wickedness shall not rest
   on the land allotted to the righteous,
so that the righteous might not stretch out
   their hands to do wrong.
Do good, O LORD, to those who are good,
   and to those who are upright in their hearts.
But those who turn aside to their own crooked ways
   the LORD will lead away with evildoers.
   Peace be upon Israel! (Ps. 125:1-5)

Additional Readings:

1 Kings 18:1-18
*Elijah condemns King
Ahab*

Ephesians 6:10-17
*The armor of God against
the powers*

Hymn: Light One Candle to Watch for Messiah, ELW 240

*Loving God, you abide with us and protect us from all evil. Surround
us with your presence and grant us peace: peace in the world, peace in
our homes, and peace in our hearts.*

Tuesday, December 16, 2008
Week of Advent 3

Acts 3:17—4:4
Peter preaches about the prophets

While Peter and John were speaking to the people, the priests, the captain of the temple, and the Sadducees came to them, much annoyed because they were teaching the people and proclaiming that in Jesus there is the resurrection of the dead. So they arrested them and put them in custody until the next day, for it was already evening. But many of those who heard the word believed; and they numbered about five thousand. (Acts 4:1-4)

Additional Readings:

2 Kings 2:9-22
Elisha receives Elijah's spirit

Psalm 125
Prayer for blessing

Hymn: Gracious Spirit, Heed Our Pleading, ELW 401

Merciful God, you bestow upon us life and salvation through your Son. Make us like Peter and John to be prophetic witnesses of Jesus' death and resurrection that all may come to believe in your redeeming word.

Mark 9:9-13
Questions about Elijah

As they were coming down the mountain, he ordered them to tell no one about what they had seen, until after the Son of Man had risen from the dead. So they kept the matter to themselves, questioning what this rising from the dead could mean. Then they asked him, "Why do the scribes say that Elijah must come first?" He said to them, "Elijah is indeed coming first to restore all things. How then is it written about the Son of Man, that he is to go through many sufferings and be treated with contempt? But I tell you that Elijah has come, and they did to him whatever they pleased, as it is written about him." (Mark 9:9-13)

Additional Readings:

Malachi 3:16—4:6   Psalm 125
Elijah and the coming one   *Prayer for blessing*

Hymn: Tree of Life and Awesome Mystery, ELW 334

Wondrous God, you raise people from death and bring them new life. Invite us to question your word, that we may constantly grow in our understanding of you. Awaken within us a more deeply rooted faith.

Psalm 89:1-4, 19-26
I sing of your love

I will sing of your steadfast love, O Lord, forever;
  with my mouth I will proclaim your faithfulness to all
    generations.
I declare that your steadfast love is established forever;
  your faithfulness is as firm as the heavens.
You said, "I have made a covenant with my chosen one,
  I have sworn to my servant David:
'I will establish your descendants forever,
  and build your throne for all generations.'"
(Ps. 89:1-4)

Additional Readings:

2 Samuel 6:1-11
*The advent of the ark of
the Lord*

Hebrews 1:1-4
*In the last days God speaks
by a son*

Hymn: Great Is Thy Faithfulness, ELW 733

Faithful God, your steadfast love endures forever. Like a father you guard and protect us; like a mother you feed and clothe us. Take us by your hand and teach us to care for one another as you care for us.

Hebrews 1:5-14
The advent of one higher than angels

For to which of the angels did God ever say,
  "You are my Son;
    today I have begotten you"?
Or again,
  "I will be his Father,
    and he will be my Son"?
And again, when he brings the firstborn into the world, he says,
  "Let all God's angels worship him."
Of the angels he says,
  "He makes his angels winds,
    and his servants flames of fire."
But of the Son he says,
  "Your throne, O God, is forever and ever,
    and the righteous scepter is the scepter of your kingdom.
  You have loved righteousness and hated wickedness;
  therefore God, your God, has anointed you
    with the oil of gladness beyond your companions."
(Heb. 1:5-9)

Additional Readings:

2 Samuel 6:12-19	Psalm 89:1-4, 19-26
The ark of God enters Jerusalem	*I sing of your love*

Hymn: As the Dark Awaits the Dawn, ELW 261

God of the angels, you anointed your Son to be greatest of all. As we wait with anticipation to celebrate the birth of your Son, anoint our hearts with the oil of gladness that we might greet him when he comes.

Saturday, December 20, 2008
Week of Advent 3

Katharina von Bora Luther, renewer of the church, 1552

John 7:40-52
The Messiah, David, and Bethlehem

When they heard these words, some in the crowd said, "This is really the prophet." Others said, "This is the Messiah." But some asked, "Surely the Messiah does not come from Galilee, does he? Has not the scripture said that the Messiah is descended from David and comes from Bethlehem, the village where David lived?" So there was a division in the crowd because of him. Some of them wanted to arrest him, but no one laid hands on him. (John 7:40-44)

Additional Readings:
Judges 13:2-24   Psalm 89:1-4, 19-26
The birth of Samson   *I sing of your love*

Hymn: O Come, O Come, Emmanuel, ELW 257

Ever-present God, you have come to be with your people. Turn us away from our own selfish understandings and create in us a space for openness, that the divisions between your people may find healing and reconciliation.

Sunday, December 21, 2008
FOURTH SUNDAY OF ADVENT

Luke 1:26-38
The angel appears to Mary

In the sixth month the angel Gabriel was sent by God to a town in Galilee called Nazareth, to a virgin engaged to a man whose name was Joseph, of the house of David. The virgin's name was Mary. And he came to her and said, "Greetings, favored one! The Lord is with you." But she was much perplexed by his words and pondered what sort of greeting this might be. The angel said to her, "Do not be afraid, Mary, for you have found favor with God. And now, you will conceive in your womb and bear a son, and you will name him Jesus. (Luke 1:26-31)

Additional Readings:

2 Samuel 7:1-11, 16
God's promise to David

Luke 1:46b-55
The Mighty One raises the lowly

Romans 16:25-27
The mystery revealed in Jesus Christ

Hymn: The Angel Gabriel from Heaven Came, ELW 265

Stir up your power, Lord Christ, and come. With your abundant grace and might, free us from the sin that would obstruct your mercy, that willingly we may bear your redeeming love to all the world, for you live and reign with the Father and the Holy Spirit, one God, now and forever.

Luke 1:46b-55
The Lord lifts up the lowly

(See the simplified form for evening prayer for this complete text on p. 398.)

"My soul magnifies the Lord,
   and my spirit rejoices in God my Savior,
for he has looked with favor on the lowliness of his servant.
   Surely, from now on all generations will call me blessed;
for the Mighty One has done great things for me,
   and holy is his name.
His mercy is for those who fear him
   from generation to generation." (Luke 1:46b-50)

Additional Readings:

1 Samuel 1:1-18
Hannah is promised a child

Hebrews 9:1-14
Christ comes as high priest

Hymn: Canticle of the Turning, ELW 723

Magnificent God, you have looked favorably upon us with rich and countless blessings. Inspire all generations to sing praises to your name and enliven our spirits to join them in the dance.

Hebrews 8:1-13
The mediator replaces the sanctuary

Now the main point in what we are saying is this: we have such a high priest, one who is seated at the right hand of the throne of the Majesty in the heavens, a minister in the sanctuary and the true tent that the Lord, and not any mortal, has set up. For every high priest is appointed to offer gifts and sacrifices; hence it is necessary for this priest also to have something to offer. Now if he were on earth, he would not be a priest at all, since there are priests who offer gifts according to the law. They offer worship in a sanctuary that is a sketch and shadow of the heavenly one; for Moses, when he was about to erect the tent, was warned, "See that you make everything according to the pattern that was shown you on the mountain." But Jesus has now obtained a more excellent ministry, and to that degree he is the mediator of a better covenant, which has been enacted through better promises. (Heb. 8:1-6)

Additional Readings:

1 Samuel 1:19-28
Hannah presents Samuel to God

Luke 1:46b-55
The Lord lifts up the lowly

Hymn: Savior of the Nations, Come, ELW 263

Majestic God, we give you thanks for the covenant of your Son. What acceptable gifts have we to offer you? Help us to grow into the diverse expressions of our very selves, a people created in your image.

Wednesday, December 24, 2008
NATIVITY OF OUR LORD

Christmas Eve

Luke 2:1-14 [15-20]
God with us

In that region there were shepherds living in the fields, keeping watch over their flock by night. Then an angel of the Lord stood before them, and the glory of the Lord shone around them, and they were terrified. But the angel said to them, "Do not be afraid; for see—I am bringing you good news of great joy for all the people: to you is born this day in the city of David a Savior, who is the Messiah, the Lord. This will be a sign for you: you will find a child wrapped in bands of cloth and lying in a manger." (Luke 2:8-12)

Additional Readings:

Isaiah 9:2-7	Psalm 96	Titus 2:11-14
A child is born for us	*Let the earth be glad*	*The grace of God has appeared*

Hymn: Angels We Have Heard on High, ELW 289

Almighty God, you made this holy night shine with the brightness of the true Light. Grant that here on earth we may walk in the light of Jesus' presence and in the last day wake to the brightness of his glory; through your Son, Jesus Christ our Lord, who lives and reigns with you and the Holy Spirit, one God, now and forever.

Thursday, December 25, 2008
NATIVITY OF OUR LORD

Christmas Day

John 1:1-14
The Word became flesh

In the beginning was the Word, and the Word was with God, and the Word was God. He was in the beginning with God. All things came into being through him, and without him not one thing came into being. What has come into being in him was life, and the life was the light of all people. The light shines in the darkness, and the darkness did not overcome it. (John 1:1-5)

Additional Readings:

Isaiah 52:7-10
Heralds announce God's salvation

Psalm 98
The victory of our God

Hebrews 1:1-4 [5-12]
God has spoken by a son

Hymn: O Come, All Ye Faithful, ELW 283

Almighty God, you gave us your only Son to take on our human nature and to illumine the world with your light. By your grace adopt us as your children and enlighten us with your Spirit, through Jesus Christ, our Redeemer and Lord, who lives and reigns with you and the Holy Spirit, one God, now and forever.

Acts 6:8—7:2a, 51-60
Stephen is stoned to death

Now during those days, when the disciples were increasing in number, the Hellenists complained against the Hebrews because their widows were being neglected in the daily distribution of food. And the twelve called together the whole community of the disciples and said, "It is not right that we should neglect the word of God in order to wait on tables. Therefore, friends, select from among yourselves seven men of good standing, full of the Spirit and of wisdom, whom we may appoint to this task, while we, for our part, will devote ourselves to prayer and to serving the word." What they said pleased the whole community, and they chose Stephen, a man full of faith and the Holy Spirit, together with Philip, Prochorus, Nicanor, Timon, Parmenas, and Nicolaus, a proselyte of Antioch. (Acts 6:1-5)

Additional Readings:

2 Chronicles 24:17-22
Zechariah is stoned to death

Psalm 17:1-9, 15
I call upon you, O God

Matthew 23:34-39
Jesus laments that Jerusalem kills her prophets

Hymn: By All Your Saints, ELW 420 (stanza 4)

We give you thanks, O Lord of glory, for the example of Stephen the first martyr, who looked to heaven and prayed for his persecutors. Grant that we also may pray for our enemies and seek the forgiveness of those who hurt us, through Jesus Christ, our Savior and Lord, who lives and reigns with you and the Holy Spirit, one God, now and forever.

Saturday, December 27, 2008
JOHN, APOSTLE AND EVANGELIST

John 21:20-25
The beloved disciple remains with Jesus

Peter turned and saw the disciple whom Jesus loved following them; he was the one who had reclined next to Jesus at the supper and had said, "Lord, who is it that is going to betray you?" When Peter saw him, he said to Jesus, "Lord, what about him?" Jesus said to him, "If it is my will that he remain until I come, what is that to you? Follow me!" So the rumor spread in the community that this disciple would not die. Yet Jesus did not say to him that he would not die, but, "If it is my will that he remain until I come, what is that to you?"

This is the disciple who is testifying to these things and has written them, and we know that his testimony is true. But there are also many other things that Jesus did; if every one of them were written down, I suppose that the world itself could not contain the books that would be written. (John 21:20-25)

Additional Readings:

Genesis 1:1-5, 26-31	Psalm 116:12-19	1 John 1:1—2:2
Humankind is created by God	*The death of faithful servants*	*Jesus, the word of life*

Hymn: The Bells of Christmas, ELW 298

Merciful God, you have revealed the mysteries of your Word made flesh through John the apostle and evangelist. Let the brightness of your light shine on your church, so that all your people, instructed in the holy gospel, may walk in the light of your truth and attain eternal life, through Jesus Christ, our Savior and Lord, who lives and reigns with you and the Holy Spirit, one God, now and forever.

Sunday, December 28, 2008
First Sunday of Christmas

The Holy Innocents, Martyrs

Luke 2:22-40
The presentation of the child

Now there was a man in Jerusalem whose name was Simeon; this man was righteous and devout, looking forward to the consolation of Israel, and the Holy Spirit rested on him. It had been revealed to him by the Holy Spirit that he would not see death before he had seen the Lord's Messiah. Guided by the Spirit, Simeon came into the temple; and when the parents brought in the child Jesus, to do for him what was customary under the law, Simeon took him in his arms and praised God. (Luke 2:25-28a)

Additional Readings:

Isaiah 61:10—62:3	Psalm 148	Galatians 4:4-7
Clothed in garments of salvation	*God's splendor is over earth and heaven*	*Children and heirs of God*

Hymn: O Lord, Now Let Your Servant, ELW 313

Almighty God, you wonderfully created the dignity of human nature and yet more wonderfully restored it. In your mercy, let us share the divine life of the one who came to share our humanity, Jesus Christ, your Son, our Lord, who lives and reigns with you and the Holy Spirit, one God, now and forever.

Monday, December 29, 2008
THE HOLY INNOCENTS, MARTYRS

(transferred from December 28)

Matthew 2:13-18
Herod kills innocent children

Now after [the magi] had left, an angel of the Lord appeared to Joseph in a dream and said, "Get up, take the child and his mother, and flee to Egypt, and remain there until I tell you; for Herod is about to search for the child, to destroy him." Then Joseph got up, took the child and his mother by night, and went to Egypt, and remained there until the death of Herod. This was to fulfill what had been spoken by the Lord through the prophet, "Out of Egypt I have called my son."

When Herod saw that he had been tricked by the wise men, he was infuriated, and he sent and killed all the children in and around Bethlehem who were two years old or under, according to the time that he had learned from the wise men. (Matt. 2:13-16)

Additional Readings:

Jeremiah 31:15-17	Psalm 124	1 Peter 4:12-19
Rachel weeps for her children	*We have escaped like a bird*	*Continue to do good while suffering*

Hymn: How Long, O God, ELW 698

We remember today, O God, the slaughter of the innocent children of Bethlehem by order of King Herod. Receive into the arms of your mercy all innocent victims. By your great might frustrate the designs of evil tyrants and establish your rule of justice, love, and peace, through Jesus Christ, our Savior and Lord, who lives and reigns with you and the Holy Spirit, one God, now and forever.

Tuesday, December 30, 2008
WEEK OF CHRISTMAS 1

Psalm 148
God's splendor is over earth and heaven

Praise the LORD!
Praise the LORD from the heavens;
   praise him in the heights!
Praise him, all his angels;
   praise him, all his host!
Kings of the earth and all peoples,
   princes and all rulers of the earth!
Young men and women alike,
   old and young together!
Let them praise the name of the LORD,
   for his name alone is exalted;
   his glory is above earth and heaven.
(Ps. 148:1-2, 11-13)

Additional Readings:

Proverbs 9:1-12
Your days will be multiplied

2 Peter 3:8-13
A thousand years as one day

Hymn: Hark! The Herald Angels Sing, ELW 270

Holy God, your name is praised in heaven and on earth. Strengthen and unite our voices, men and women together, young and old alike, that we might proclaim your name from the heights of every mountain.

John 8:12-19
I am the light

Again Jesus spoke to them, saying, "I am the light of the world. Whoever follows me will never walk in darkness but will have the light of life." Then the Pharisees said to him, "You are testifying on your own behalf; your testimony is not valid." Jesus answered, "Even if I testify on my own behalf, my testimony is valid because I know where I have come from and where I am going, but you do not know where I come from or where I am going. You judge by human standards; I judge no one. Yet even if I do judge, my judgment is valid; for it is not I alone who judge, but I and the Father who sent me." (John 8:12-16)

Additional Readings:

1 Kings 3:5-14
God grants a discerning mind

Psalm 148
God's splendor is over earth and heaven

Hymn: Love Has Come, ELW 292

God of the journey, you lead your people out of darkness. Let the light of your love shine before us to direct us in your ways that we may more perfectly love your whole creation.

Lesser Festivals and Commemorations

January 1 – Name of Jesus Every Jewish boy was circumcised and formally named on the eighth day of his life. Already in his infancy, Jesus bore the mark of a covenant that he made new through the shedding of his blood on the cross.

January 2 – Johann Konrad Wilhelm Loehe Wilhelm Loehe was a pastor in nineteenth-century Germany. From the small town of Neuendettelsau he sent pastors to North America, Australia, New Guinea, Brazil, and the Ukraine.

January 15 – Martin Luther King Jr. Martin Luther King Jr. is remembered as an American prophet of justice among races and nations. Many churches hold commemorations near Dr. King's birth date of January 15, in conjunction with the American civil holiday honoring him.

January 17 – Antony of Egypt Antony was one of the earliest Egyptian desert fathers. He became the head of a group of monks that lived in a cluster of huts and devoted themselves to communal prayer, worship, and manual labor.

January 17 – Pachomius Another of the desert fathers, Pachomius was born in Egypt about 290. He organized hermits into a religious community in which the members prayed together and held their goods in common.

January 18 – Confession of Peter; *Beginning of the Week of Prayer for Christian Unity* The Week of Prayer for Christian Unity is framed by two commemorations, the Confession of Peter and the Conversion of Paul. On this day the church remembers that Peter was led by God's grace to acknowledge Jesus as "the Christ, the Son of the living God" (Matt. 16:16).

January 19 – Henry When Erik, King of Sweden, determined to invade Finland for the purpose of converting the people there to Christianity, Henry went with him. Henry is recognized as the patron saint of Finland.

January 21 – Agnes Agnes was a girl of about thirteen living in Rome, who had chosen a life of service to Christ as a virgin, despite the Roman emperor Diocletian's ruling that had outlawed all Christian activity. She gave witness to her faith and was put to death as a result.

January 25 – Conversion of Paul; *End of the Week of Prayer for Christian Unity* As the Week of Prayer for Christian Unity comes to an end, the church remembers how a man of Tarsus named Saul, a former persecutor of the early Christian church, was led to become one of its chief preachers.

January 26 – Timothy, Titus, Silas On the two days following the celebration of the Conversion of Paul, his companions are remembered. Timothy, Titus, and Silas were missionary coworkers with Paul.

January 27 – Lydia, Dorcas, Phoebe On this day the church remembers three women who were companions in Paul's ministry.

January 28 – Thomas Aquinas Thomas Aquinas was a brilliant and creative theologian who immersed himself in the thought of Aristotle and worked to explain Christian beliefs in the philosophical culture of the day.

February 2 – Presentation of Our Lord Forty days after the birth of Christ the church marks the day Mary and Joseph presented him in the temple in accordance with Jewish law. Simeon greeted Mary and Joseph, responding with the canticle that begins "Now, Lord, you let your servant go in peace."

February 3 – Ansgar Ansgar was a monk who led a mission to Denmark and later to Sweden. His work ran into difficulties with the rulers of the day, and he was forced to withdraw into Germany, where he served as a bishop in Hamburg.

February 5 – The Martyrs of Japan In the sixteenth century, Jesuit missionaries, followed by Franciscans, introduced the Christian faith in Japan. By 1630, Christianity was driven underground. This day commemorates the first martyrs of Japan, twenty-six missionaries and converts, who were killed by crucifixion.

February 14 – Cyril, Methodius These brothers from a noble family in Thessalonika in northeastern Greece were priests who are regarded as the founders of Slavic literature. Their work in preaching and worshiping in the language of the people is honored by Christians in both East and West.

February 18 – Martin Luther On this day Luther died at the age of sixty-two. For a time, he was an Augustinian monk, but it is primarily for his work as a biblical scholar, translator of the Bible, reformer of the liturgy, theologian, educator, and father of German vernacular literature that he is remembered.

February 23 – Polycarp Polycarp was bishop of Smyrna and a link between the apostolic age and the church at the end of the second century. At the age of eighty-six he was martyred for his faith.

February 25 – Elizabeth Fedde Fedde was born in Norway and trained as a deaconess. Among her notable achievements were the establishment of the Deaconess House in Brooklyn and the Deaconess House and Hospital of the Lutheran Free Church in Minneapolis.

March 1 – George Herbert Herbert was ordained a priest in 1630 and served the little parish of St. Andrew Bremerton until his death. He is best remembered, however, as a writer of poems and hymns such as "Come, my way, my truth, my life" and "The King of love my shepherd is."

March 2 – John Wesley, Charles Wesley The Wesleys were leaders of a revival in the Church of England. Their spiritual methods of frequent communion, fasting, and advocacy for the poor earned them the name "Methodists."

March 7 – Perpetua, Felicity, companions In the year 202 the emperor Septimius Severus forbade conversions to Christianity. Perpetua, a noblewoman, Felicity, a slave, and other companions were all catechumens at Carthage in North Africa, where they were imprisoned and sentenced to death.

March 10 – Harriet Tubman, Sojourner Truth Harriet Tubman helped about 300 slaves to escape via the Underground Railroad until slavery was abolished in the United States. After slavery was abolished in New York in 1827, Sojourner Truth became deeply involved in Christianity, and in later life she was a popular speaker against slavery and for women's rights.

March 12 – Gregory the Great Gregory held political office and at another time lived as a monk, all before he was elected to the papacy. Having also established a school to train church musicians, Gregorian chant is named in his honor.

March 17 – Patrick Patrick went to Ireland from Britain to serve as a bishop and missionary. He made his base in the north of Ireland and from there made many missionary journeys, with much success.

March 19 – Joseph The Gospel of Luke shows Joseph acting in accordance with both civil and religious law by returning to Bethlehem for the census and by presenting the child Jesus in the temple on the fortieth day after his birth.

March 21 – Thomas Cranmer Cranmer's lasting achievement is contributing to and overseeing the creation of the Book of Common Prayer, which remains (in revised form) the worship book of the Anglican Communion. He was burned at the stake under Queen Mary for his support of the Protestant Reformation.

March 22 – Jonathan Edwards Edwards was a minister in Connecticut and has been described as the greatest of the New England Puritan preachers. Edwards carried out mission work among the Housatonic Indians of Massachusetts, and became president of the College of New Jersey, later to be known as Princeton University.

March 24 – Oscar Arnulfo Romero Romero is remembered for his advocacy on behalf of the poor in El Salvador, though it was not a characteristic of his early priesthood. After several years of threats to his life, Romero was assassinated while presiding at the eucharist.

March 25 – Annunciation of Our Lord Nine months before Christmas the church celebrates the annunciation. In Luke the angel Gabriel announces to Mary that she will give birth to the Son of God, and she responds, "Here am I, the servant of the Lord."

March 29 – Hans Nielsen Hauge Hans Nielsen Hauge was a layperson who began preaching in Norway and Denmark after a mystical experience that he believed called him to share the assurance of salvation with others. At the time itinerant preaching and religious gatherings held without the supervision of a pastor were illegal, and Hauge was arrested several times.

March 31 – John Donne This priest of the Church of England is commemorated for his poetry and spiritual writing. Most of his poetry was written before his ordination and is sacred and secular, intellectual and sensuous.

April 4 – Benedict the African Although Benedict was illiterate, his fame as a confessor brought many visitors to him, and he was eventually named superior of a Franciscan community. A patron saint of African Americans, Benedict is remembered for his patience and understanding when confronted with racial prejudice and taunts.

April 6 – Albrecht Dürer, Matthias Grünewald, Lucas Cranach These great artists revealed through their work the mystery of salvation and the wonder of creation. Though having remained a Roman Catholic, at Dürer's death Martin Luther wrote to a friend, "Affection bids us mourn for one who was the best." Several religious works are included in Grünwald's small surviving corpus, the most famous being the Isenheim Altarpiece. Lucas Cranach was widely known for his woodcuts, some of which illustrated the first German printing of the New Testament.

April 9 – Dietrich Bonhoeffer In 1933, and with Hitler's rise to power, Bonhoeffer became a leading spokesman for the Confessing Church, a resistance movement against the Nazis. After leading a worship service on April 8, 1945, at Schönberg prison, he was taken away to be hanged the next day.

April 10 – Mikael Agricola Agricola began a reform of the Finnish church along Lutheran lines. He translated the New Testament, the prayerbook, hymns, and the mass into Finnish and through this work set the rules of orthography that are the basis of modern Finnish spelling.

April 19 – Olavus Petri, Laurentius Petri These two brothers are commemorated for their introduction of the Lutheran movement to the Church of Sweden after studying at the University of Wittenberg. Together the brothers published a complete Bible in Swedish and a revised liturgy in 1541.

April 21 – Anselm This eleventh-century Benedictine monk stands out as one of the greatest theologians between Augustine and Thomas Aquinas. He is perhaps best known for his "satisfaction" theory of atonement, where God takes on human nature in Jesus Christ in order to make the perfect payment for sin.

April 23 – Toyohiko Kagawa Toyohiko Kagawa's vocation to help the poor led him to live among them. He was arrested for his efforts to reconcile Japan and China after the Japanese attack of 1940.

April 25 – Mark Though Mark himself was not an apostle, it is likely that he was a member of one of the early Christian communities. The gospel attributed to him is brief and direct and is considered by many to be the earliest gospel.

April 29 – Catherine of Siena Catherine of Siena was a member of the Order of Preachers (Dominicans), and among Roman Catholics she was the first woman to receive the title Doctor of the Church. She also advised popes and any uncertain persons who told her their problems.

May 1 – Philip, James Philip and James are commemorated together because the remains of these two saints were placed in the Church of the Apostles in Rome on this day in 561.

May 2 – Athanasius At the Council of Nicea in 325 and when he himself served as bishop of Alexandria, Athanasius defended the full divinity of Christ against the Arian position held by emperors, magistrates, and theologians.

May 4 – Monica Almost everything known about Monica comes from Augustine's *Confessions*, his autobiography. Her dying wish was that her son remember her at the altar of the Lord, wherever he was.

May 8 – Julian of Norwich Julian was most likely a Benedictine nun living in an isolated cell attached to the Carrow Priory in Norwich, England. When she was about thirty years old, she reported visions that she later compiled into a book, *Sixteen Revelations of Divine Love*, which is a classic of medieval mysticism.

May 9 – Nicolaus Ludwig von Zinzendorf Drawn from an overly intellectual Lutheran faith to Pietism, at the age of twenty-two Count Zinzendorf permitted a group of Moravians to live on his lands. Zinzendorf participated in worldwide missions emanating from this community and is also remembered for writing hymns characteristic of his Pietistic faith.

May 14 – Matthias After Christ's ascension, the apostles met in Jerusalem to choose a replacement for Judas. Though little is known about him, Matthias had traveled among the disciples from the time of Jesus' baptism until his ascension.

May 18 – Erik Erik, long considered the patron saint of Sweden, ruled there from 1150 to 1160. He is honored for efforts to bring peace to the nearby pagan kingdoms and for his crusades to spread the Christian faith in Scandinavia.

May 21 – Helena Helena was the mother of Constantine, a man who later became the Roman emperor. Helena is remembered for traveling through Palestine and building churches on the sites she believed to be where Jesus was born, where he was buried, and from which he ascended.

May 24 – Nicolaus Copernicus, Leonhard Euler Copernicus formally studied astronomy, mathematics, Greek, Plato, law, medicine, and canon law and is chiefly remembered for his work as an astronomer and his idea that the sun, not the earth, is the center of the solar system. Euler is regarded as one of the founders of the science of pure mathematics and made important contributions to mechanics, hydrodynamics, astronomy, optics, and acoustics.

May 27 – John Calvin Having embraced the views of the Reformation by his mid-twenties, John Calvin was a preacher in Geneva, was banished once, and later returned to reform the city with a rigid, theocratic discipline. Calvin is considered the father of the Reformed churches.

May 29 – Jiři Tranovský Jiři Tranovský is considered the "Luther of the Slavs" and the father of Slovak hymnody. He produced a translation of the Augsburg Confession and published his hymn collection *Cithara Sanctorum* (Lyre of the Saints), also known as the Tranoscius, which is the foundation of Slovak Lutheran hymnody.

May 31 – Visit of Mary to Elizabeth Sometime after the Annunciation, Mary visited her cousin Elizabeth, who greeted Mary with the words, "Blessed are you among women," and Mary responded with her famous song, the Magnificat.

June 1 – Justin Justin was a teacher of philosophy and engaged in debates about the truth of Christian faith. Having been arrested and jailed for practicing an unauthorized religion, he refused to renounce his faith and he and six of his students were beheaded.

June 3 – The Martyrs of Uganda King Mwanga of Uganda was angered by Christian members of the court whose first allegiance was not to him but to Christ. On this date in 1886, thirty-two young men were burned to

death for refusing to renounce Christianity. Their persecution led to a much stronger Christian presence in the country.

June 3 – John XXIII Despite the expectation upon his election that the seventy-seven year old John XXIII would be a transitional pope, he had great energy and spirit. He convened the Second Vatican Council in order to open the windows of the church. The council brought about great changes in Roman Catholic worship and ecumenical relationships.

June 5 – Boniface Boniface led large numbers of Benedictine monks and nuns in establishing churches, schools, and seminaries. Boniface was preparing a group for confirmation on the eve of Pentecost when he and others were killed by a band of pagans.

June 7 – Seattle The city of Seattle was named after Noah Seattle against his wishes. After Chief Seattle became a Roman Catholic, he began the practice of morning and evening prayer in the tribe, a practice that continued after his death.

June 9 – Columba, Aidan, Bede These three monks from the British Isles were pillars among those who kept alive the light of learning and devotion during the Middle Ages. Columba founded three monasteries, including one on the island of Iona, off the coast of Scotland. Aidan, who helped bring Christianity to the Northumbria area of England, was known for his pastoral style and ability to stir people to charity and good works. Bede was a Bible translator and scripture scholar who wrote a history of the English church and was the first historian to date events *anno Domini* (A.D.), the "year of our Lord."

June 11 – Barnabas Though he was not among the Twelve mentioned in the gospels, the book of Acts gives Barnabas the title of apostle. When Paul came to Jerusalem after his conversion, Barnabas took him in over the fears of the other apostles who doubted Paul's discipleship.

June 14 – Basil the Great, Gregory of Nyssa, Gregory of Nazianzus, Macrina The three men in this group are known as the Cappadocian fathers; all three explored the mystery of the Holy Trinity. Basil's Longer Rule and Shorter Rule for monastic life are the basis for Eastern monasticism to this day, and express a preference for communal monastic life over that of hermits. Gregory of Nazianzus defended Orthodox trinitarian and Christological doctrine, and his preaching won over the city of Constantinople. Gregory of Nyssa is remembered as a writer on spiritual life and the contemplation of God in worship and sacraments. Macrina was the older sister of Basil and Gregory of Nyssa, and her teaching was influential within the early church.

June 21 – Onesimos Nesib Onesimos, an Ethiopian, was captured by slave traders and taken from his Galla homeland to Eritrea, where he was bought, freed, and educated by Swedish missionaries. He translated the Bible into Galla and returned to his homeland to preach the gospel there.

June 24 – John the Baptist The birth of John the Baptist is celebrated exactly six months before Christmas Eve. For Christians in the Northern Hemisphere, these two dates are deeply symbolic, since John said that he must decrease as Jesus increased. John was born as the days are longest and then steadily decrease, while Jesus was born as the days are shortest and then steadily increase.

June 25 – Presentation of the Augsburg Confession On this day in 1530 the German and Latin editions of the Augsburg Confession were presented to Emperor Charles of the Holy Roman Empire. The Augsburg Confession was written by Philipp Melanchthon and endorsed by Martin Luther and consists of a brief summary of points in which the reformers saw their teaching as either agreeing with or differing from that of the Roman Catholic Church of the time.

June 25 – Philipp Melanchthon Though he died on April 19, Philipp Melanchthon is commemorated today because of his connection with the Augsburg Confession. Colleague and co-reformer with Martin Luther, Melanchthon was a brilliant scholar, known as "the teacher of Germany."

June 27 – Cyril Remembered as an outstanding theologian, Cyril defended the orthodox teachings about the person of Christ against Nestorius, who was at that time bishop of Constantinople. Eventually it was decided that Cyril's interpretation, that Christ's person included both divine and human natures, was correct.

June 28 – Irenaeus Irenaeus believed that only Matthew, Mark, Luke, and John were trustworthy gospels. As a result of his battles with the gnostics he was one of the first to speak of the church as "catholic," meaning that congregations did not exist by themselves, but were linked to one another throughout the whole church.

June 29 – Peter, Paul One of the things that unites Peter and Paul is the tradition that says they were martyred together on this date in A.D. 67 or 68. What unites them even more closely is their common confession of Jesus Christ.

July 1 – Catherine Winkworth, John Mason Neale Many of the most beloved hymns in the English language are the work of these gifted poets. Catherine Winkworth devoted herself to the translation of German hymns into English, while John Mason Neale specialized in translating many ancient Latin and Greek hymns.

July 3 – Thomas Alongside the doubt for which Thomas is famous, the gospel according to John shows Thomas moving from doubt to deep faith. Thomas makes one of the strongest confessions of faith in the New Testament, "My Lord and my God!" (John 20:28).

July 6 – Jan Hus Jan Hus was a Bohemian priest who spoke against abuses in the church of his day in many of the same ways Luther would a century later. The followers of Jan Hus became known as the Czech Brethren and later became the Moravian Church.

July 11 – Benedict of Nursia Benedict is known as the father of Western monasticism. Benedict encourages a generous spirit of hospitality. Visitors to Benedictine communities are to be welcomed as Christ himself.

July 12 – Nathan Söderblom In 1930, this Swedish theologian, ecumenist, and social activist received the Nobel Prize for peace. Söderblom organized the Universal Christian Council on Life and Work, which was one of the organizations that in 1948 came together to form the World Council of Churches.

July 17 – Bartolomé de Las Casas Bartolomé de Las Casas was a Spanish priest and a missionary in the Western Hemisphere. Throughout the Caribbean and Central America he worked to stop the enslavement of native people, to halt the brutal treatment of women by military forces, and to promote laws that humanized the process of colonization.

July 22 – Mary Magdalene The gospels report Mary Magdalene was one of the women of Galilee who followed Jesus. As the first person to whom the risen Lord appeared, she returned to the disciples with the news and has been called "the apostle to the apostles" for her proclamation of the resurrection.

July 23 – Birgitta of Sweden Birgitta's devotional commitments led her to give to the poor and needy all that she owned while she began to live a more ascetic life. She founded an order of monks and nuns, the Order of the Holy Savior (Birgittines), whose superior was a woman.

July 25 – James James was one of the sons of Zebedee and is counted as one of the twelve disciples. James was the first of the Twelve to suffer martyrdom and is the only apostle whose martyrdom is recorded in scripture.

July 28 – Johann Sebastian Bach, Heinrich Schütz, George Frederick Handel These three composers did much to enrich the worship life of the church. Johann Sebastian Bach drew on the Lutheran tradition of hymnody and wrote about two hundred cantatas, including at least two for each Sunday and festival day in the Lutheran calendar of his day. George Frederick Handel was not primarily a church musician, but his great work *Messiah* is a musical proclamation of the scriptures. Heinrich Schütz wrote choral settings of biblical texts and paid special attention to ways his composition would underscore the meaning of the words.

July 29 – Mary, Martha, Lazarus of Bethany Mary and Martha are remembered for the hospitality and refreshment they offered Jesus in their home. Following the characterization drawn by Luke, Martha represents the active life, and Mary, the contemplative.

July 29 – Olaf Olaf is considered the patron saint of Norway. While at war in the Baltic and in Normandy, he became a Christian, then returned to Norway, declared himself king, and from then on Christianity was the dominant religion of the realm.

August 8 – Dominic Dominic believed that a stumbling block to restoring heretics to the church was the wealth of clergy, so he formed an itinerant religious order, the Order of Preachers (Dominicans), who lived in poverty, studied philosophy and theology, and preached against heresy.

August 10 – Lawrence Lawrence was one of seven deacons of the congregation at Rome and, like the deacons appointed in Acts, was responsible for financial matters in the church and for the care of the poor.

August 11 – Clare At age 18, Clare of Assisi heard Francis preach a sermon. With Francis's help she and a growing number of companions established a women's Franciscan community, called the Order of Poor Ladies, or Poor Clares.

August 13 – Florence Nightingale, Clara Maass Nightingale led a group of thirty-eight nurses to serve in the Crimean War, where they worked in appalling conditions. She returned to London as a hero and there resumed her work for hospital reform. Clara Maass was born in New Jersey and served as a nurse in the Spanish-American War, where she encountered the horrors of yellow fever. Later responding to a call for subjects in research on yellow fever, Maass contracted the disease and died.

August 14 – Maximilian Kolbe, Kaj Munk Confined in Auschwitz, Father Kolbe was a Franciscan priest who gave generously of his meager resources, and finally volunteered to be starved to death in place of another man who was a husband and father. Kaj Munk, a Danish Lutheran pastor and playwright, was an outspoken critic of the Nazis. His plays frequently highlighted the eventual victory of the Christian faith despite the church's weak and ineffective witness.

August 15 – Mary, Mother of Our Lord The honor paid to Mary as mother of our Lord goes back to biblical times, when Mary herself sang "from now on all generations will call me blessed" (Luke 1:48). Mary's song speaks of reversals in the reign of God: the mighty are cast down, the lowly are lifted up, the hungry are fed, and the rich are sent away empty-handed.

August 20 – Bernard of Clairvaux Bernard was a Cistercian monk who became an abbot of great spiritual depth. Through translation his several devotional writings and hymns are still read and sung today.

August 24 – Bartholomew Bartholomew is mentioned as one of Jesus' disciples in Matthew, Mark, and Luke. Except for his name on these lists of the Twelve, little is known.

August 28 – Augustine As an adult Augustine came to see Christianity as a religion appropriate for a philosopher. Augustine was baptized by Ambrose at the Easter Vigil in 387, was made bishop of Hippo in 396, and was one of the greatest theologians of the Western church.

August 28 – Moses the Black A man of great strength and rough character, Moses the Black was converted to Christian faith toward the close of the fourth century. The change in his heart and life had a profound impact on his native Ethiopia.

September 2 – Nikolai Fredrik Severin Grundtvig Grundtvig was a prominent Danish theologian of the nineteenth century. From his university days he was convinced that poetry spoke to the human spirit better than prose, and he wrote more than a thousand hymns.

September 9 – Peter Claver Peter Claver was born into Spanish nobility and was persuaded to become a Jesuit missionary. He served in Cartagena (in what is now Colombia) by teaching and caring for the slaves.

September 13 – John Chrysostom John was a priest in Antioch and an outstanding preacher. His eloquence earned him the nickname "Chrysostom" ("golden mouth"), but he also preached against corruption among the royal court, whereupon the empress sent him into exile.

September 14 – Holy Cross Day The celebration of Holy Cross Day commemorates the dedication of the Church of the Resurrection in 335 on the location believed to have been where Christ was buried.

September 16 – Cyprian During Cyprian's time as bishop many people had denied the faith under duress. In contrast to some who held the belief that the church should not receive these people back, Cyprian believed they ought to be welcomed into full communion after a period of penance.

September 17 – Hildegard of Bingen Hildegard lived virtually her entire life in convents, yet was widely influential. She advised and reproved kings and popes, wrote poems and hymns, and produced treatises in medicine, theology, and natural history.

September 18 – Dag Hammarskjöld Dag Hammarskjöld was a Swedish diplomat and humanitarian who served as secretary general of the United Nations. The depth of Hammarskjöld's Christian faith was unknown until his private journal *Markings* was published following his death.

September 21 – Matthew Matthew was a tax collector, an occupation that was distrusted, since tax collectors were frequently dishonest and worked as agents for the Roman occupying government; yet it was these outcasts to whom Jesus showed his love. Since the second century, tradition has attributed the first gospel to him.

September 29 – Michael and All Angels The scriptures speak of angels who worship God in heaven, and in both testaments angels are God's messengers on earth. Michael is an angel whose name appears in Daniel as the heavenly being who leads the faithful dead to God's throne on the day of resurrection, while in the book of Revelation, Michael fights in a cosmic battle against Satan.

September 30 – Jerome Jerome translated the scriptures into the Latin that was spoken and written by the majority of people in his day. His translation is known as the Vulgate, which comes from the Latin word for "common."

October 4 – Francis of Assisi Francis renounced wealth and future inheritance and devoted himself to serving the poor. Since Francis had a spirit of gratitude for all of God's creation, this commemoration has been a traditional time to bless pets and animals, creatures Francis called his brothers and sisters.

October 4 – Theodor Fliedner Fliedner's work was instrumental in the revival of the ministry of deaconesses among Lutherans. Fliedner's deaconess motherhouse in Kaiserswerth, Germany, inspired Lutherans all over the world to commission deaconesses to serve in parishes, schools, prisons, and hospitals.

October 6 – William Tyndale Tyndale's plan to translate the scriptures into English met opposition from Henry VIII. Though Tyndale completed work on the New Testament in 1525 and worked on a portion of the Old Testament, he was tried for heresy and burned at the stake.

October 7 – Henry Melchior Muhlenberg Muhlenberg was prominent in setting the course for Lutheranism in the United States by helping Lutheran churches make the transition from the state churches of Europe to independent churches of America. Among other things, he established the first Lutheran synod in America and developed an American Lutheran liturgy.

October 15 – Teresa of Ávila Teresa of Ávila (also known as Teresa de Jesús) chose the life of a Carmelite nun after reading the letters of Jerome. Teresa's writings on devotional life are widely read by members of various denominations.

October 17 – Ignatius Ignatius was the second bishop of Antioch in Syria. When his own martyrdom approached, he wrote in one of his letters, "I prefer death in Christ Jesus to power over the farthest limits of the earth . . . . Do not stand in the way of my birth to real life."

October 18 – Luke Luke, as author of both Luke and Acts, was careful to place the events of Jesus' life in both their social and religious contexts. Some of the most loved parables and canticles are found only in this gospel.

October 23 – James of Jerusalem James is described in the New Testament as the brother of Jesus, and the secular historian Josephus called James the brother of Jesus, "the so-called Christ." Little is known about James, but Josephus reported that the Pharisees respected James for his piety and observance of the law.

October 26 – Philipp Nicolai, Johann Heermann, Paul Gerhardt These three outstanding hymnwriters all worked in Germany in the seventeenth century during times of war and plague. Philipp Nicolai's hymns "Wake, awake, for night is flying" and "O Morning Star, how fair and bright!" were included in a series of meditations he wrote to comfort his parishioners during the plague. The style of Johann Heermann's hymns (including "Ah, holy Jesus") moved away from the more objective style of Reformation hymnody toward expressing the emotions of faith. Paul Gerhardt, whom some have called the greatest of Lutheran hymnwriters, lost a preaching position at St. Nicholas's Church in Berlin because he refused to sign a document stating he would not make theological arguments in his sermons.

October 28 – Simon, Jude Little is known about Simon and Jude. In New Testament lists of the apostles, Simon the "zealot" or Cananaean is mentioned, but he is never mentioned apart from these lists. Jude, sometimes called Thaddeus, is also mentioned in lists of the Twelve.

October 31 – Reformation Day By the end of the seventeenth century, many Lutheran churches celebrated a festival commemorating Martin Luther's posting of the Ninety-five Theses, a summary of abuses in the church of his time. At the heart of the reform movement was the gospel, the good news that it is by grace through faith that we are justified and set free.

November 1 – All Saints Day The custom of commemorating all of the saints of the church on a single day goes back at least to the third century. All Saints Day celebrates the baptized people of God, living and dead, who make up the body of Christ.

November 3 – Martín de Porres Martín was a lay brother in the Order of Preachers (Dominicans) and engaged in many charitable works. He is recognized as an advocate for Christian charity and interracial justice.

November 7 – John Christian Frederick Heyer, Bartholomaeus Ziegenbalg, Ludwig Nommensen Heyer was the first missionary sent out by American Lutherans, and he became a missionary in the Andhra region of India. Ziegenbalg was a missionary to the Tamils of Tranquebar on the southeast coast of India. Nommensen worked among the Batak people, who had previously not seen Christian missionaries.

November 11 – Martin of Tours In 371 Martin was elected bishop of Tours. As bishop he developed a reputation for intervening on behalf of prisoners and heretics who had been sentenced to death.

November 11 – Søren Aabye Kierkegaard Kierkegaard, a nineteenth-century Danish theologian whose writings reflect his Lutheran heritage, was the founder of modern existentialism. Kierkegaard's work attacked the established church of his day—its complacency, its tendency to intellectualize faith, and its desire to be accepted by polite society.

November 17 – Elizabeth of Hungary This Hungarian princess gave away large sums of money, including her dowry, for relief of the poor and sick. She founded hospitals, cared for orphans, and used the royal food supplies to feed the hungry.

November 23 – Clement Clement is best remembered for a letter he wrote to the Corinthian congregation still having difficulty with divisions in spite of Paul's canonical letters. Clement's letter is also a witness to early understandings of church government and the way each office in the church works for the good of the whole.

November 23 – Miguel Agustín Pro Miguel Agustín Pro grew up among oppression in Mexico and he worked on behalf of the poor and homeless. Miguel and his two brothers were arrested, falsely accused of throwing a bomb at the car of a government official, and executed by a firing squad.

November 24 – Justus Falckner, Jehu Jones, William Passavant Not only was Falckner the first Lutheran pastor to be ordained in North America, but he published a catechism that was the first Lutheran book published on the continent. Jones was the Lutheran church's first African American pastor and carried out missionary work in Philadelphia, which led to the formation there of the first African American Lutheran congregation (St. Paul's). William Passavant helped to establish hospitals and orphanages in a number of cities and was the first to introduce deaconesses to the work of hospitals in the United States.

November 25 – Isaac Watts Watts wrote about six hundred hymns, many of them in a two-year period beginning when he was twenty years old. When criticized for writing hymns not taken from scripture, he responded that if we can pray prayers that are not from scripture but written by us, then surely we can sing hymns that we have made up ourselves.

November 30 – Andrew Andrew was the first of the Twelve. As a part of his calling, he brought other people, including Simon Peter, to meet Jesus.

December 3 – Francis Xavier Francis Xavier became a missionary to India, Southeast Asia, Japan, and the Philippines. Together with Ignatius Loyola and five others, Francis formed the Society of Jesus (Jesuits).

December 4 – John of Damascus John left a career in finance and government to become a monk in an abbey near Jerusalem. He wrote many hymns as well as theological works, including *The Fount of Wisdom*, a work that touches on philosophy, heresy, and the orthodox faith.

December 6 – Nicholas Nicholas was a bishop in what is now Turkey. Legends that surround Nicholas tell of his love for God and neighbor, especially the poor.

December 7 – Ambrose Ambrose was baptized, ordained, and consecrated a bishop all on the same day. While bishop he gave away his wealth and lived in simplicity.

December 13 – Lucy Lucy was a young Christian of Sicily who was martyred during the persecutions under Emperor Diocletian. Her celebration became particularly important in Sweden and Norway, perhaps because the feast of Lucia (whose name means "light") originally fell on the shortest day of the year.

December 14 – John of the Cross John was a monk of the Carmelite religious order who met Teresa of Ávila when she was working to reform the Carmelite Order and return it to a stricter observance of its rules. His writings, like Teresa's, reflect a deep interest in mystical thought and meditation.

December 20 – Katharina von Bora Luther Katharina took vows as a nun, but around age twenty-four she and several other nuns who were influenced by the writings of Martin Luther left the convent. When she later became Luther's wife, she proved herself a gifted household manager and became a trusted partner.

December 26 – Stephen Stephen, a deacon and the first martyr of the church, was one of those seven upon whom the apostles laid hands after they had been chosen to serve widows and others in need. Later, Stephen's preaching angered the temple authorities, and they ordered him to be put to death by stoning.

December 27 – John John, the son of Zebedee, was a fisherman and one of the Twelve. Tradition has attributed authorship of the gospel and the three epistles bearing his name to the apostle John.

December 28 – The Holy Innocents The infant martyrs commemorated on this day were the children of Bethlehem, two years old and younger, who were killed by Herod, who worried that his reign was threatened by the birth of a new king named Jesus.

Prayers

Various intercessions may be spoken at this time. The prayer provided in this book for each day may also be used.

The following prayer is especially appropriate for morning.
Almighty and everlasting God,
you have brought us in safety to this new day.
Preserve us with your mighty power,
that we may not fall into sin nor be overcome in adversity.
In all we do, direct us to the fulfilling of your purpose;
through Jesus Christ our Lord.
Amen.

The Lord's Prayer

Our Father in heaven,
   hallowed be your name,
   your kingdom come,
   your will be done,
      on earth as in heaven.
Give us today our daily bread.
Forgive us our sins
   as we forgive those
      who sin against us.
Save us from the time of trial
   and deliver us from evil.
For the kingdom, the power,
   and the glory are yours,
   now and forever. Amen.

Blessing

Let us bless the Lord.
Thanks be to God.

Almighty God,
the Father, + the Son, and the Holy Spirit,
bless and preserve us.
Amen.

Additional materials for daily prayer are available in Evangelical Lutheran Worship *(pp. 295–331) and may supplement this simple order.*

A SIMPLIFIED FORM
FOR EVENING PRAYER

When used for group prayer, a leader may speak the words printed in boldface type.

Opening
Jesus Christ is the light of the world,
the light no darkness can overcome.
Stay with us, Lord, for it is evening,
and the day is almost over.
Let your light scatter the darkness
and illumine your church.

Psalmody
The psalmody may begin with Psalm 141, Psalm 121, or another psalm appropriate for evening. Psalms provided in this volume for each week may be used instead of or in addition to the psalms mentioned.

A time of silence follows.
A hymn may follow (see the suggested hymn for each day).

Readings
One or more readings for each day may be selected from those provided in this volume.
The reading of scripture may be followed by silence for reflection.

The reflection may conclude with these or similar words.
Jesus said, I am the light of the world.
Whoever follows me will never walk in darkness.

Gospel Canticle

The song of Mary may be sung or said.
My soul proclaims the greatness of the Lord,
my spirit rejoices in God my Savior,
for you, Lord, have looked with favor on your lowly servant.
From this day all generations will call me blessed:
you, the Almighty, have done great things for me,
and holy is your name.
You have mercy on those who fear you,
from generation to generation.
You have shown strength with your arm
and scattered the proud in their conceit,
casting down the mighty from their thrones
and lifting up the lowly.
You have filled the hungry with good things
and sent the rich away empty.
You have come to the aid of your servant Israel,
to remember the promise of mercy,
the promise made to our forebears,
to Abraham and his children forever.

Prayers

Various intercessions may be spoken at this time. The prayer provided in this book for each day may also be used.

The following prayer is especially appropriate for evening.
We give thanks to you, heavenly Father,
through Jesus Christ your dear Son,
that you have graciously protected us today.
We ask you to forgive us all our sins, where we have done wrong,
and graciously to protect us tonight.
For into your hands we commend ourselves:
our bodies, our souls, and all that is ours.
Let your holy angels be with us,
so that the wicked foe may have no power over us.
Amen.

The Lord's Prayer

Our Father in heaven,
    hallowed be your name,
    your kingdom come,
    your will be done,
        on earth as in heaven.
Give us today our daily bread.
Forgive us our sins
    as we forgive those
        who sin against us.
Save us from the time of trial
    and deliver us from evil.
For the kingdom, the power,
    and the glory are yours,
    now and forever. Amen.

Blessing

Let us bless the Lord.
Thanks be to God.

The peace of God,
which surpasses all understanding,
keep our hearts and our minds in Christ Jesus.
Amen.

Additional materials for daily prayer are available in Evangelical Lutheran Worship *(pp. 295–331) and may supplement this simple order.*